PRAISE FOR

'Working-parent guilt? Digitally distracted? *Spacemaker* will remind you of what's really important to live a fulfilling, happy and healthy life, and how to achieve it.'
— **CATH ANDREW,** HEAD OF HUMAN RESOURCES, STARBUCKS AUSTRALIA

'A stimulating and practical guide for leaders who crave time to think and reflect on what matters most.'
— **DR YVONNE THOMPSON CBE,** FOUNDER/CEO, WINTRADE GLOBAL; AUTHOR; INTERNATIONALLY RECOGNISED CAMPAIGNER FOR EQUALITY, DIVERSITY AND INCLUSIVITY IN THE WORKPLACE

'Daniel's philosophy and tools have helped me create the sanctuary of space. If you want to take control of your life, read this book.'
— **EVANGELISTA ALBERTINI**, CEO, HYDRO TASMANIA

'Daniel's productivity tools and habits have helped me to organise myself, and others, off the football field. Read this book!'
— **JACK RIEWOLDT**, AUSTRALIAN RULES FOOTBALLER, PREMIERSHIP VICE-CAPTAIN, ALL-AUSTRALIAN AND COLEMAN MEDALLIST

'*Spacemaker* is a compelling journey into the roots of human productivity. It's a gem.'
— **ALAN HIRSCH**, AWARD-WINNING AUTHOR

'The most productive people I know are the ones who are able to create the most space to think and rest. This book will show you how.'
— **JORDAN RAYNOR**, BESTSELLING AUTHOR OF *REDEEMING YOUR TIME*

'I loved this book so much that I am paying my kids to read it. Read it. Live it. You won't regret it.'
— **SIMON HOLLEY**, TEAM LEADER, CATALYST NETWORK

'Highly practical and super helpful, but be warned: Daniel Sih does not just present a series of techniques for decluttering our schedules; he wants us to remake ourselves into different people.'
— **MICHAEL FROST**, BESTSELLING AUTHOR

'A rebellious book to help us busy people reflect, take action and make space!'
— **JANE HILLIARD**, FOUNDING DIRECTOR, DESIGNFUL

'Daniel's story of making space in his busy life is one we can all gain from – an easy to read, clear guide for a busy person.'
— **RICHARD STOKES**, CEO, AUSTRALIAN BOARDING SCHOOLS ASSOCIATION

'Finally! A practical, real-world guide for anyone truly desiring a healthy and balanced relationship with technology. Pick up *Spacemaker* if you're serious about finding joy and fulfilment away from the screen.'
— **BRANDON SCHAEFER**, FOUNDER/CEO, FIVE CAPITALS COACHING

'Read this book as fast as possible, preferably with your phone turned off.'
— **MISSY WALLACE**, MANAGING DIRECTOR, REDEEMER CITY TO CITY, NEW YORK

'A new and rich way of carving out space for the things that really matter.'
— **MARK SAYERS**, SENIOR LEADER, RED CHURCH; PODCAST HOST; BESTSELLING AUTHOR

SPACE
MAKER

HOW TO
UNPLUG, UNWIND & THINK CLEARLY
IN THE DIGITAL AGE

DANIEL SIH

MOVEMENTS
PUBLISHING

First published in 2021 by 100 Movements Publishing
www.100Mpublishing.com
Copyright © 2021 by Daniel Sih

www.100Mpublishing.com
www.movementleaderscollective.com
www.catalysechange.org

ISBN 978-1-7355988-6-4 (paperback)

Cover design and interior illustrations by Tom Smith / commmotion.co
Interior design by Revo Creative Ltd.

100 Movements Publishing
An imprint of Movement Leaders Collective
Cody, Wyoming

To my friend and business partner, Tim Hynes,
who shares a vision for a world with more space.

Nobody can switch worlds unless an alternative world is made richly available with great artistry, care and boldness.

WALTER BRUEGGEMANN

CONTENTS

INTRODUCTION

I first met Amy in a bustling café in Sydney.[1] She contacted me to help her reorganise her overflowing inbox and online to-do lists. A finance executive in a global fashion company, Amy had everything – a dream job, a city apartment, a wonderful husband and two beautiful children. But Amy had a nagging feeling that something was amiss. Life should have been perfect, but it wasn't.

After hearing Amy's story, it soon became apparent that email and to-do lists were not her greatest challenge. Amy was addicted to the churn of activity and constant distraction associated with a professional lifestyle. Like many of us, she had forgotten how to be unbusy. Increasingly reliant on her devices, Amy was losing her capacity to stop and breathe. Her life was a flurry of online activity – emails, social media and other applications – as well as juggling the constant demands of family life. Amy rarely stopped to think or plan anymore, let alone rest deeply.

Concerned by her relentless tiredness, Amy's husband suggested she work fewer nights and switch off her devices after dinner. He was frustrated by her lack of presence and wanted to help her regain some vitality. Amy agreed but struggled to follow through, hiding her online behaviours from her family. She found herself habitually in the bathroom scanning emails, and sneaking out of bed to complete PowerPoint presentations. Late one night, Amy's husband returned home to find her fast asleep. Only she wasn't. Her iPad was still warm, and she was pretending to be asleep. Caught red-handed in the act of overworking, Amy felt like a naughty schoolkid. She had broken a promise to her family and to herself, compelling her to reassess her priorities and her habits.

For Amy, this was a defining moment in her life. She needed to rethink the meaning of work, the value of rest, and the rhythms required to be productive.

WHAT IS THIS BOOK ABOUT?

Every book begins with a question. In my case, it's a question that's been burning within my heart, in different forms, for nearly a decade.

It nags at me as I crash on the couch, exhausted after a huge week at work. It speaks to me whenever I lift my head from my smartphone, having missed a moment with my children. It tugs at my mind as I struggle to sleep, overwhelmed by the responsibilities of leading a company and my team through a minefield of change.

How do I make space in the clutter of life to be highly productive and deeply human?

This question is both simple and complex. It raises a host of related questions surrounding work and rest, online addiction and connectivity. How do I embrace the brilliance of technology and all that it has to offer without becoming consumed? How do I compete in a global economy without losing my capacity to rest and think? How do I reorder my time and my patterns to experience a healthy and whole life? How do I unplug, unwind and think clearly in the digital age?

SPACE AND CLUTTER

This book is essentially about space – the meaning and making of space.

Space is the pause between sentences, the gap in our schedules, the rare moments in time where we have nothing to do. It involves resting, thinking, breathing and being. It is uninterrupted time to notice our surroundings, to determine our priorities, to focus on one thing. It is the ability to slow down and address our inner world. It is time away from distraction to master our thoughts, strengthen our resolve and become our better selves.

These moments are like gold if we use them wisely. For me, space is strolling along the path near my house, picking blackberries. It is sitting beside my office window, enjoying the warmth of the sun. Space is a quiet moment alone with a novel or a rowdy moment with my children as they goof around at breakfast. It is unbroken time to develop business strategy, to build relationships with my team or to edit a chapter of a book. Space unlocks meaning. Without space, we cannot be productive. It enables us to ponder, plan, set direction and live deliberately.

What then, is the opposite of space?

Clutter.

Clutter is so ubiquitous to modern living that we struggle to describe its accumulative effect on our lives. We use words like *busy* and *drowning* and *stressed* to describe how we are feeling, yet the root cause is clutter. Clutter is an overflowing inbox that never seems to relent. It is waking in the middle of the night with a head full of to-dos. It is the feeling you get when you finish a frantic work week and groan at the thought of your weekend commitments. There is so much to do in the digital age: projects, blogs, apps, games, travel, texts. Rather than lacking opportunity, we lack both the time to think and the attention required to focus. We are wired and distracted much of the time.

CLUTTER   SPACE IN THE CLUTTER

Space, in contrast, is an increasingly rare commodity. It may not be commonplace to speak of space, yet deep down, we know we need more. If we are to frequently experience space, we will need to address our love affair with new media: our smartphones, tablets and other internet-enabling devices. Rather than allowing always-on devices to dictate the texture of every moment, we can make adjustments to reform our relationship with the online world. In a culture of clutter, space rarely, if ever, happens by accident. By exploring the ideas and assumptions behind our habits, we can increase our capacity to think as independent people and therefore make space.

THIS BOOK IS FOR SPACEMAKERS

As I consult around the world, I meet leaders, managers, executives, politicians, working parents and business owners who have a deep desire for more space. They are hardworking, intelligent and relationally competent people. They care deeply about their families, their teams and their communities, and are genuinely seeking to make a difference in the world. They also spend a lot of their life online. They may be overworked and over-committed, but they are willing to learn, grow and make necessary changes to improve their life.

I call these people *Spacemakers*.

It is not a requirement to be busy and over-stretched to gain value from this book, but my assumption is that you are regularly on your devices, engaged in roles that thrust you into a world of constant connectivity with ever-increasing distraction.

THIS BOOK IS PERSONAL

In many ways, this book has been written for myself and for others like me.

A few years ago, I found myself working three jobs, pushing myself so hard across work and life that my health suffered, both physically and mentally. As a driven leader, I have always loved working, but I started to experience breathing difficulties related to anxiety, stress and lack of sleep. I was almost always tired and wired. I only knew one speed – super-fast – with no mechanism to pause, mentally slow down or simply be. Following my doctor's orders, I accepted a two-week period of stress leave, but this didn't resolve the underlying issues. I lacked cadence in my life and needed to radically reorient the way I lived and worked.

This near burnout experience was formative for me. It encouraged me to cherish space and to redesign my time both online and offline. I found a coach and asked my closest friends to keep me accountable to a series of life-giving habits. In doing so, I discovered the productivity of rest. I discovered the power of silence. I discovered the value of habitually unplugging from my devices to think, plan and give attention to my inner life. None of these rhythms have stopped me from getting things done. In contrast, they have enabled me to pursue meaningful goals with excellence, including starting a company, building a house and leading a series of community initiatives.

As a productivity consultant, I now have the pleasure of helping other people discover the patterns that have so richly helped me. *Spacemaker* is a personal book because it represents passions and perspectives that have shaped my life. Many of the hard-won lessons in this book are not my own but gems of wisdom gained from others. I am deeply thankful for the hundreds of coaching conversations that have shaped this book. I also attribute many of the philosophical and practical insights in these pages to my Christian faith, which informs my way of seeing the world. However, *Spacemaker* is written for anyone who longs for space, irrespective of background or belief. My hope is that my personal stories and spiritual perspectives will encourage you in your own journey towards a more space-filled life.

Despite being a productivity expert, I am not immune to stress and tiredness. I too struggle at times to enjoy a balanced and healthy life. There are seasons where there is more space, and seasons where slowing down is a constant battle. I have attempted to be honest about this in the pages to come, as one of my personal commitments is to teach only those practices that I apply myself. So, throughout the book there are stories of both success and failure, some light-hearted and others deeply personal. I hope to encourage you to achieve your goals along the way.

PARADIGM, PRINCIPLES AND PRACTICES

Many books have been written about the challenges of the digital world, so what's different about this one?

Digital habits and behaviours can be hard to adjust, requiring a comprehensive evaluation of our world view. In order to shift ingrained behaviours, we need both a personal *why* and a practical *how*. We need to understand the big ideas and broad principles influencing our relationship with the online world (our *why*), as well as practical and specific tools to translate our renewed thinking into action (the *how*). Whereas most books tend to focus on either the *why* OR the *how*, *Spacemaker* will move systematically from theory to practice, exploring the paradigm, moving to the principles, and landing with the practices.[2]

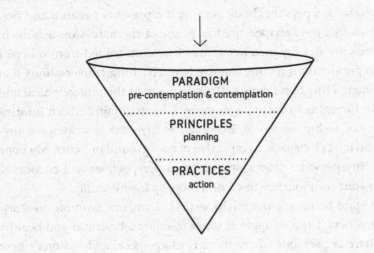

HOW TO GET THE MOST OUT OF THIS BOOK

There are a number of ways to read this book, both fast and slow. I encourage you to explore the whole book, but if you want to access the practices more rapidly, you can skip forward to the fourth part.

Part one introduces the concept of space and pace, explaining how a spacemaking approach enhances productivity.

Part two explores the paradigm of spacelessness. Why is digital technology so seductive? How does neuroplasticity influence our behaviour? In what ways do power, freedom and choice impact our capacity to disconnect?

Part three describes a set of timeless principles to help you rethink your priorities. Why set limits and assign rest as a predictable pattern?

Why embrace silence and solitude? Why make space to cultivate relationships away from a screen?

Part four outlines a series of practices to help you unplug from your devices as a rhythm. There are annual, weekly and daily habits to help you think deeply, rest fully and spend more time with loved ones.

Also included in the appendices is a summary of the principles in practice, to encourage personal planning and application.

DO YOU NEED MORE SPACE?

Imagine if you could be both productive and rested by living an ordered, rhythmical life. What if unplugging was not simply a means of surviving week by week but a strategy to produce your best work?

Interested? Then join me on a journey to uncover the making of space in our busy lives.

PART I

MAKING
SPACE

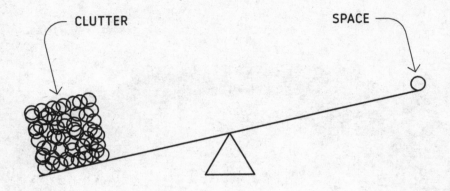

CLUTTER

SPACE

It's what you learn after you know it all that counts.

COACH JOHN WOODEN

CHAPTER 1

SPACE AND PACE

Several years ago, I was renovating my home and struggling to drill through concrete with my battery-powered drill. The battery kept smoking, and I needed more grunt. I needed *The Ken*.

It wasn't called The Ken back then, but it is now.

The Ken is a super-powerful electric drill, which I borrowed from a friend named Ken. He warned me that the drill was fast and hard to use.

This was an understatement.

Most drills come with various speed settings, but The Ken has only one. When I squeezed the trigger, the chuck rotated so quickly that I needed to brace my arm to maintain precision. No matter how much I practised, The Ken made a huge mess and was impossible to control.

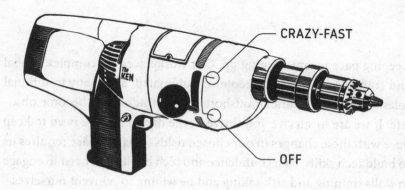

I still have this power tool sitting in my shed as Ken didn't seem to want it back. Whenever I see The Ken gathering dust on my shelf, it reminds me of the importance of cadence and rhythm. An on-switch without slower speed settings is limited. Faster is not always better, particularly if we lack the capacity to slow down and shift gears. Those who achieve space know this and unplug as a habit to maximise their productivity.

When it comes to personal effectiveness, opposites are important. If we don't stop to unwind, we achieve little. Highly effective people give equal attention to opposing realities. They create a rhythmical lifestyle of activity and inactivity, connection and disconnection. For simplicity, I call this pattern *keeping pace and making space*. Pace and space are the yin and yang of personal productivity. They require skill and attention, and we must value and practise both habits if we are to live a healthy, meaningful life.

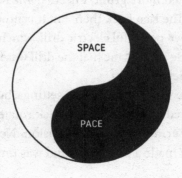

KEEPING PACE

Keeping pace means keeping up. Our workplaces are complex, global and competitive. Jobs are becoming automated, and many traditional roles are moving online or offshore. Entire trades have become obsolete. If we are to survive and thrive in the digital age, we need to keep pace with these changes in our chosen fields. Keeping pace requires us to build tech skills, tech confidence and tech habits. We need to engage in skills training and risk-taking and be willing to reinvent ourselves.

In my line of business, keeping pace means adopting skills and systems to maximise output against effort. I have an online system to coordinate timetables and to communicate with my staff. Apps are used to mind-map ideas, store passwords and manage money. I upload blog posts and download podcasts. Software updates help me stay afloat in a cloud-based environment. Such practices consume most of my time and head space, and enable me to achieve my goals.

MAKING SPACE

Making space is about slowing down; a conscious choice to unplug and unwind.

Space does not mean meditation and mindfulness, although these can be useful tools. Space is anything that helps us to stop, reflect and regenerate. Spacemakers pay attention to their habits and motivations. They think before they react, plan before they do, rest before they work. Space can be inactive – lying in a park staring up at the sky – or active – running along a beach or skiing down a mountain. We can find space in a meaningful conversation or alone in deep thought. The secret is to find space as a habit, resting deeply at a soul level, rather than being stuck in high gear.

A SUCCESSFUL STRATEGY

There are many books written to help people keep pace in a busy world. They teach you to do more, know more and add more to your already full life. Yet in my experience, doing less is sometimes more productive than doing more. Many of my clients are ruthlessly organised yet unproductive. They adopt every new app and lifehack that promises effectiveness but are unable to focus or prioritise. They tackle too many projects and jump at every notification. The root cause is not a lack of pace but space.

In recent times, 'productivity' has become synonymous with 'pacemaking'. Workplaces subconsciously communicate the idea that adding without subtracting is effective. They want more projects, more policies, more services – never less. In my own business, most of our contracted services are to help people 'keep pace' – building teams, redesigning meetings, developing strategy – all busy stuff!

Companies rarely invest in the unconventional habits of 'making space', teaching staff to do less, not more. This is not surprising; buying a donut for its hole instead of the sugar-coated ring is counter-intuitive (even if the hole has fewer calories). Visionary companies, such as activewear giant, Lululemon Athletica, are beginning to see the world differently. They have created a winning culture by urging staff to set personal goals (one-year, three-year and ten-year goals) and supporting them to succeed. Staff are encouraged to take part in activities such as yoga and meditation within working hours. The head office provides reading materials to inspire personal growth, and staff have access to board games, gym facilities and a healthy-living café to encourage health and wholeness.[1] Space and pace in balance – it works!

In almost every field of employment, making space is a good investment. Take email for example. Workplaces that eliminate email notifications, discourage out-of-hours communication and reduce email volume, save money and improve efficiency.[2] When individual workers process their inbox less often, rather than continuously, they experience less stress without losing responsiveness.[3]

As will be argued and explored in this book, balancing pace and space is a winning strategy. I believe it is the secret to sustained productivity and getting the *right* things done. So why do so few of us have space to focus? Why are we wired, tired and distracted? Let's find out.

PART II
THE
PARADIGM

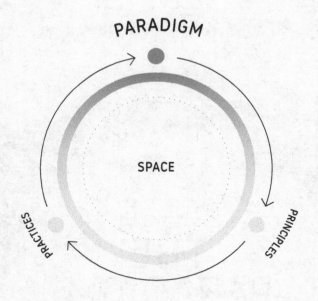

PARADIGM

SPACE

PRINCIPLES

PRACTICES

Have you ever had a dream, Neo, that you were so sure was real? What if you were unable to wake from that dream – how would you know the difference between the dream world and the real world?

MORPHEUS

The energy in the room was electric. Steve Jobs, founder of Apple, walked on stage before a huge audience of adoring Macworld fans, wearing his trademark black turtleneck, blue jeans and white sneakers. Behind him was an enormous screen. It was January 2007, and Jobs knew he was about to change the world.

Rumour had been circulating that Apple had invented a game-changing product that would yet again transform the technology industry. In his now-famous speech, Jobs reminded his listeners he was in the business of revolution. The Macintosh had transformed the computing industry in 1984. The iPod had transformed the music industry in 2001. Apple now had a product of even greater significance. 'It's an iPod, a phone, an internet communicator ... these are not three separate devices. And we are calling it iPhone! Today Apple is going to reinvent the phone.'[1] And they did.

When the history books are written, 2007 will be remembered as a defining moment in technological history. Apple's iPhone created a cultural earthquake that rivalled the release of the Gutenberg printing press in 1440 – an invention that democratised knowledge, and pre-empted the Age of Enlightenment, the development of modern science and universal education.[2] The iPhone redefined how we access information and use our time. En masse, we have shifted the way we live and work, think and behave. Now it is almost impossible to live without a mini-computer in our pocket – and in this way, digital technology has changed our *paradigm* of the world. Jobs did not simply revolutionise the phone. He redefined our experience of being human.[3]

TRADING TIME

Seismic shifts are occurring across all generations, yet one group in particular exemplifies what happens when we trade space for clutter. iGen are the newest generation of young people to enter the workforce. Born between 1995 and 2012, they do not remember a time before tablets and smartphones, and had an Instagram account by the time they entered secondary school. iGeners are smart, capable, anxious, distracted and obsessed by their phones.

According to generational researcher Jean Twenge, generational changes occur along a continuum in a gradual and predictable way.

Characteristics, such as those differentiating Gen X from Millennials, present as modest hills and valleys when graphed over time. Only after several years might a set of trends become significant and consistent enough to warrant 'a new generation'.

Until recently.

Around 2012, Twenge and her team observed significant, discontinuous changes in teen behaviour and emotional experience, compared with previous generations. These variations were replicated across numerous high-quality national surveys tracking change across America. Twenge was at a loss to explain what she was observing. The data was remarkable. In her own words:

> The gentle slopes of the line graphs became steep mountains and sheer cliffs, and many of the distinctive characteristics of the Millennial generation began to disappear. In all my analyses of generational data – some reaching back to the 1930s – I had never seen anything like it.[4]

Since 2012, the behaviour of young people has changed dramatically. iGeners spend much less time with their friends, are less likely to hang out at shopping centres, go to the cinema, attend parties or date one another. iGeners sleep less than previous generations. They worry about emotional safety and are more likely to experience loneliness, anxiety, depression and suicidal ideation. In almost every respect, iGeners look, think and act differently to young people a few years before them.

What happened in 2012 to cause such a dramatic shift in teen behaviour? It wasn't the Great Recession in America, between 2007 to 2009. Global competition does not explain the shift, as teens spend fewer hours on homework and have better work opportunities than Millennials before them. According to Twenge's deep dive into the research, a single invention set iGen in motion: the iPhone. The data began to shift at 'exactly the moment when the proportion of Americans who owned a smartphone surpassed 50 percent'.[5] From this moment onwards, young people started to change their behaviour, trading time with friends for time alone on a screen, leading the way for generations before and after them.

Irrespective of gender, ethnicity and socio-economic background, iGeners spend most of their leisure hours online. Secondary school seniors, for example, spend an average of six hours a day multitasking on new media, texting (2¼ hours a day), browsing the internet (2 hours a day), gaming (1½ hours a day) and using video chat (½ an hour a day).[6] Since 2012, iGen has been trading traditional pursuits associated with increased happiness with online activities, resulting in an overall increase in unhappiness. The following image is a visual representation of Twenge's research, showing the correlation between activities that make you happier and unhappier.

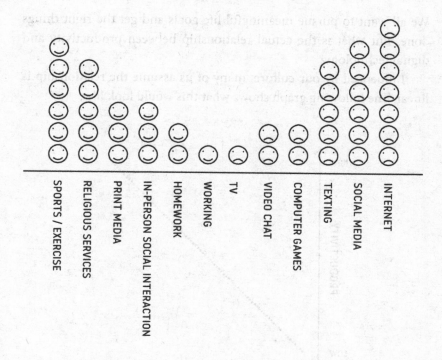

The problem is not with iGen, who are remarkably creative and socially aware, but with *digital technology overuse* (which we will explore in depth later on). Twenge summarises: 'Teens who spend more time on screen activities are more likely to be unhappy, and those who spend more time on non-screen activities are more likely to be happy. There's not a single exception: all screen activities are linked to less happiness, and all non-screen activities are linked to more happiness.[7]

This trade-off is not isolated to younger people. The average US adult, for example, spends an average of twelve hours a day using digital media.[8] As digital usage goes up, time pursuing other activities goes down, including interests that improve happiness. No matter our age, if we over-play our digital technology card, we almost always lose our sense of balance. The result: spacelessness.

PRODUCTIVITY AND DIGITAL TECHNOLOGY

We all want to pursue meaningful life goals and get the right things done. But what is the actual relationship between productivity and digital technology?

Influenced by our culture, many of us assume the relationship is linear. The following graph shows what this would look like.

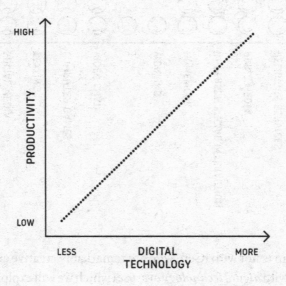

The narrative goes like this: if you want to be productive, you need to invest in digital technology. Adopt as much as possible for yourself and your team. Get a phone, tablet, laptop and smartwatch, and your pro-ductivity will increase. Download work and lifestyle apps. Improve your skills, your savvy and your connectivity, and your efficiency will soar.

In other words, digital technology is always good. The more you have, the more productive you will be. But is this true?

With infinite time, this might be so. But time is limited, as is atten-tion, energy and our capacity to focus. The more time we spend online, the less time we have for other pursuits. It's simple maths.

Rather than a linear relationship, where technology delivers limit-less productivity, let's consider an alternative line graph – the convex plateau. In this graph, an early investment in digital technology im-proves productivity, yet over time, with more technology, your gains taper. You experience the law of diminishing returns and receive mini-mal benefits for your ongoing investments.

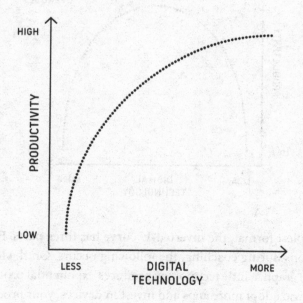

In coaching leaders from around the world, it would seem that a convex graph is closer to the truth. Buy a touch screen and your productivity increases. Invest in an online calendar, cloud storage and a series of pro-ductivity apps, and your outcomes improve again. Yet over time, as you over-invest in digital technology, your gains plateau. Buy a smartwatch, a second monitor, another twenty apps, and the law of diminishing returns kicks in. More is more … to a point. And then you plateau.

Although the convex plateau is closer to the truth, it is not the full picture. There is a reality beyond the plateau which we must grapple with – a point where more technology actually *reduces* personal productivity. In mathematical terms, this is depicted by an inverted-U curve, a commonly used model to explain how life works. We see inverted-U curves in health (too little and too much food impact mortality), in parenting (low- and high-income earners find it harder to raise well-adjusted children) and in education (very large and small class sizes impact teaching outcomes).

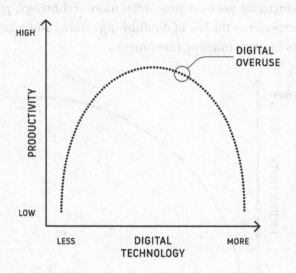

In its simplest format, the inverted-U curve has three parts. From my observations during coaching, the following occurs. On the left-hand side of the graph, a little technology produces exponential productivity gains. As you adopt more apps and invest in devices, your productivity increases, until you reach the centre of the curve where the line graph plateaus. You have reached the point of diminishing returns. Keep going, pursuing even more time online, and the trade-off takes effect. You descend down the right-hand side of the inverted-U curve and become unproductive. Instead of a net gain, you experience a net loss.

Doing and having more diminishes your space, and along with it, your ability to get the right things done.

Although the inverted-U curve is found across many areas of life, it is counter-intuitive to how we think and act. As Malcolm Gladwell argues in *David and Goliath*, 'inverted-U curves almost never fail to take us by surprise, and one of the reasons we are so often confused about advantages and disadvantages is that we forget when we are operating in a U-shaped world'.[9]

My point is this: to be a Spacemaker, we must examine our habits and practices through the lens of the inverted-U curve. A certain level of online activity will boost productivity. But not in excess. We must aim for the productive middle.

RECALIBRATING OUR HABITS

For many of us, the way to boost our productivity is to be smarter in how we use our time online *and* aim to spend less time online. This is difficult to achieve in a culture that pushes us to the right of the inverted-U curve. Like iGen, we are trending towards media overuse and are less productive as a result. Distraction and oversaturation are the new normal, as we slide en masse down the right-hand side of the inverted-U curve.

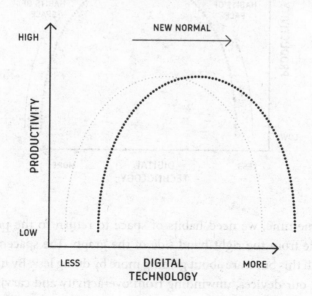

I regularly coach leaders caught in this maelstrom. Executives tell me they are working longer hours and achieving fewer meaningful goals than ever before. They feel distracted, reactive, and time poor, bombarded by information day and night. These are symptoms of digital overuse, where doing and having more is producing poorer outcomes.

HABITS OF PACE AND SPACE

In line with this concept, the most productive people develop habits on both sides of the inverted-U curve, habits of pace and space.

Pace begins by mastering the fundamental technologies required for our roles. For most people, this begins with email, word processing, using an online calendar, to-do lists, cloud-based project tools and other programs specific to one's profession. Without these core skills, we suffer from a lack of productivity; the curse of the left-hand side of the inverted-U curve.

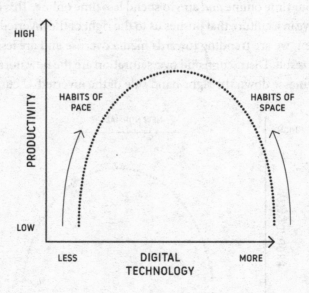

At the same time, we need habits of space to return to the productive middle from the right-hand side of the graph. The spacemaking practices in this book are about gaining more by doing less. By unplugging from our devices, unwinding from overactivity and carving out time to think deeply, we can increase our productivity, as well as our happiness.

BEGINNING WITH A PHILOSOPHY OF TECHNOLOGY

Doing less may be effective, but it's hard to achieve in practice. It is one thing to value simplicity, yet another to choose space over clutter each day. As a Spacemaker, we will need to look beyond simple productivity hacks and reflect deeply on why we do what we do.

In *Digital Minimalism*, Cal Newport argues the following:

> Minor corrections, willpower, tips, and vague resolutions are not sufficient by themselves to tame the ability of new technologies to invade your cognitive landscape – the addictiveness of their design and the strength of the cultural pressures supporting them are too strong for an ad hoc approach to succeed. … what you need instead is a full-fledged *philosophy of technology use*, rooted in your deep values, that provides clear answers to the questions of what tools you should use and how you should use them and, equally important, enables you to confidently ignore everything else.[10]

Having worked with hundreds of leaders suffering from spacelessness, my conclusion is similar. Technology is seductive, and habits are hard to change. Without a deep conviction and robust understanding of technology, it is almost impossible to adopt and sustain a spacemaking approach.

If we are to make space and overcome digital clutter, we will need to think deeply about our beliefs, our values, our drives and compulsions. In other words, we need a philosophy of technology – a paradigm.

CHAPTER 2

TECHNOLOGY

Have you ever felt overwhelmed in a crowd of strangers?

That was me a few years ago, an introvert attending a toddler's birthday party. Imagine lots of noise, coddling parents, dirty nappies … and no escape plan.

Luckily, I met Matt.

He appeared as uncomfortable as I was, so I went over to say hello. Screaming toddlers make hard work of small talk, yet we ended up deeply engaged in conversation about the impact of mobile phones and popular culture.

Matt didn't own a mobile phone. As his friends and colleagues scrambled to upgrade their smartphones, Matt avoided purchasing even a basic model. Despite working in the professional world, he resisted the pressure to 'keep up with the Joneses', a difficult position to sustain, as he remained genuinely out of range whenever away from his home or office. By choosing not to engage in majority culture, Matt experienced life as an outsider looking in, perceiving rapid shifts in people's attitudes, beliefs and behaviours over time. I found his observations to be fascinating. Matt noticed that his friends and family had become less able to commit to plans, less willing to turn up on time and less able to 'hang out' (without gravitating towards their phones and devices). Those around him seemed to be more distractible and less reliable.

In Matt's own words (paraphrased from memory):

People are reluctant to book a time to hang out with me when they hear I don't have a phone. They question me; 'How will

I contact you if I'm running late or can't make it anymore?' It just makes me mad. I feel like saying, 'Well, it's simple … just make a time and turn up.' It didn't used to be this way. Now that everyone has a phone, they keep their options open all the time.

Matt acknowledged there are many benefits to having a smartphone, such as sharing moments with grandparents or meeting friends in a spontaneous way. Yet this conversation, shared more than a decade ago, opened my eyes to the disadvantages of an always-on culture. What is the silent impact of digital technology in my life? What ideas and assumptions are embedded within my devices, and how do they shape my identity and my habits?

OUR ENVIRONMENTS SHAPE US

Winston Churchill famously stated: 'We shape our buildings; thereafter they shape us.'* Churchill was more than a shrewd politician. A keen observer of human behaviour, he intuitively understood that physical environments shape personhood – how we see and understand ourselves.

Several years ago, I climbed to the top of one of the oldest cathedrals in Australia, in the heart of Melbourne. I was part of a tour group, and from our viewing platform, we could see the entire city. One hundred years ago, our tour guide explained, the cathedral was the largest building in Melbourne. Towering above the skyline, the cathedral called people from all over to celebrate as a congregation. A bastion of religion, this building was designed to be awe-inspiring.

---

* In 1943, following the bombing of the Commons Chamber during the Blitz, the British parliament debated whether to maintain or modify the original design. Winston Churchill argued that the shape of the old chamber (rectangular rather than semi-circular in design) was responsible for the two-party system, which is the essence of British parliamentary democracy. Hence his statement: 'We shape our buildings; thereafter they shape us.' See 'Churchill and the Commons Chamber', UK Parliament.

A congregational member entering such a grandiose building might expect to feel insignificant – a reminder of the holiness, mystery and otherness of God. The cathedral size and scope communicated power, magnificence and transcendence. These ideas were embedded into the architecture and shaped the values, habits and identity of the community.

The land surrounding the cathedral is now the central business district. Newer, taller skyscrapers overshadow its spires. Religion has been replaced by production, and crosses with brand logos. The skyline is littered with cranes, erecting glass towers with even greater engineering prowess. Postmodern Australians feel at home in this concrete landscape with its icons and corporate images. The city skyline reminds us of salaries and suits, sushi and smashed avocado, motivating us to produce, achieve and consume. Our values shape our physical environments, which in turn, inform our behaviours. The skyscraper tells a different story to the cathedral. It embodies a different set of ideas and communicates different messages that impact how we think and act, altering our collective identity.

Just as our physical environments communicate messages, so do our digital environments. From a neurological perspective, online ecosystems are far more potent than bricks and mortar. To explore this concept further, we need to rewind a few decades to the era of sex, drugs and rock and roll.

KENNEDY'S SECRET WEAPON

It was 1960, a volatile time in American history. With the Cold War in full swing, fear of nuclear fallout was widespread. Vietnam was heating up with troops heading overseas. Rosa Parks had refused to give up her seat on the bus, sparking non-violent civil rights protests across the country. The election was looming. America was desperate for a capable leader.

Alongside this heady mix of war and civil unrest, a young, unknown senator from Massachusetts surprised the world by becoming the thirty-fifth president of the United States of America. Rising from obscurity, he was not expected to win the election. His name was John F. Kennedy.

Affectionately known as JFK, Kennedy is most widely remembered for his assassination in 1963. Yet his rise to power is also noteworthy. His Republican opponent, Richard Nixon, was an experienced lawmaker. Strong on foreign policy, the incumbent vice president was odds-on favourite to win. Kennedy was less experienced and suffered from ill health. But he did have a trick up his sleeve – a secret weapon that Nixon overlooked. Kennedy was great on television.

When the first US televised presidential debate was held on 26 September 1960, the entire country tuned in. Nine out of ten families were connected to the airways, and fifty-two million television sets were in use across North America.[1] During this now-famous debate, Kennedy looked confident and relaxed in front of the camera. Sporting a youthful tan, he smiled directly at his global audience, whereas Nixon was pale and sweated under the lights. A seasoned politician, Nixon addressed reporters in the audience. To those watching on 'the tube', Nixon's side glances made him look shifty and untrustworthy. He didn't make eye contact with the American public and failed to win their trust.

The 1960 televised debate shifted politics forever, demanding new skills to lead a nation. No longer elected on character and experience alone, politicians needed to perform well on television, a precursor to Twitter. It would eventually be movie stars and social media influencers, not lawyers and community leaders, who would rise to the top.

THE MEDIUM IS THE MESSAGE

The year after Kennedy's televised assassination in 1963, a philosopher called Marshall McLuhan pioneered the study of media by publishing his seminal book, *Understanding Media: The Extensions of Man*.[2] McLuhan, who coined the term 'the medium is the message', noticed something about the nature of media that his contemporaries had not yet recognised. Television was causing a buzz, and intellectuals found themselves debating its benefits and drawbacks. For progressives, the tube was liberating. For conservatives, it was lewd and scandalous. Yet most of the debate focused on the content of the shows played by the networks, rather than on the medium itself (the physical technology). In McLuhan's mind, it was the machine itself, not the programs, that fundamentally changed the American psyche. The medium had changed values and behaviours in subtle but significant ways. For example, rather than face each other at the dinner table, families oriented themselves around a box. This altered social interaction, shifting how families understood themselves and communicated with each other. The machine also disrupted authority, bringing external influence into the living room. This changed the nature of neighbourhoods and therefore communities. Enthralled by the new technology, families were becoming passive and consumptive in how they used their time.

Nicholas Carr, author of *The Shallows*, summarises McLuhan's argument in this way:

> In the long run a medium's content matters less than the medium itself in influencing how we think and act. As our window onto the world, and onto ourselves, a popular medium moulds what we see and how we see it – and eventually, if we use it enough, it changes who we are, as individuals and as a society.[3]

The tools we use, and the ideas embedded within them, profoundly shape who we are and how we see the world.

IDEAS SHAPE US

John Culkin, a contemporary of McLuhan, famously stated: 'We become what we behold. We shape our tools and then our tools shape us.'[4] Every new technology is founded on a set of ideas. We may not recognise these ideas, yet they influence us nonetheless.

Consider the mobile phone before it became 'smart'. Originally a commercial tool, the mobile phone allowed business people to continue working when out of the office. It was designed to promote greater freedom, flexibility and availability. When the mobile phone arrived, it was large and heavy as a brick, yet it improved workplace productivity. By removing the hard boundary between people and their offices, this technology forever changed the interplay between work and life.

Research has found that 97 per cent of Australians now own a mobile phone and are deeply impacted by the ideas embedded within the device.[5] We are no longer limited by geography. In my business, mobility gives me the freedom to work in different places, with different people. Our accountant, website developer and copy-editor all live and work in different cities. I work from home, and no longer rent a physical office. It's fantastic, but there are downsides to being 'free' from an office. Longer hours, never-ending emails and a loss of work-life balance are just a few. There is a shadow side to workplace mobility. As the business owner joke goes: 'Running a business gives me 100 per cent flexibility to work wherever I want whenever I want ... so long as it's seventy hours a week!'

In a similar way, the smartphone was built on an idea to integrate multiple applications in a single handheld device. It combines existing technologies and hosts multiple applications at the same time. In other words, the smartphone is built for multitasking. But are we? If McLuhan and Culkin are right, and 'we become what we behold', then it would be logical for a multitasking device to impact our head and our habits. Our devices are always available, constantly switching, and rarely silent. Is it any surprise that many of us feel overwhelmed? Constant partial attention is the *expected* consequence of using a device built on the idea of multitasking.

Media theorist Tim Challies, author of *The Next Story*, writes:

A technology will eventually and inevitably do what it was created to do. Yet we, the consumers, rarely know exactly what the technology was created to do. If we can find the original purpose for a technology, we will not be surprised when we learn how it will soon begin to change and shape us ... The wise consumer of technology will realise that the technology he uses today, the technology he has come to love and depend on, will have unintended consequences in his life and in the world around him. He will look not just to the technology itself but to the function for which it was created, the problem it was originally supposed to address.[6]

TECHNOLOGY WEARS ITS BENEFITS ON ITS SLEEVE

Herein lies our challenge.

With every new technology, there are positive and negative effects, shaped by the ideas embedded within the medium. Our culture has a positive bias towards the new, and this leaves us unprepared for negative effects that inevitably emerge. New is good, we say. It brings benefits and opportunities. We might balk at price or debate our favourite brands, yet rarely do we question the inherent value (and likely consequences) of technological innovation at a fundamental level. This is changing, as more people awaken to the draining effects of hyperconnection, yet our societal bias still shapes the narrative.

Tim Challies suggests that 'advertisers lure us in with a long list of benefits and claims of better lives, but they only tell us half the story. We fall into this trap, time after time, for the simple reason that a technology tends to wear its benefits on its sleeve – while the drawbacks are buried deep within.'[7] This, I believe, is worth repeating. Technology tends to wear its benefits on its sleeve, while the drawbacks are buried deep within. It takes a thirty-second advert to promote a new product, but much longer to consider – and discover from experience – its negative effects.

What we need, I suggest, is a circuit breaker – an ability to stop, unplug and reflect for long enough to understand ourselves and our devices. Pausing requires time and space to think deeply and ask probing questions: Who am I? Who do I want to be? Do my habits reflect my values? What are the consequences of continuing the way I am going? Do I like who I am becoming, and how do I make space to become a better version of me?

PIONEERS AND THEIR CHILDREN

A low-tech approach to parenting is increasingly common among Silicon Valley's elite. It appears that the pioneers of the digital age understand the drawbacks inherent in their own technologies more than we do, and are therefore highly conscious in how they consume their own products.

Steve Jobs, founder of Apple, did not allow his children to own an iPad. He strictly limited his children's use of technology and insisted that they eat together, discussing books and history at mealtimes. When speaking to *The New York Times* journalist Nick Bilton about the iPad's release, Jobs stated: 'They haven't used it. We limit how much technology our kids use at home.'[8]

Bill Gates, founder of Windows, didn't give his children a mobile phone until they were fourteen years old, stating, 'we often set a time after which there is no screen time, and in their case that helps them to get to sleep at a reasonable hour'. Google CEO Sundar Pichai, who limits his own phone and computer use, strictly monitors his family's screen time. As does Snapchat's CEO, Evan Spiegel, who allows his stepson a total of ninety minutes of screen time per week.[9] Apple CEO Tim Cook doesn't want his nephew to access social media,[10] and Chris Anderson, co-founder of 3D Robotics, suggests, 'We have seen the dangers of technology firsthand. I've seen it in myself, and I don't want to see that happen to my kids.'[11]

Other Silicon Valley executives, such as the chief technology officer of eBay, send their children to low-tech schools such as Waldorf School of the Peninsula, in California. This school, built on a pedagogy of creativity and imagination, bans all screens from the classroom and strongly discourages technology use at home. While their parents are developing next generation information technologies, the children of Silicon Valley's elite are using pens and paper, knitting needles and mud.[12]

Professor of communications studies, Everett Rogers, proposed the diffusion of innovations theory to explain how, why and at what rate new ideas and technologies spread. This model, commonly known as the *early adopter* curve, is helpful to explain what is happening in Silicon Valley.

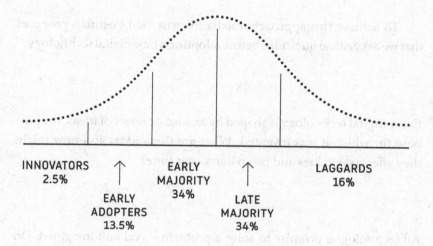

INNOVATORS
2.5%

EARLY
ADOPTERS
13.5%

EARLY
MAJORITY
34%

LATE
MAJORITY
34%

LAGGARDS
16%

Inventions begin with an *innovator* or *pioneer*. Pioneers observe changes in their environment that others can't yet see and respond by creating novel solutions to those problems. Once a new technology is developed, *early adopters* jump on board, followed by an *early majority*. By the time the *late majority* get involved, a new technology has passed its tipping point. It is no longer novel, but normative, and well established in society.[13]

Because of their nature, true pioneers continue to reinvent, seeking to overcome limitations in their original ideas. They critique their own inventions and identify problems before the majority experience them. Perhaps then, it shouldn't surprise us that the inventor of the iPad set limitations on its use; that Jobs understood his own ideas better than we do – calculating the impact of both the medium and the message.

THE CONSIDERED ADOPTER

When it comes to making space in the digital world, I propose that we embrace an attitude of critical thinking – the posture of the considered adopter. That is, one who does not rush out for the next shiny thing, but isn't overly sceptical either. Every technology has benefits and limitations that influence people in subtle ways. And so a conscious consumer is objective, considered and intentional.

To achieve this approach, media theorist Neil Postman proposes that we ask critical questions before adopting a new digital technology:[14]

WHY WAS THIS TECHNOLOGY INVENTED?

Every digital technology is shaped by an idea or series of ideas: the purpose for which it was invented. What are these ideas and how might they affect our values and behaviours over time?

WHAT PROBLEMS DO THESE TECHNOLOGIES SOLVE?

All technologies promise to solve a problem – real and imagined. Do we really need a waterproof phone or a camera with more pixels? Is this an actual problem that we experience, or is it an imagined one?

WHAT NEW PROBLEMS ARE LIKELY TO ARISE BY USING THIS TECHNOLOGY?

Are the costs greater than the benefits? An example of this for me is Netflix. I have been slow in adopting this popular streaming service, considering the costs to be greater than the benefits. By costs, I don't mean price, but the impact on my time and attention.

Some other helpful questions to analyse a new technology are:

- Does this technology serve a greater goal or align with a personal value?
- Is this technology the best way to achieve my purposes?
- What limitations will I set when using this technology, to maximise benefits and minimise drawbacks?

IN SUM

- Technology, as wonderful as it is, shifts our patterns in unexpected ways. (Remember the story of mobile-less Matt.)

- Physical environments communicate messages, and so do digital environments. Our environments shape us, even as we shape our environments. (Remember the cathedral and skyline of brand logos.)

- The medium is the message (Marshall McLuhan). Our digital tools impact our beliefs and behaviours beyond the content of the downloaded apps. (Remember the televised presidential debate of 1960.)

- We become what we behold (John Culkin). Over time, the ideas embedded within a technological medium influence our head, heart and habits. The mobile phone altered thinking about work and life, and the smartphone reduced our capacity to focus on one thing at a time.

- There are positive and negative effects with every invention, but negative ones take longer to surface. Pioneers understand this and are savvier in how they use their inventions.

- We can be a considered adopter rather than an uninformed consumer.

CHAPTER 3

PLASTICITY

I used to be a physiotherapist. It was a fantastic career and allowed me to meet and treat a variety of interesting people from every walk of life.

One day, a woman named Susan shuffled into my outpatient clinic, walking in the most unusual way.[1] Her head was rotated to one side as she side-stepped like a crab towards me.

Injured in a high-speed car crash three years prior, Susan had worn a collar to protect her neck, and over time her head had drifted to one side – 30 degrees to the left. It is difficult to engage in normal life with your head off-centre. Susan's eyes were constantly strained, her body was contorted and her balance unsteady.

Even more unusual was Susan's lack of physical awareness. It surprised her when I mentioned her head was fixed to one side, and she couldn't explain why. Susan's friends had told her she 'walked a little bit funny', and she had a gnawing sense that she was 'off-kilter'. Perplexed and curious, I examined Susan's range of movement to see how restricted her neck was. I expected to find significant stiffness, but she was able to turn her head to both the left and right. There was some pain as she rotated but no *physical* reason her head should be off-centre.

Following a battery of tests, I concluded that Susan's problem was not stiffness or pain, but perception (which in medical terms, we call *proprioception*). Our brain creates a mental picture of our body, an internal map, that guides how we move each day. Every joint in our body has sensory nerves, which inform our brain about the position of the joint in its surrounding environment. This is why we can walk in the dark without falling over, or drive without looking at the steering wheel. In Susan's case, something was amiss in the way her brain interpreted her neck and head position in relation to her body. Abnormal had become normal. Her internal map was distorted.

To test my theory, I tried an experiment. Standing in front of a mirror, I asked Susan to close her eyes and turn her neck to the left and to the right, as far as she could go. I then asked her to reposition her head to a 'straight' position, without opening her eyes. Susan's head ended up where it normally sat – 30 degrees rotated to the left. According to her internal map, this position *was* straight, but when she opened her eyes, the mirror showed her a different story. We practised correcting Susan's neck position in front of a mirror again and again, to help her recalibrate what 'straight' felt like. Over time, Susan gradually corrected her posture without a mirror. Her walking improved, her pain reduced and she began to live a normal life. It was a great outcome.

Susan's story highlights a fascinating and important reality – our brain is changeable and adapts whenever we habitually behave in a particular way. To begin with, Susan's neck was straight, but the use of a collar had slowly shifted it 30 degrees to the left. For Susan (and her brain), the changes were imperceptible – her internal map drifted off course without her knowing it.

Sometimes our perception of reality can shift without us noticing. The digital world is changing the way in which our brains develop, process and perceive information. This is worth exploring.

OFF-CENTRE

I recently hung a large painting in my house, located eight metres above a staircase, while balancing on a ladder. It wasn't a straightforward task. I probably shouldn't have attempted to do it alone.

The frame was heavy, and the first time I connected the string to the hook, it hung off-centre. I had to climb up and down the ladder several times to make slight adjustments – a little to the left, a little to the right. Still not straight!

On my fifth attempt, the painting was roughly spot on (a term I once learnt from a builder), but to make it perfect, I decided to make one last adjustment. As I lifted the string to shift the frame, I over-reached and tilted the whole painting about 40 degrees in the opposite direction!

Here's the strange thing. The immediate thought that popped into my head wasn't an expletive. Instead, my automatic cognitive response was to think *Command-Z,* coupled with an automatic twitch of two fingers in my left hand. (For non-IT geeks, Command-Z is a keyboard shortcut to 'undo' a mistake on a Mac computer.)

At the time, I knew this was ridiculous. My brain had subconsciously confused a real-life situation with an online keyboard shortcut. After so many hours engaged in the digital world, typing and retyping this book, my brain and my automatic responses seemed to be temporarily confused. (I do secretly hope that someone will invent a shortcut to automatically un-tilt a painting one day!)

Why did this happen? And what is going on in my brain to act in this way?

WHAT IS PLASTICITY?

Neuroplasticity is a fancy term that simply means that our brain is malleable, constantly reshaping itself to adapt to our conditions. The human brain is plastic.

When neurobiologists suggest that the brain can change, they are referring to both the structure and function of nerve connections and its complex biochemistry. Neurons and chemical synapses develop in the brain to reinforce habitual behaviour. The more you participate in a particular activity, the more your brain adapts to these conditions.[2] Conversely, when a thought pattern or behaviour becomes infrequent, fewer cells reinforce that activity. Synapses weaken, and neurons shrink or die. The old saying, 'use it or lose it', turns out to be true. The brain is a dynamic, adaptive and highly responsive organ that is constantly changing in accordance with our needs.[3]

Think of neuroplasticity in this way. Imagine your brain is a series of complex and interconnected hiking trails. At first, it is difficult to clear a path through the mountainous undergrowth. Over time, the more people who walk a path, the more traversable it becomes. A well-used path becomes clearer and wider, creating even greater opportunities for increased traffic. If this continues, signage, seating and viewing platforms may be warranted. In some circumstances, where foot traffic is heavy and frequent, a boardwalk might be added, or even concrete for multi-use access.

Conversely, when a walking path becomes unused, shrubs and weeds creep in. The surface becomes boggy, rocky and uneven. This makes the path less attractive and less accessible. Without visitors, the path will eventually become overgrown, overrun, and cease to exist at all. Such is the way of the brain, with its constant growing and replacing of neurons, in line with our activity.

We all have habits. Habits and the repetitive actions required to develop them form the basis of neuroplasticity. For example, when I was a teenager I learnt the piano. Despite being undisciplined, I accumulated hundreds of hours of practice over a decade. Because of this activity, my brain developed accordingly. Areas of my brain devoted to music recognition and melody, finger dexterity and rhythm, increased with repetition. Scales, chords, even specific songs became encoded as synapses in my brain. One particular song – 'Nocturne in E-flat major' by Frédéric Chopin – was very difficult to learn. I practised this piece of music again and again until I could play it by memory. The more I practised, the more I developed and expanded the 'Chopin' regions of my brain.

I haven't played the piano for twenty years, and those neuronal pathways have now disappeared. I can no longer play 'Nocturne in E-flat major' (with or without sheet music). The closest I come to moving my fingers on a keyboard is when I type words on a laptop. Chopin has been replaced by Google, Mozart by Microsoft, and Schubert by Skype. Our neural pathways are constantly changing based on our behaviours.

THE DIGITAL MIND

I'm grateful for my lifestyle; I live in Tasmania, one of the most beautiful places in the world, and yet the internet means I can still easily access information, connect with others and consult globally. In the middle of winter, when it's dark and dreary, I wake up, ruffle my hair, put on a business shirt, and log on to coach a client in New York, Toronto or London. On the face of it, I'm a professional consultant, helping executives to achieve their goals. Behind the professional facade, behind the screen, I'm a daggy* Tasmanian. Casual as ever in warm pyjama trousers and woollen Ugg boots, I am embracing the technological revolution.

Part of me also feels uncomfortable about my over-reliance on the cloud. Almost everything I do requires a phone, tablet or laptop – from checking the weather, booking a meeting, coaching a client to communicating with my kids. My lifestyle is so deeply intertwined with the internet that to lose my phone would be to lose a part of myself. I used to think that this was just a feeling. I now understand it to be a biological reality.

The brain of a person raised in the age of print, who primarily digested books and physical reading materials, is markedly different from the brain of a person who learns through interactive screens, including images and videos.[4] If my brain had been scanned as a child and rescanned today, research suggests it would look physically different *in response* to my lifestyle choices. This is especially true given my rapid shift towards heavy online activity over the last eight years. The parts of my brain devoted to typing and swiping must now be huge, in contrast to reduced areas for music, or reading printed text.

In *The Shallows*, Nicholas Carr questions the gravitational pull of the internet.

> Over the last few years I've had an uncomfortable sense that someone, or something, has been tinkering with my brain, remapping the neural circuitry, reprogramming the memory. My mind isn't going – so far as I can tell – but it's changing.

---

* *Daggy*, for those outside of Australia, is an affectionate term that describes being unstylish and uncool (in an 'I'm proud to be uncool' type of way). It's good to be daggy.

I'm not thinking the way I used to think. I feel it most strongly when I'm reading. I used to find it easy to immerse myself in a book or a lengthy article. My mind would get caught up in the twists of the narrative or the turns of the argument, and I'd spend hours strolling through long stretches of prose. That's rarely the case anymore. Now my concentration starts to drift after a page or two. I get fidgety, lose the thread, begin looking for something else to do. The deep reading that used to come naturally has become a struggle.[5]

INTERNET PRACTICE

Before internet usage surged in the COVID-19 pandemic, the average Australian was already spending 9.4 hours a day in front of a screen (cumulative total). This is more than one-third of our nation's entire life spent in front of a computer, tablet, phone or television. To put this in perspective, we spend more time on a screen than we do eating, commuting, working and exercising combined. We also spend more time on screens than we do asleep (that is, 7.3 hours a night, on average).[6] As a blogger, online coach and small-business owner, there are times when my workplace habits require even more time online, especially when writing. That's a lot of time in front of a screen, 'practising' the internet.

Some habits are easier to form than others. When I was young, piano practice was a battle. My parents did their best, but I am a fighter by nature. During my teenage years, I argued bitterly to avoid music practice. Their expectations were not excessive, but some days twenty minutes seemed like an eternity.*

Imagine if I had dedicated as much time to practising the piano as I now spend 'practising' digital media? Nine hours a day playing an

---

* My wife and I recently purchased a second-hand piano and enrolled our children into lessons. I hope the expression 'what goes around comes around' is not universally true. That said, given the tenacity of my children, my wife and I are bracing ourselves for civil war!

instrument would have had a significant impact on my musical development and ability.

Imagine if the entire Australian population dedicated a third of their life to practising a musical instrument in the same way we 'practise' our screens. How might society change as a result? To start, it would need to build a thousand new Sydney Opera Houses to cater for developing orchestras. Parliament would need a 'minister for music' to manage the exploding arts and the shift in our values, resources and growth. Australians would be a harmonic people (pun intended) – a society built on sound! Music would define the country, but time dedicated to composition would come at a cost. Health, education, social services and sports would become less significant; not by design, but through neglect.

This example is ridiculous, but it demonstrates a point. Few of us consider our online behaviour to be 'practice' in the same way we practise music, martial arts or a manual trade, but neuroplasticity does not discriminate between repetitive tasks. The more we use our devices, the more adept we become at using them. The more we practise, the more we crave. The more we crave, the more we use. Is it any surprise that three in five Australians have 'concerns or negative feelings' about their screen time use?[7] Is it any surprise that our always-on behaviours might leave us feeling disoriented, distracted and unbalanced?

Even still, there is hope, because our biochemistry has a remarkable ability to remodel itself in response to our behaviour.

THE MYTH OF MULTITASKING

The most common symptom of excessive 'internet practice' is multitasking. Multitasking involves rapid, dynamic switching from one task to the next. From a neurological perspective, multitasking is not a desirable attribute. We are not designed to multitask.

The human brain is not biologically capable of processing two or more attention-rich activities at once. We can hum while doing the dishes, which is largely automated, but we can't perform algebra while engaging in a meaningful conversation. When we use a phone and laptop simultaneously, we are shifting from one input to the next without focusing deeply on anything.[8] By habitually exposing ourselves to digitally-enriched environments, we are reducing our capacity to concentrate and analyse information. According to the late Stanford University professor Clifford Nass, 'the neural circuits devoted to scanning, skimming, and multitasking are expanding and strengthening, while those used for reading and thinking deeply, with sustained concentration, are weakening or eroding'.[9] We may think it is an achievement to attempt multiple tasks at the same time, but in reality we are less effective than if we were to focus on just one thing.

Researchers have observed a reduction in grey matter density in the brains of people who regularly multitask – in a part of the medial frontal lobe called the *anterior cingulate cortex* (ACC).[10] The ACC is associated with motivation and emotional regulation, which explains, from a biological perspective, why heavy media multitaskers find it near impossible to differentiate between relevant and irrelevant information.[11] They demonstrate reduced levels of emotional and cognitive control,[12] poorer academic performance,[13] and are at greater risk of developing mood disorders.[14] In other words, when we scan our Facebook newsfeed while texting a friend, it's damaging to our health. It shrinks the grey matter in our brains, which in turn, reduces our ability to think deeply, regulate difficult emotions and concentrate.

I'm not a neuroscientist. My area of interest is personal productivity. If you gave me a human brain to play with (admittedly an unusual thing to do), I wouldn't have a clue where to find the anterior cingulate cortex. But I do see changes in my own habits and the habits of my clients. Almost all of my clients engage in the online world more than they did a decade ago. They routinely use handheld devices and are more likely to use multiple devices at the same time. As multitasking increases, our capacity to think deeply and focus on one task for a sustained length of time diminishes. If we dive deeply into digital technology, without reflecting on our behaviours, we become 'suckers for irrelevancy' – leading busy, reactive and ultimately unproductive lives.[15]

PRACTISE MAKING SPACE

Everything we do online has neurological consequences. Whenever we swipe a screen or browse a search engine, we alter the biochemical makeup of our brains. This isn't a problem – it is how we reduce the mental effort required to perform repetitive actions. Neuroplasticity only becomes a problem when we reinforce unhealthy behaviours – spending hours switching between multiple tasks discontinuously. Do this, and we lose our capacity to sit still, stay focused and pay attention to what matters most. These neuroplasticity changes are not healthy or desirable. They represent clutter, not space, in the inner workings of our minds.

Many of the most life-enriching experiences are not found in front of a screen. It is critical to unplug from time to time, to rebuild neglected neural pathways and rebalance the scorecard. Again, we return to the value of space. Silence, deep thinking, contemplation and self-reflection require practice and repetition. Relationships also require practice – the ability to start a conversation with a stranger, make a joke, maintain eye contact, communicate feelings or empathise with another person without an emoji. To master these essential human skills, we need to habitually unplug from our devices. We need to make space to enjoy quieter moments.

Spacemaking is not coincidental. It is not a fortuitous accident that occurs whenever the phone runs flat. Unplugging as a habit is an intentional practice designed to retrain the brain to think in different ways. It is a deliberate choice to counteract the hyperactive pace of digital living in exchange for something better. I appreciate how difficult this can be, which is why in part four of this book you will find practical guidance on how to begin unplugging. Be encouraged. It *is* possible to change your habits and neural pathways. But to do so will require embracing a wide variety of skills that don't require a screen. Why not start in small ways? Enjoy a cup of tea without the phone. Take your niece to the park. Bring out a board game. Play a musical instrument. Write in your journal. Pray with a friend. Laugh out loud. Marvel at the intricate patterns of moss on a rock. Cook a new recipe. Concentrate on a puzzle. Cry on someone's shoulder. Read a difficult book. Sleep, rest and re-energise your brain.

We all need a mirror – an external point of reference to snap us back to reality. Unplugging can be our point of reference. If we feel concerned by the amount of time we are online, we can switch modes and shift habits. By doing this, we can broaden the neural pathways in our brain, to focus, pause and feel human.

IN SUM

- The human brain is malleable and adapts to our conditions. The biology of our brain changes whenever we repeat an action habitually. (Remember a walking trail can become a multi-use path in response to repeated use.)

- Our habits have neurological consequences. Sometimes we are surprised by these consequences because they happen imperceptibly over time. (Remember Susan and her rotated neck, and my 'Command-Z' response when hanging a painting.)

- The digital world is changing how our brains process and perceive information. This can be positive, but not if we over-practise the internet. (Remember my ponderings about swapping internet and piano practice.)

- Multitasking has negative consequences for our brain and behaviours. By losing grey matter, we reduce our ability to think deeply, regulate difficult emotions and concentrate.

- Neuroplasticity is a wonder of human biology and can work in our favour. Rather than spend too much time practising the internet, we can embrace a broad variety of activities to increase our health and happiness.

SOMETHING TO THINK ABOUT

How much 'internet practice' do you get each day? Imagine swapping thirty minutes of the internet to master a different skill – what would you choose to do?

CHAPTER 4

POWER

In 1961, President John F. Kennedy boldly announced to the world that America would 'land a man on the moon and return him safely to the earth before the decade was out'.[1] It was a radically ambitious goal to unite a nation and inspire collective action.

NASA was massively underprepared. They lacked the computer technology to navigate a spacecraft moving at thirty kilometres per second to a precise location on an orbiting moon. They lacked propulsion – the velocity needed to break free of the earth's gravitational pull. And they lacked life-support technologies required to keep an astronaut alive in zero gravity.[2] In every regard, NASA was ill-equipped and underpowered from the beginning. It would be a massive feat to overcome such obstacles without digital computing and their related technologies.

Imagine how much easier things might have been had NASA owned a smartphone. Remarkably, the iPhone contains more processing power than the entire computing juggernaut used to land humanity on the moon. In theory, my ageing iPhone could simultaneously guide many hundreds of Apollo rockets across space. It is 120,000,000 times faster and can process instructions 80,800,000 times more rapidly than the computing mainframe that guided Neil Armstrong in 1969.[3] That's incredible. Almost all of us have a supercomputer of enormous capacity in our pockets, and yet we barely raise an eyebrow.

Some power is invisible. It is so familiar to us that we fail to recognise it. Digital power is one such reality. Through our devices, we have vast access to knowledge, influence and reach, yet many of us aren't even aware of the power at our fingertips. Not only are smartphones powering satellites, they are opening up opportunities in every professional field – enabling remote health care, tracking disease outbreaks, navigating self-driving cars, detecting chemical warfare attacks, protecting rainforests from illegal logging.[4] Digital power is everywhere. What was once extraordinary is now commonplace.

By power, I am not referring to political, socio-economic or social constructs, but the power made available through our screens. By understanding and acknowledging such power – the power in our pockets – we are more likely to appreciate what we have, what we hold, and in doing so, handle it wisely.

Let's explore this further.

WHAT IS POWER?

Andy Crouch, author of *Playing God,* suggests we differentiate two distinct expressions of power – power that is *coercive* and power that is *creative*.[5] Coercive power is well understood. Lord Acton in the nineteenth century reportedly noted, 'Power corrupts, and absolute power corrupts absolutely'.[6] That's the nature of coercive power and those who wield it. Such power is gained at the expense of others. It dictates, controls and manipulates. It relies on force and fear. In contrast, positive forms of power are creative, generous and sacrificial. Creative power is 'the ability to make something of the world'.[7] If we inspire and influence using relationships, rather than control, everyone can benefit. By using skills and knowledge to better the lives of others, we share wins. Unlike coercive power, creative power has the capacity to expand and multiply, without reducing the power of others. The more you share it, the more it grows.

As we shall explore, having power is not always a bad thing. In fact, it can be tremendously helpful. If we are willing to acknowledge the power in our own lives, reflect on our motivations and generously share what we have, we are well placed to use power for good. We can make, rather than unmake, something of the world. This is particularly relevant when accessing the power of our devices.

TO WRESTLE WITH POWER

Bilbo Baggins knew what it meant to hold an article of power in his hands. He knew the beauty and allure of such an object and wrestled daily with its gravitational pull.

In J. R. R. Tolkien's iconic trilogy, *The Lord of the Rings*, Bilbo expresses his struggle with the ring of power:

> It would be a relief in a way not to be bothered with it any more. It has been so growing on my mind lately. Sometimes I have felt it was like an eye looking at me. And I am always wanting to put it on and disappear, don't you know; or wondering if it is safe, and pulling it out to make sure. I tried locking it up, but I found I couldn't rest without it in my pocket. I don't know why. And I don't seem able to make up my mind.[8]

Bilbo is an unlikely hero. In Tolkien's world, Hobbits were unassuming, incorruptible halflings who rarely strayed from the Shire. Unlike dwarves, elves and humans – who tended to lust for control – Hobbits were simple, unassuming folk. They resisted the temptation to take power for themselves and therefore were found worthy of carrying the ring. Tolkien's story may be fantasy but it speaks of humanity and reminds us of higher virtues, such as integrity, goodness and simplicity. At the same time, Tolkien also illuminates the darkness of the human condition.

Like Bilbo's ring, our devices amplify and extend the human condition. Our media use magnifies our motivations, drives and compulsions. A healthy inner-life – mental, emotional and spiritual – amplifies our capacity to love, learn and lead through our screens. The same is true for the worst of humanity – our narcissism, fear and resentments find an equally strong voice online. By examining ourselves and acknowledging the power extended through our devices, we can become more responsible wielders of such power.

USING POWER FOR GOOD

Power comes in many forms – knowledge, wealth, physical strength, social status – anything that enables us to exert influence positively or negatively. In this way, most of us have power, in varying degrees. When I first explored this idea in my own life, I realised just how many resources I had at my disposal – professional networks, qualifications, good health, broad relationships. I'd never considered myself a particularly powerful person, but as I stepped back and assessed my life, I became increasingly aware not only of the power I held, but also of the responsibility to use that power for the good of others.*

Around this time, a friend of mine approached me with a problem. Robert had held the same job for more than a decade and felt trapped in his career.[9] He wanted to become a manager but lacked the human resources experience needed to become a team leader. When the 'perfect job' came up – a newly created position to lead his existing team – Robert didn't get an interview. His written application barely addressed the selection criteria and showed gaps in his experience. After Robert shared his frustrations with me, it became obvious that my friend needed help.

I knew Robert well and was confident that, if given the chance, he would become a strong team leader. When the job was re-advertised, I coached Robert and used my knowledge to draw out leadership stories from his past. Together, we rewrote his job application, using the language of leadership. I coached my friend to answer behavioural

---

* In writing this example, I acknowledge that my experience is one of advantage as a straight, educated, middle-class and able-bodied male. From a position of power rather than powerlessness, I don't pretend to understand the experiences of those who battle against structural inequality and discrimination because of their gender, ethnicity, religion, education or beliefs. I am deeply grateful for the opportunities that I have been given.

questions that might arise at interview. I acted as a referee to use my influence to strengthen his application.

In the end, it was Robert's persistence and character that awarded him the job, but my power that unlocked his ambition. Sharing my power with Robert was not dominating or controlling, but life-affirming. It felt good to help a friend out, no strings attached. My power and knowledge expanded his power by opening up his career. Robert might even pay this gesture forward, helping others in a similar way.

This is the nature of power as a positive force. Whenever we give away time, knowledge, energy, money or relational currency, others benefit, and everyone's power is magnified. The same is true in the digital world.

THE MULTIPLICATION EFFECT OF DIGITAL POWER

At the height of the COVID-19 pandemic, during a lengthy, enforced lockdown, I went for a mountain bike ride to clear my head. This turned out to be a bad idea. I returned from hospital with multiple lacerations, a dislocated finger and a fractured kneecap. Stuck in a brace for over three months, I was forced to spend much of my time working, sleeping and eating in one room. I was physically incapacitated, frustrated and trapped at home.

But never powerless.

I still had access to digital power! Armed with a laptop and an internet connection, this period of enforced inactivity gave me an opportunity to pursue a creative idea.

For a number of months before my accident, I had been ruminating on how to help others affected by COVID-19. With the world in crisis, people were feeling isolated, fearful and anxious. Through my past experiences in building faith communities, I felt inspired to create a framework to gather people in small groups using Zoom. The intention was to create a movement of hope-filled communities, online, to practise thankfulness, share challenges, help neighbours and pray together.

Stuck in my bedroom with nothing else to do, I developed a training course and shared my idea with others. A remote team of leaders gathered around me, and over the next few months we trained more than six hundred people to start more than one hundred and twenty Hope Groups. We gave our resources away for free. Momentum developed, and others began to translate and use my training in other languages. Before long, we had groups world-wide, meeting in person as well as online. Stories flooded in from people giving and receiving help as a result of this initiative. A single mother, who was unemployed, gave a generous gift of cinema tickets to encourage people in her street. A family living in Kenya made blankets for orphans. A lady in lockdown wrote an encouraging let-ter to her neighbour, sent by paper aeroplane over the fence. By the time I was able to get back on my mountain bike, Hope Groups had launched on every continent (excluding Antarctica, of course), in places as diverse as Mongolia, Colombia, Scotland, Congo, USA and the Cayman Islands.

This is a simplification of a longer story, with other factors in-volved in our success – a bit of faith, an angel investor, the right people appearing at the right time – but without digital power, none of this would have been possible. My laptop unlocked my imagination, al-lowing me 'to make something of the world'. I acknowledge that not everyone has my skills or networks, but almost anyone can contribute in a positive way. We can give, serve and encourage others using our devices. This might involve a positive message, a kind word, the brav-ery to speak up, or indeed, the discernment to hold our tongue. We almost all have access to power in the digital age, in some form, and with it a responsibility to use it wisely.

DIGITAL POWER GONE SOUR

Not all digital power, of course, enhances society. Aleksandr Solzhenitsyn once suggested: 'The line dividing good and evil cuts through the heart of every human being.'[10] The world is not divided into good and bad people. Rather, we each have the capacity for love and violence, and depending on our circumstances, to act in great and terrible ways. This reality is reflected in the online world.

It isn't hard to think of individuals or companies who have harnessed the power of technology for selfish gain. Democratising knowledge and decentralising communication have exposed the best and worst of humanity. Read the news, and you are likely to notice powerful people using digital platforms to 'unmake' the world. More concerning still, as outlined in Cal Newport's *Digital Minimalism*, is the addictive design of social media and search engine tools. Many of the companies we trust use psychology and behavioural science to monetise our addictions. By adding reward-loops and dopamine-inducing notifications, we end up spending more time eyeballing products, expanding our data profile, and therefore, increasing our monetary value for targeted advertising.[11] This is, of course, coercive power, advantaging those who control the cloud. Lord Acton, I imagine, would protest.

POWER AND RESPONSIBILITY

'With great power comes great responsibility', so the saying goes.[12]

When I first learnt to drive a car, my mother warned me: 'Always remember that driving is a privilege. A car is a powerful machine, and it can kill people.' Mum wanted me to drive responsibly, stay sober and concentrate on the road. Her intention in warning me was not to scare but to prepare me, as she transferred greater freedom and responsibility. I needed to be aware of this power and use it with respect and proficiency.

Likewise, as we expand our reach through digital communication, we must become cognisant of the responsibility that comes with that. If we fail to respect our devices, they have a way of acting harmfully against us and others. There are few disadvantages to being cautious, or at the very least, handling our power tools with care. The alternative is to dive in rashly and get caught off guard, trapped in an addictive cycle that is neither healthy for us nor the ones we love. Digital trappings are often hidden from view – as the expression goes, 'the most dangerous enemy is the one you cannot see'. It's both wise and realistic to be aware that each and every one of us is impacted by the centripetal force of our smartphones. Digital proficiency, like driving a car, can only be strengthened by respecting and taking responsibility for such power.

THE POWER TO TAME OURSELVES

Jurassic Park is not just a book about dinosaurs. In contrast to Spielberg's Hollywood adaptation, Michael Crichton's original book is about power and control. Sure, there are plenty of dinosaurs, yet these are side-attractions to the main narrative.

For those unfamiliar with the story, Jurassic Park is a giant amusement park, built on a remote island, celebrating the advances of genetic science. Dinosaurs are reproduced in a laboratory by harnessing the blood of fossilised mosquitos. The park's creator, John Hammond, is both a visionary and an entrepreneur, who has no difficulty fusing business with science. Science creates dinosaurs, and business promotes these discoveries to the world.

Crichton's other central character is the brilliant yet habitually ignored chaos scientist, Ian Malcolm. Malcolm acts as the prophet of the story; he predicts problems before they occur and explains the meaning behind unfolding events. He and Hammond are at loggerheads from the beginning – Malcolm warns against manipulating living systems as if they were a commodity. Following the devastating rampage of an escaped herd of Velociraptors, Malcolm provides a poignant discourse about progress and power:

> Most kinds of power require a substantial sacrifice by whoever wants the power. There is an apprenticeship, a discipline lasting many years. Whatever kind of power you want. President of the company. Black belt in karate. Spiritual guru. Whatever it is you seek, you have to put in the time, the practice, the effort. You must give up a lot to get it. It has to be very important to you. And once you have attained it, it is your power. It can't be given away; it resides in you. It is literally the result of discipline.
>
> Now, what is interesting about this process is that, by the time someone has acquired the ability to kill with his bare hands, he has also matured to the point where he won't use it unwisely. So that kind of power has a built-in-control. The discipline of getting the power changes you so that you won't abuse it.

But scientific power is like inherited wealth: attained without discipline. You read what others have done and you take the next step. You didn't earn the knowledge for yourselves, so you don't take any responsibility for it. You stand on the shoulders of geniuses to accomplish something as fast as you can, and before you even know what you have done, you have patented it, and packaged it, and slapped it on a plastic lunchbox.[13]

According to Crichton, the way a person attains their power is important. Power that is owned and internalised, as a result of struggle and discipline, can be kept in check – this is *tamed power*. The other is *inherited power* – attained without discipline or cost. Both forms of power look similar from the outside but differ in substance. One is restrained and the other exploited. Inherited power is seductive and often uncontrollable – it enables people to achieve great things without requiring them to understand why they can do what they do.

At the end of *Jurassic Park* (the movie), John Hammond acknowledges the error of his ways. He escapes in a helicopter and enjoys one last glimpse of his island paradise as it shimmers in the sun. In Crichton's original story, Hammond's exit is far less Hollywood-esque. Rather than learning his lesson, Hammond clings to control until the very end. Alone in a rainforest, he is poisoned and slowly disembowelled by a pack of prehistoric birds the size of chickens.[14] Although a bit gruesome, Crichton's message is simple: those who do not understand the power given to them are prone to being undone.

I cannot help but see parallels in our own time. We can predict the weather, text family in China, order activewear online, without sacrificing anything. Digital power is inherited power. For the consumer, it does not take years to develop, learn or appropriate. It does not require hard work or sacrifice and has none of the built-in control mechanisms associated with self-mastery. Our devices may not disembowel us (that would be most unusual), but they do give us influence, at times, greater than our maturity to handle such power. If we are to master our devices, rather than the other way round, we must respect digital power and use it selectively, to create and serve, rather than simply take and consume.

POWER DOWN TO POWER UP

There is a paradox to power, particularly digital power. 'The true power that is available to us, the power that multiplies power, lies on the other side of the choice to empty ourselves of power.'[15] According to Andy Crouch, those who wield power wisely are the ones who understand it most and need it least. In my mind, this is why we unplug. Such a separation is healthy and life-giving. By letting go of power, Spacemakers come to respect it more fully. We power down to power up. By unplugging from our devices, we optimise our ability to make something good of the world – to give, serve and create.

IN SUM

- Most of us have access to power, through digital tools. (Remember NASA had less computing power than an iPhone when they sent 'a man to the moon'.)

- Power can and should be used for good. (Remember how I shared my power to advance a friend's career and also used a laptop to launch a movement.)

- Humans have the potential to help and harm. By acknowledging this, we become better wielders of digital power. (Remember Bilbo Baggins and his ring of power.)

- With great power comes great responsibility. The freedom afforded to us by digital media must be balanced with personal responsibility. (Remember how my mother warned me about driving safely.)

- Digital power is inherited power, acquired without practice, personal sacrifice or self-mastery. Such power is readily misused unless we tame ourselves. (Remember Jurassic Park and the prophecy of Ian Malcolm.)

- Power down to power up. There is value in unplugging from our devices, to make something good of the world.

SOMETHING TO THINK ABOUT

In what ways do you have power? And how might you use digital power to help others?

CHAPTER 5

FREEDOM AND CHOICE

You may have heard of the Five Monkeys experiment.

Behavioural scientists put five monkeys in a cage. In the centre of the cage was a ladder, and at the top of the ladder hung a delicious bunch of bananas. There was nothing unusual about this enclosure except for a set of sprinklers at the top of the cage.

Whenever a curious or hungry monkey climbed the ladder, scientists activated the sprinkler system and drenched the primates with cold water. This was an unpleasant experience, and after repeating this once, twice, and three times, our sensible monkeys stopped pursuing bananas.

Then the experiment gets interesting. Scientists removed one monkey from the cage and replaced it with a new monkey. As predicted, it didn't take long for the new monkey to spot the bananas and start climbing the ladder. The response from the rest of the pack was merciless. They pulled and scratched, aggressively jumping on the climbing monkey to stop it from reaching the bananas. After experiencing an adverse response on a number of occasions, the new monkey adapted to pack rules. The ladder was out of bounds. The monkey stopped pursuing bananas.

Next, a second original monkey was removed and replaced by another new monkey. Same response. The entire group dragged the new monkey away from the ladder.

Eventually, all five monkeys were replaced. None of the original group remained in the cage. The new pack of monkeys avoided climbing the ladder and eating bananas, even though none of them had been soaked with water. Ladder avoidance became normative behaviour; an engrained culture so to speak.

Why were bananas out of bounds? Why were ladders avoided? If these monkeys could speak, they might struggle to explain their behaviour: 'Ladders and bananas? I'm not really sure why we avoid them. We're monkeys, I suppose. That's just how we do things around here!'[1]

REASON IS BASED ON STORY

You and I don't perceive the world as it is. We perceive the world as we see it. This may sound like a technicality, but it is important for us to grasp.*

Most of us think of ourselves as rational beings; individuals who value logic and reasoning and who see the world objectively. Yet in reality, no one is objective. We make decisions, day by day, based on a set of untested ideas and assumptions that form our world view. This world view is built on beliefs, not just facts. At the heart of it all is story.

Think of an onion with rings (without thinking of the ogre Shrek). At the centre of the onion is our *story* – a series of foundational ideas and beliefs that help us make sense of who we are and why we exist. Some of these are existential in nature – we are 'meaningless dust', 'part of the universe', or 'made in the image of God'. Others are personal, involving place, family, gender, ethnicity. Many of our stories are hard to articulate. They are influential and yet invisible. Our deep stories shape our world view and determine how we think, reason and act.[2]

The next onion ring is *reasoning*, our determination of what is

---

* In *Thinking, Fast and Slow*, Nobel Prize-winner, Daniel Kahneman, explains how two systems in your brain are constantly fighting over control of your behaviour and actions: *fast thinking* (system 1) and *slow thinking* (system 2). We are over-confident in how we assess our own logic and judgement. We struggle to think statistically, jump to conclusions, make associations and use shortcuts to bypass objective analysis – influenced by our beliefs and background (London: Penguin Books, 2011).

rational and irrational, based on our story. There are 'facts' all around me. I have a window on my right. The air is warm. My hair is black.

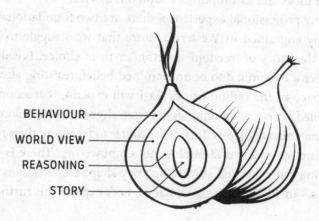

BEHAVIOUR
WORLD VIEW
REASONING
STORY

We cannot pay attention to every fact, so we must choose and use information selectively. Two people may notice the same set of facts and interpret them differently because of their foundational assumptions. One woman may wear a bikini at the beach, and another a full-length burkini.[3] For the former, bare skin is an expression of independence, autonomy and femininity. For the latter, covered skin represents modesty, purity and dignity. Who is right? Who is wrong? Who is logical or illogical? Both and neither.[4] Our stories inform our logic and reasoning, which in turn, creates a world view.*

I have spent years seeking to understand why we are reluctant or unable to make space in the clutter of digital life. Why is it so difficult to unwind digital habits that, a decade ago, were non-existent? Why do we open our phones first thing in the morning and last thing at night? Why do we habitually fill our lives with more rather than less? The answer to these questions, although multi-faceted, necessitates understanding our stories. Space is rarely created through habit

---

* Philosophers use different terminology to describe the impact of beliefs on behaviour. I have simplified a number of complex ideas to avoid getting bogged down in an explanation of dogma, plausibility structure and mythology. I have added further thoughts in the endnotes for interested readers.

change alone. Our stories, left unexamined, create inertia to meaningful change. To make and maintain space, we must tackle and dethrone invisible ideas and assumptions within our stories.

In my professional experience, there are two foundational stories so deeply engrained in Western culture that we struggle to identify them – the 'story of freedom' and the 'myth of choice'. Freedom and choice are a dynamic duo of unexamined belief, resisting attempts to make space in the online world. As I will explain, if freedom is *unconstrained liberty*, then unplugging from digital media is suppressive rather than advantageous. If choice *equates to* freedom, then reducing our online options is undesirable, not empowering. There is value in examining our inherited stories, for they shape our attitudes and behaviours – including our digital habits. Let's explore this further.

THE FREEDOM NARRATIVE

We all desire freedom, but what exactly is it? And what does it mean to be truly free?

Freedom is a complex idea, defined by the Oxford Dictionary as 'the power or right to act, speak, or think as one wants'.[5] When using the term, I am not referring to freedom in a legal manner – discussing human rights, freedom of speech or freedom of association. These fundamental civil liberties are enshrined in law and, although important, are beyond this discussion. When I talk about freedom, and the story of freedom, I am referring to our private world – the way we use our time, money and attention in our own lives. We might call this personal autonomy or personal freedom. It is the freedom to act and make choices, as individuals, within the broader framework of the law.

Although this may stand as a technical definition, it fails to capture the heartbeat of what freedom means to you and me. Freedom is sacred and personal. It is our right to choose a career, move cities, eat vegan, choose a partner, or wear red with pink. Freedom, as a story of unrestricted autonomy, is deeply engrained in our psyche in the West.

We are raised in this narrative at a young age, and it influences how we think, act and consume.

THE STORIES WE TELL OUR CHILDREN

All cultures share stories with their children. Fables and parables reinforce the collective beliefs and values of a people, generation by generation. In traditional cultures, elders use song and poetry, history and mythology, to communicate meaning. Identity is forged around a campfire; stories from the past inform the future. The same is true in our culture, although the medium is different – our stories are pre-packaged, animated and accompanied by a catchy sing-a-long soundtrack. These are, of course, the movies released every holiday season by Disney, Pixar and others film studios, communicating a message about what it means to be free.

At first glance, every Disney movie tells a different story. Some feature princesses; others cars, fish, planes, dogs or robots. Yet the story behind the story, the big story that drives most Hollywood movies, is what I call the 'freedom narrative'. Here's the plot: the story begins with a central character, constrained by their family, their village or their tradition. A conflict occurs, and they escape; sometimes in rebellion (like in *Brave*, *Tangled*, *Inside Out* and *Moana*), or more often after a parental figure dies or is assumed dead (think *Frozen*, *Up*, *Finding Dory* and *Big Hero 6*). This creates a vacuum or liminal space where the hero becomes 'free' to discover who they really are. Next is an adventure, where they are tested internally and externally, followed by an awakening, where they discover their 'true self'. Once self-actualised, the hero returns home to rescue, restore or renew the mindset of the community they left. Sometimes a guy and girl (or two fish) fall in love, but in modern Disney movies that's not always the case. In every situation, however, an enlightened community lives happily ever after.[6]

Sounds familiar? This is the freedom narrative – the story of communities being saved by individuals who unshackle themselves from cultural constraint. They follow their heart. They trust their feelings.

They break the rules, and in doing so, become free. This story has been told and retold so continually that we barely see it anymore. If you want to be healthy and happy, you must shape your own path. Do what you want, when you want, without limitation ... and you will be free.

Freedom, in this way, is not just the removal of unreasonable bondages – such as poverty and slavery – but the elimination of all restrictions from one's path. It means to 'break free' from all community expectations, institutions, rules and regulations. Freedom, in this narrow definition, leaves little room for self-control, delayed gratification, community responsibility, parental obedience, boredom, relational resilience and moral restraint. I still love Disney movies and watch them with my kids. But these stories shape us. There are drawbacks to doing whatever feels right.*

DEBT, HEALTH AND RELATIONSHIPS

As appealing as it might sound, no one can actually live like *Frozen*'s Elsa. Unless you have genuine superpowers, it is unfathomable to 'let it go' and 'slam the door' on all personal limitations.[7] It doesn't work in practice. No one can lead an organisation, build a family, develop self-mastery or love for a lifetime, without a great degree of personal sacrifice and intentional constraint.[8]

Take money for example. I could say, it's my life, so I'll max out my credit card, take an overseas holiday and buy that mountain bike I've always dreamed of. Does this lead to freedom? Maybe, until fleeting independence is replaced by the long, drawn-out experience of debt.

Then, of course, there's physical health. 'Following your heart' is a recipe for overeating, particularly if it becomes modus operandi. Sleep, exercise and healthy eating are essential for long-term health. None

---

* The freedom narrative, at a societal level, does include two caveats: 1) I cannot break the law of my country, and 2) My individual actions should not limit another person's individual freedom, as they are equally sacrosanct. The interesting aspect of this second caveat is that it reinforces the idea that the individual comes first, with the community considered second. It also results in culture wars between groups of 'individuals' with conflicting interests.

of these habits are easy. They require a loss of short-term freedom in order to achieve longer-term gain. It may be easier to sit on a sofa and eat snacks all day, yet eventually these behaviours rob us of the ability to think clearly, move painlessly and live adventurously.

The freedom narrative is also misleading in the arena of love. Love, by its very nature, is self-limiting. Meaningful relationships require consistency, discipline and self-imposed restraint. An open, loose and carefree partnership may sound appealing, yet such relationships rarely last. Monogamous relationships, in contrast, built on mutual commitment and self-sacrifice, have been shown to increase life-expectancy, mental health and long-term happiness.[9] We wash dishes, put the toilet seat down, entertain our father-in-law and forego after-work drinks as a means of giving and receiving love. The cost is significant, but the benefits are extraordinary. In this way, 'true love' breaks the Disney freedom formula. Freedom is enhanced whenever two parties voluntarily limit their choices, relinquishing aspects of personal freedom for the good of the other.

Everything in life is a trade-off. Freedom is not eating what you want but choosing to eat in a way that promotes long-term health. Freedom is not spending what you want but prioritising your spending based on what matters most. Freedom is not doing what you want but strategically limiting your choices to pursue meaningful goals, dreams and relationships. This is true in almost every area of life, including our relationship with the online world.

FREEDOM IN THE ONLINE WORLD

I remember a conversation with a marketing executive called Stuart.[10] He was stressed, over-worked and in desperate need of more space. We reviewed his habits, including his online behaviours, and agreed to carve out more time to think, rest and reflect. To make space, I suggested that Stuart consider putting away his phone for a period of time at the weekend, to remove the temptation to check email constantly. This didn't go down well. In fact, Stuart found it offensive. Asking Stuart to limit his online activity was akin to challenging his personal autonomy. I was confronting his personal freedom narrative, and it was not appreciated. No doubt, many of us would feel the same way if someone challenged us to make such a radical change. Our belief in our right to remain 'always-on' is so deeply engrained that to consider limiting our options can be offensive.

If we understand freedom to be the absence of constraint, then limiting our options is to limit ourselves. If, however, freedom necessitates self-control and self-denial, then a series of well-designed restrictions is desirable.

THE CHOICE NARRATIVE

Alongside the ideology of freedom is a parallel and equally powerful dogma – the value of unlimited choice. Choice and freedom are kissing cousins. One myth does not exist without the other.

According to Barry Schwartz, in his TED talk on the paradox of choice, freedom is 'the official dogma of all Western industrialised societies'. All societies seek to maximise the welfare of their citizens. Western societies, however, believe that the way to enhance welfare is to maximise individual freedom through maximising individual choice. Schwartz explains the connection in this way:

> The more choice people have, the more freedom they have, and the more freedom they have, the more welfare they have. This, I think, is so deeply embedded in the water supply that it wouldn't occur to anyone to question it. And it's also deeply embedded in our lives.[11]

Schwartz argues that at the heart of our world view is a deep-seated belief that more choice equals more freedom. Conversely, and by extension, less choice implies less freedom. Saying yes to more options will increase our happiness, whereas reducing choice reduces happiness. This formula, if true, has significant implications for how we approach spacemaking in the digital age. Do we need more choice to remain happy and healthy, or could the opposite be true?

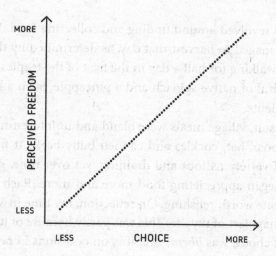

LIVING SIMPLY

In my early twenties, I spent some time in a rural village in Vanuatu, on the remote island of Malakula, as part of a youth leadership development program. As one of only two 'white-fella' on the island, I learnt and spoke Bislama (a dialect of pidgin English) and acclimatised to life without electricity, communications and running water. As part of the tribe, I hunted fresh meat by spearing wild boar, captured fruit bats and collected mud cockles in knee-deep mud. We gathered fruit and vegetables as necessary, planting corn, manioc, taro and bush-spinach deep in the jungle. It was a fascinating experience. I learnt to eat fresh game, boiled in water, with the hair still attached. I discovered that cockles replace salt when wrapped in banana leaves. I ate char-grilled corn and wood-fired coconut for the first time. I devoured fresh mangos. It was paradise.

That said, nothing in village life was particularly easy. There was no communication with the outside world, so I was isolated from family and friends. There was no hospital on the island. The nearest shop was half a day's walk away, and even then, the only supplies available were sugar, salt, canned meat, dry crackers and a smattering of spices. Not much in the way of choice! As a result, a surprising high percentage of each day revolved around finding and collecting food. We ate only what we managed to harvest that day, as determined by the season. I remember walking for half a day in the heat of the tropics just to harvest a handful of native spinach and a pineapple. Such a hard way to find ingredients.

As a result, village meals were bland and uninteresting. Our only meat was boar, bat, cockles and canned bully beef. At first, I found this lack of variety tedious and draining, yet over time, my attitudes shifted. I began appreciating food more and more. Each meal was a gift, every bite worth relishing. On reflection, my time in Vanuatu was one of the happiest of my life. This was partly because of its simplicity. The lack of choice was *liberating*. Sure, on occasions I craved familiar foods like pizza, porridge and pancakes (not together, of course), but even then, the ordinariness of my cravings surprised me. I learnt to celebrate small things, to be grateful. Despite the lack of choice in food and entertainment, I felt surprisingly free.

Then I returned home to Australia.

Travellers commonly prepare themselves for culture shock when visiting another country, yet rarely do we prepare ourselves for the shock of returning home. I remember the first time I entered a supermarket after returning from my adventures away. It felt like a movie – the type of movie where someone is abducted by aliens and transported to a distant planet. The ecosystem of a supermarket is perplexing. It resembles a factory more than a farm. Meat and vegetables are available in-season and out-of-season, day and night. Food is accessible, pre-cut and pre-packaged from around the world. The quantity and variety of choice is truly mind-boggling. I remember seeing a huge row of beef, chicken, pork and other gourmet meats, packaged for my pleasure. Someone had raised these animals, transported them, killed, cut and wrapped them in clean polystyrene containers, to save me the trouble of hunting in the jungle for a day. It was so convenient.

Yet, everything was also more complicated. All I needed was milk and a box of cereal. In Vanuatu, milk was not an option. In Australia, I had a choice of full-cream, low fat or skinny milk, ethical or home brand. Do I buy one litre and return in a few days, or save money by buying in bulk? There's also fresh bread next to the milk fridge – that could be nice. Actually, maybe I should change my mind altogether and buy a croissant for breakfast instead? But what type of croissant? There is plain or chocolate. If I choose a plain croissant, do I buy cheese and ham or jam? So much choice!

This was nearly two decades ago. Nowadays my supermarket has exploded with an ever-increasing range of milk, including rice milk, almond milk, soya milk, macadamia milk, coconut milk, chocolate/strawberry/vanilla-flavoured milk, condensed milk, milk powder, non-homogenised milk and lactose-free milk. They also have combination milk options in various forms, such as low sugar, low salt, low GMO, long-life, organic and non-organic milk, across multiple brands and home brands.* The variety is exciting, but also exhausting. It takes up brain space, creates distraction and somehow leaves me less appreciative of what I have.

THE PARADOX OF CHOICE

Choice, in the digital age, is almost unlimited.

At the time of writing, the World Wide Web had 6.26 billion web pages.[12] That's more than one web page for every person who lives on the planet. English Wikipedia has 6,230,786 articles covering everything from Aspirin to Zoolander.[13] If you give yourself the 'freedom' to choose from this unlimited array of options, you can quite literally spend the rest of your life browsing.

Barry Schwartz argues that our culture has moved beyond a point where choice is healthy. In fact, the opposite is true: 'There is no question that some choice is better than none, but it doesn't follow that more choice is better than some choice. There's some magical amount. I don't know what it is. I'm pretty confident that we have long since passed the point where options improve our welfare.'[14] This sounds like

---

* It is worth acknowledging that the Western narrative of personal freedom and choice is not available to everyone who stands in the milk aisle. Access to wealth impacts our practical choices. There are many for whom the only *actual* option is the three-litre home brand milk.

another inverted-U curve to me. Too little choice is a barrier to thriving. Too much choice is equally counterproductive. In the middle is the sweet spot – a healthy balance between accessibility and simplicity. Having overreached as a culture, re-correcting our course is a brave, necessary step.

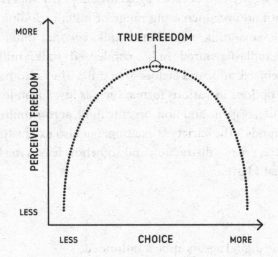

With more choice comes higher expectation. We demand more and enjoy less. We are overloaded by options and paralysed by indecision. We struggle to eliminate non-essentials and experience the fear of missing out. Beyond a certain point, choice stops being freeing and starts enslaving. Too much choice, and we erode our capacity to enjoy a simple, thankful life.

THE CHOICE TO BE PRESENT

Some parents are saints. Especially when they drive their children to after-school sports clubs. Rain or shine, they slice oranges, lace up boots, taxi their kids to a variety of grassy fields and cheer from the sidelines. It's great for the children but can be tough on the parent as a spectator.

Getting my children to their games (on time) is hard enough, but watching attentively can be harder. There are dozens of options to keep me entertained while standing on the sidelines. I can take out my phone to play Scrabble, respond to a text, or tweet #earningdadpoints for kudos. I can scan the news, check emails or respond to a thread on Slack. I try to restrain from doing these things (most of the time) and focus on the game at hand. But isn't this the downside of un-limited choice? Rather than be present in the moment, I must *choose* to be present in the moment. I am forced to decide what to give my attention to, which is draining. What if I make the wrong decision? What if there is a better option? Unlimited choice creates an allusion of personal freedom by promising more, but in doing so, reduces the simplicity of living.

Life by its very nature is mundane. Sure, there are bursts of excite-ment and adventure, yet the everyday-ness of life is something we all need to grapple with. It can be tedious to make sandwiches for lunch, pay bills or wait for a train. It can be harder still to live in the moment, without distraction. Sometimes you stand on the sidelines and noth-ing happens. Sometimes there's a goal and everyone cheers. It can be hard to limit our choices, but in doing so, we experience the fullness of ordinary moments.

THE CHOICE TO LIVE FOR THE GOOD OF OTHERS

An early Christian saint, Paul of Tarsus, wrote extensively about choice and freedom in his recorded letters to converts in Asia Minor. Freed from the rules of Judaism and Roman superstitions, Paul saw that first-century believers did not understand their new-found freedom. In this context, he writes: "'I have the right to do anything,' you say – but not everything is beneficial. "I have the right to do anything" – but not everything is constructive. No one should seek their own good, but the good of others.'[15] In other words, just because someone has the ability to do anything they want, whenever they want, it does not mean that they should activate these choices. Freedom, true freedom, is not the freedom to do anything, but the ability to limit actions to those that are constructive, valuable, loving and purposeful. I have the 'right' to escape online every time I feel tired, bored or uncomfortable, yet is this beneficial? Will it improve my ability to connect with, and positively influence, my colleagues, family and friends? Or will it achieve the opposite?

Our culture tells us that choice equals freedom, and that more choice equals more freedom. Closely related is the freedom narrative – the desire and expectation that we might live without personal constraint. Together, the ideologies of choice and freedom create a potent belief system that affect how we live, work and swipe. Adopted without nuance, our cultural stories limit our ability to limit ourselves.

As Spacemakers, we think differently. We pay attention to our stories and consider our baseline narratives. We recognise that true freedom is gained, not by getting everything we desire, but by giving up certain rights in the pursuit of meaningful goals, dreams and relationships. Limiting choices and embracing liberating constraints is a way to make space and find freedom in the digital world. By doing so, we can prioritise our energy on whatever we love and value the most, which, as we shall explore next, is the basis of digital love.

IN SUM

- As tribal people, we adopt the stories of our culture, acting in line with 'how we do things around here'. (Remember the story of the five monkeys and the bananas.)

- Our stories are influential. We start with a story, add reasoning and form a world view. (Remember onion rings.)

- Two cultural stories, in particular, influence our digital habits: the story of freedom and the myth of choice. Together, they limit our ability to limit ourselves.

- Perhaps true freedom is not the absence of limitation, but the decision to constrain our options for the greater good. (The Disney narrative, 'let it go', does not deliver in the real world.)

- Some choice enhances human happiness, but unlimited choice reduces life satisfaction. (Remember 'no milk' in Vanuatu, and mundane moments at kids sports clubs.)

- Freedom and choice are important, but we can re-examine how these play out in our culture. Less choice can be life-giving. Less freedom can be liberating. By nuancing our thinking, and our story, we can make space in the digital world.

SOMETHING TO THINK ABOUT

Has there ever been a time when too much freedom, or unlimited choice, has been problematic for you?

CHAPTER 6

LOVE

I remember the day we first met.

It was Christmas time, and we found ourselves sitting side by side on a bench seat, next to a busker playing the violin. She didn't say much at first, just polite conversation, yet the more we interacted, the more I liked her. I'd be lying if I told you we took things slowly. She was smart, creative and captivating. She took my mobile number, and the rest is, well, history.

That was more than a decade ago. Since then, we've laughed and cried, argued and made up. We don't always agree with one another, but I can't image my life without her.

I often wonder about that time we first met – was it love at first sight? Probably not. Yet from the moment I unwrapped her immaculately designed packaging and caressed her embossed Apple logo, I knew she would change my life forever.

A LOVE RELATIONSHIP

Although tongue in cheek, I really do remember the first time I unwrapped my first iPhone. I signed up for a twenty-four-month contract, sat down on that bench amid the hustle and bustle of people, and carefully unwrapped my new gadget. It didn't feel like a relationship back then, but it does now. And I really cannot imagine my life without it.

In the digital age, love and technology are intertwined. For many of us, engaging in the online world can feel personal, individual and connected – like a relationship. We may not 'fall in love' with our phones in a literal sense, but we do adore what they allow us to do. We are emotional beings, moved by feelings, not just reasoning. This is why so many of us 'love' our screens. They enable us to pursue our passions and desires, such as our hunger for success, popularity, security, wealth, entertainment or achievement. In this way, love and screens go hand in hand. We can love *through* our screens, and adore *through* our devices. No wonder it is hard to unplug – because unplugging is *emotional*. It requires that we break our digital attachments, for a time, to examine who and what we truly love.

EYES THAT CANNOT SEE

To explore our emotions further, let's go back in time. Imagine that we are in ancient Mesopotamia around 900 BC. A man cuts down a tree from the forest. He uses handmade tools to carve a wooden statue for himself in the shape of a bird, goat or fish. He places it in his hut, welcoming his new god with incense and vows. He does this in the hope that his family will receive peace, wealth and blessing from the gods.

After a time, this object is no longer inanimate but alive. The man gives honour to his artwork. He attributes meaning and identity to it. He bows down and makes this wood his idol. As enlightened twenty-first-century citizens, we may observe this curious ritual and think, 'Mate, that's not a god. That's a piece of wood you carved out of a tree!' And although this may be accurate, the primitive man is closed to such rationale. He cannot hear our opinion, see our perspective or consider our point of view because his creation has become his god. To this man and his household, this statue is now a living reality and promises to fulfil his greater needs. It is the filter through which he views reality. And the more he adores his handiwork, the more he begins to mirror the very thing he worships.

This is the story behind Psalm 115, an ancient Hebrew poem that shines light on our tendency to adore our own creations.[1]

Why do the nations say,
'Where is their God?'

Our God is in heaven;
he does whatever pleases him.
But their idols are silver and gold,
made by human hands.
They have mouths, but cannot speak,
eyes, but cannot see.
They have ears, but cannot hear,
noses, but cannot smell.
They have hands, but cannot feel,
feet, but cannot walk,
nor can they utter a sound with their throats.
Those who make them will be like them,
and so will all who trust in them.

For context, this sacred poem is recited by Jews and Christians as an affirmation of monotheism, the belief in a singular God. Beyond this, however, the psalmist is providing a cogent explanation of the human condition, which has particular relevance in the digital age. We are not as modern as we might like to assume – demonstrated by my translation of this poem.

Our idols are lithium, cobalt, glass,
made by human hands.
We have cameras, but cannot see.
Siri, but cannot speak.
We have touchscreens, but cannot feel.
5G mobility, but cannot walk.
Those who make them will be like them,
and so will all who trust in them.

Few of us worship idols made of wood anymore, but let's not be fooled – the desire to adore is very much present today. Like our Mesopotamian man, we take something useful, give it meaning and elevate it to the heavens. We can pour in our loves and our longings, dreams and desires, giving heartfelt attention to the objects of our affection. As we do so, it is possible to find ourselves closing our eyes, our minds and our hearts to alternative perspectives. We can struggle to recognise the cult-like devotion in our own rituals. Are we really so advanced? Are we really so logical? Have our digital habits truly matured beyond this Mesopotamian man?

LOVE AND WORSHIP

Love is one of our highest motivations. Love induces us to step out of our comfort zones. Love propels us towards others. Love compels us to worship.

As modern twenty-first-century people, we may think we are beyond worship, but the late postmodern novelist David Foster Wallace begged to differ. In his watershed commencement address at Kenyon College, he delivered these words:

> In the day-to-day trenches of adult life there is no such thing as not worshipping. Everybody worships. The only choice we get is what to worship. … If you worship money and things – if they are where you tap real meaning in life – then you will never have enough. Never feel you have enough. It's the truth. Worship your own body and beauty and sexual allure and you will always feel ugly, and when time and age start showing, you will die a million deaths before they finally plant you. … Worship power – you will feel weak and afraid, and you will need ever more power over others to keep the fear at bay. Worship your intellect, being seen as smart – you will end up feeling stupid, a fraud, always on the verge of being found out. And so on.[2]

As humans, we each have a propensity to worship someone or something, as an act of love. Each of us yearns for a sense of meaning. We want to love and to be loved. We desire a cause and a purpose and to connect deeply with someone or something beyond ourselves – either through our relationships or through our work, goals and dreams. Isn't this the stuff of worship?

Fyodor Dostoevsky, author of *The Brothers Karamazov*, famously wrote: 'So long as man remains free he strives for nothing so incessantly and so painfully as to find someone to worship.'[3] This is not an observation about religion but love. It is the recognition that, deep down, most of us are driven to adore, connect and relate in divine ways, as an expression of our humanity. In this way, Wallace's treatise on worship is sound. Each of us, somewhere along the line, decides to put our trust, our hope and our security into something, whether it be a person, object or an ideology. These subconscious choices drive our behaviour, shape our habits and determine our direction in life.

Our online activities are not exempt; almost any human desire can be expressed online. There is nothing wrong with liking our devices and valuing what they enable us to do. But when 'love' becomes dehumanising – negatively impacting our relationships, mental health or participation in society – we move away from intimacy and into addiction.*

UNCONSCIOUS WORSHIP

The challenge with worship is that we often struggle to recognise what we worship and when we are doing it. We can be blind to our own motivations. According to Wallace, it is possible to worship anything, and often we are unaware that we are even worshipping: 'The insidious thing about these forms of worship is not that they're evil or sinful; it is that they are unconscious. They are default-settings. They're the kind of worship you just gradually slip into, day after day, getting more and more selective about what you see and how you measure value without ever being fully aware that that's what you're doing.' If our worship remains unexamined, Wallace argues, then it is possible to worship just about *anything*. This is not always in our best interest.

---

* Though the concept of worship may be foreign to some readers, it is helpful when seeking to understand the motivations of the human heart – not everything can be explained by physiology alone. I was tempted to choose a safer word, such as *addiction*, which is easier to measure and quantify, but it is not the same idea. It is worship that drives addiction.

Take relationships for example – whether it be with our children, partner, parents, friends or teachers. People are easy to worship. In the language of psychology, this can lead to co-dependency and emotional dependence. It is good to love our children, but when we derive our raison d'être from our relationship with them, we will end up disappointed. Then there's materialism – a love of physical objects, such as cars, houses, model train collections or antique pottery. We can spend our lives chasing after and investing in these things, but they rarely deliver the long-term satisfaction we seek.

We worship ideas – political, religious, financial and ideological – finding ultimate meaning in philosophies and frameworks. We also worship celebrity, brands, sports teams, travel experiences, drugs, wine, jobs, trees, sexuality, renewable energy, tolerance, communities. Many of these things are good things. Some are great things. Yet if unexamined, or worshipped by default, they make terrible masters. They own us instead of us owning them – as is the case with unexamined power – taking more and giving less over time.

Now of course, not everything we do or love is worship. It is wholly possible to love someone (or something) deeply without worshipping them. We can value people and relish material objects. When it comes to worship, the key question to ask ourselves is this: 'What or who is the functional master of my heart?'[4] In other words, what do I love so much that it defines me? What do I orientate my life around when no one is watching? What captivates my thinking, day in and day out, shaping my everyday choices?

Once you discover these things, you discover who or what you worship.

ON THE TRAIN

During the course of writing this book, I have taken time to observe my own behaviour and that of those around me. How are we spending our time? What is captivating us? What are the functional masters of our hearts? It is amazing what I have noticed by stopping to look.

I'm on a train and observe a bunch of private-school boys in a four-booth compartment. They wear the same uniform. I smell sweaty shoes and cheap deodorant. They sit down, dump their bags and everyone pulls out their phone. No one talks, except for an occasional mumble. They pull out headphones and stream videos for an hour. Occasionally someone will laugh or show an amusing clip to a friend. They generally avoid eye contact with one another. I glance outside my nearest window. Silver Wattle trees are flowering yellow and the sun is radiant, yet none of the boys take notice. They are absorbed in their screens ...

Next, I'm at the dentist. The waiting room is clean and friendly. Before habitually pulling out my phone, I momentarily observe my surroundings. The wall is adorned with multicultural pictures of people with unnaturally white teeth. There's a mother with her child sitting next to me. The mother is playing a game on her phone. Her child has a tablet and is watching a movie. They don't interact with each other the whole time. I hope that the dentist doesn't use fluoride foam on my teeth this time. It smells like artificial strawberries and has a bad aftertaste. I go back to using my phone ...

Next, I'm on the tenth floor of a high-rise building, listening to an executive bemoan the health of his team. As a consultant, I have been brought in to develop and execute strategy. Brr-brr. My client's phone vibrates for the third time during our meeting, and he quickly scans his message. I don't really mind. It gives me a chance to check my inbox. He returns to our conversation but seems distracted by whatever he's just read on his device. Brr-brr. This time it's me. Only ten minutes until my next meeting ...

These are but a few observations – not research or science but a snapshot of what I see around me every day. Our collective behaviours are changing. One moment we were on a train, talking with friends; the next, solitary automatons, engrossed online. When did this happen? I'm not exactly sure. But somewhere along the way, a great number of us made a subconscious decision to move our habits, rituals and passions online, in the form of digital worship.

GROUND-FLOOR AND TOP-FLOOR PROJECTS

Although it is possible to worship anything, not everything is worth worshipping. It is possible to love some things way too much. Theological blogger, Steve McAlpine, uses the analogy of 'top- and ground-floor projects' to examine our existential behaviours. The top floor is for awe and wonder. Reserved for the transcendent, it is here that we keep our most precious things. We enter the top floor whenever we ponder deeper questions like 'Where did I come from?', 'Why do I exist?' and 'Where am I ultimately going?' Ground-floor projects, in contrast, are secular not sacred. They include personal projects and goals – career, family, pleasure, experiences. We work hard for a promotion. We invest in shares. We shop at IKEA. These self-fulfilment projects are important. They take up the majority of our time and provide both happiness and meaning. They live on the ground floor – unless we push them up one level.

It seems to me that Western society is not sure how to use the top floor. Most of us spend little time thinking about otherworldliness – why worry about the existential when there's nappies to be folded, renovations to complete or coffee to be had … But ultimate significance must be found one way or another, so we find ourselves gravitating towards worship nonetheless. As a result, ground-floor projects are pushed up one level. Money, children, travel, sex, all compete for transcendent meaning. I believe this is to our detriment, mostly, because it's exhausting but also uncompromising. If we make career our god, we can sacrifice health and family on the altar of overwork. If we put our children on a pedestal, we can struggle to provide loving correction. If we elevate economics to the divine, we can devalue people and treat the environment as a commodity. In McAlpine's words: 'We now have several generations of well off, well-educated Westerners who are constantly in therapy, because they know that the huge amount of self-fulfilment projects upon which they embark should satisfy them but they are not.'[5] Now of course, nothing is set in stone. We can move our ground-floor projects up and down, depending on our season of life, so long as we are aware of them in the first place – acknowledging that we may, in fact, be worshipping. We can only do this by keeping our eyes open to who or what we are pushing to the top floor and remaining conscious of how our decisions are playing out over time – particularly in our relationship with digital technology.

DIGITAL WORSHIP

If it is true that we gravitate towards love expressed as worship, then it's only natural we will find a *way* to worship – through rituals, liturgy, songs or sacred icons. This is where worship and the online world intersect.

Most of us are more religious than we like to acknowledge. We start and end the day with digital routines that are laden with meaning. We may call these habits, but they are rituals nonetheless, designed to attain whatever we value most. As noted earlier, we 'love' our devices for what they enable us to do. This is why we panic whenever we lose our phones. This is why we struggle to unplug. Our screens capture our imagination, as religious relics have always done.

Let me give you a few examples, although I'm sure you can think of more. If our greatest yearning is social acceptance, we might dedicate hours on Instagram to manicure the 'right' public image. Everyone likes a good selfie, but when 'likes' are what we live for, we enter the arena of worship. The same is true for almost every desire, or longing or love. Our desire to be a better parent can be satiated through forums and blogs. Our hunger for sexual fulfilment is replete with online options. We can worship the cult of home interiors or escape from life with an entertainment binge. If success is more our thing, there are productivity apps to consume, and wealth to accumulate electronically. Many of these activities are positive and life-giving unless they become our gods. This is where emotional awareness comes in. When a passion becomes all-consuming, draining or compulsive, it's time to recognise what those things are doing to our hearts and our relationships. When the activities we cherish most are also the ones we resent, then it may be time to unplug.

THE PATH BACK AGAIN

So perhaps it's time to take a step back from our digital activities, to examine ourselves, warts and all. We might take some time to observe the impact of our digital habits on our identities, our desires and our direction. We might even identify the loves and longings behind our behaviours. As Wallace concludes: 'None of this is about morality, or religion, or dogma, or big fancy questions of life after death. ... It is about simple awareness – awareness of what is so real and essential, so hidden in plain sight all around us, that we have to keep reminding ourselves to stay conscious and alive, day in and day out.'[6] Such awareness, as Wallace describes, is worth fighting for, and for this we need space. We need time out to think. We need moments to breathe. We need lives that are deliberate, uncluttered and oriented around our deepest values. And to do that, we will need to take time out to examine our hearts and our passions and to redesign our habits in line with who or what we are choosing to love.

For we are first and foremost lovers, propelled towards love.

IN SUM

- Love is one of our highest motivations; it drives our habits.

- Love and technology are intertwined. We may not 'fall in love' with our phones in a literal sense, but we do adore what they allow us to do. (Remember the Mesopotamian man who made a statue out of wood and gave it meaning.)

- Worship is a useful concept for anyone seeking to understand the motivations of the human heart. It is possible to worship anyone and anything. We do this consciously and unconsciously, drifting towards adoration unknowingly. (Remember David Foster Wallace and his commencement speech.)

- Although it is possible to worship anything, not everything is worth worshipping. To discover who or what we worship, we must answer the question: 'What or who is the functional master of my heart?' (Remember the analogy of ground-floor and top-floor projects.)

- Self-awareness is important if we are to identify the loves and longings that are shaping our lives. What do I love so much that it defines me? What do I orientate my thoughts and choices around when no one is watching? (Remember my observations on the train, and how we are spending our time.)

- To be a Spacemaker, we need to be aware of who and what we worship and to avoid giving transcendent meaning to our devices. We also need to be intentional about why we are engaging in the online world.

SOMETHING TO THINK ABOUT

Think about one digital activity that you would hate to eliminate from your life. Why is it important to you, and how does it reflect a deeper love?

EMBRACE THE PARADIGM

Over the last few chapters, we've examined our relationship with the online world at a foundational level. Embracing the paradigm is essential if we are to see lasting habit change. We've explored the messages of media, the role of neuroplasticity, the challenge of inherited power, the narratives of choice and freedom, and the impact of love as worship. I have argued, using biology, sociology, theology and philosophy, that *more is not necessarily better* when it comes to making space in the digital age.

Digital technology is miraculous, valuable, and life-changing, if we use it wisely. And by wisely, I mean not continuously, for there is value and meaning in unplugging from time to time. Our devices are powerful, relational and habit-forming. Without awareness and intentionality, we may drift towards overconsumption, which inevitably results in spacelessness.

More technology does not make us indefinitely more productive. There is a limit to how effective we can be. If we start to slide down the right-hand side of the inverted-U curve, into hyperactivity, reaction and distraction, we lose the gains we desire most – higher productivity, greater happiness and increased purpose.

Awareness of why and how we are filling our life is the first step in spacemaking. As we examine our heart, our motivations and our habits, we can build awareness, be intentional and ruthlessly declutter.

PARADIGM
ON A PAGE

We all need a paradigm – an overarching framework to help us make space in the digital age. Here's what we've covered so far.

Technology: The ideas embedded within our technologies impact our beliefs and behaviours, beyond the downloadable content. It is wise to consider what impact these ideas have on our habits.

Plasticity: The human brain is malleable and adapts to our conditions. Digital multitasking has negative consequences for our brain and behaviours. Neuroplasticity can work in our favour if we practise and reinforce helpful habits online.

Power: Most of us have access to digital power through our screens. The freedom afforded to us by digital media must be balanced with personal responsibility. We tame power by letting go of digital power, as a way of taming ourselves.

Freedom and Choice: As human beings, our actions are influenced by our stories. Two cultural narratives, in particular, influence our digital habits: the story of freedom and the myth of choice. Together, they limit our ability to limit ourselves.

Love: Love is an engine that drives our digital habits. We may not 'fall in love' with our phones in a literal sense, but we do adore what they allow us to do. To unplug is difficult, because it involves breaking emotional and relational bonds with our devices that arise from digital worship.

MAKE IT
HAPPEN

Below are three questions to help you stop, reflect and gain the most
from what you have explored.

What *3 significant insights* have arisen from what you have read so far?

What *2 practical actions* will you commit to doing soon?

What *1 big question* do you still have?

PART III
THE PRINCIPLES

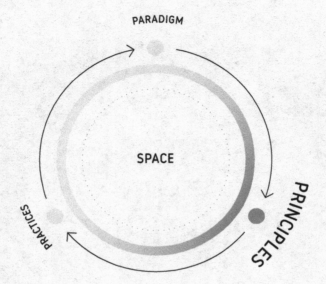

PARADIGM

SPACE

PRINCIPLES

PRACTICES

*If you go against the grain of the
universe, you get splinters.*

H. H. FARMER

I nearly gave up on this book. I hit a barrier and shelved my manuscript for more than a year. I didn't have writer's block. I wasn't struggling with motivation. I wasn't out of ideas. Rather, I ran out of space. Let me explain.

Spacemaker began with a simple dream. After slowing down and making space, I wanted to help others do the same. Originally a twenty-page e-book, my ideas soon morphed into a fully fledged paperback. I stayed up late drafting chapters. I used lunch breaks to research articles. I took annual leave to fast-track progress, entering 'monk mode' for weeks at a time. At the same time, I was running a business, volunteering in a church, and raising a young family with little spare time. Throwing in writing a book left me stretched beyond capacity. Of course, the irony of the situation wasn't lost on me. After a particularly stressful week, my ten-year-old daughter commented, 'Dad, you're writing a book about putting down your computer, but you're always on your computer.'

Ouch. I was writing about space, and yet felt spaceless myself.

It all came to a head one particular evening. After a tiring day, I came home in a shocking mood, started an argument with my wife, stormed out the room and kicked a hole in our bedroom door.

Yes, a hole!

Normally level-headed and self-controlled, I stood there, perplexed, staring at the hole in our door. There was no denying that something was wrong. I was no longer fun to be around; I was no longer patient; and I was no longer happy. And I definitely wasn't living by the principles contained within this book. I felt hypocritical and could no longer write with integrity. So I made a decision to close my files, archive my manuscripts and put my final chapters on ice.

Shelving my book felt like a little death. But how can one deny a hole in a bedroom door? Winston Churchill once suggested that 'writing a book is an adventure. To begin with, it is a toy and an amusement; then it becomes a mistress, and then it becomes a master, and then a tyrant.'[1] Yes indeed! Conceding that my book and I were becoming tyrants, I apologised to my family and rebooted my rhythms. I made space to think about my priorities and adjusted my habits accordingly.

I spent quality time with my wife, built a zip line for my kids and caught up on sleep, rest and exercise. This book was dead, but life was full again.

Now obviously, I did end up finishing and publishing this book. But my second approach to writing was entirely different. Rather than rush against the clock, I progressed my final chapters in a sustainable way. I regained my composure. Rather than write *about* my principles, I wrote *from* my principles, and that made all the difference.

Principles matter. They inspired me to start a book and compelled me to change my approach to writing it. They are, in many ways, the reason why *Spacemaker* exists.

WHAT ARE PRINCIPLES?

The late Stephen Covey wrote a lot about principles. He described principles as timeless, 'self-evident, self-validating natural laws. … When we centre our lives on correct principles, we become more balanced, unified, organised, anchored, and rooted.'[2] Unlike values, which are individualised and self-defined, principles are objective and external. They transcend cultures, apply in multiple contexts and are adaptable to different situations.

For example, the golden rule of relationships, 'do to others as you would have them do to you', is a universal principle. It is both consistent and flexible. In one situation, we might 'do to others' by praising a colleague in public. In another situation, we might challenge their actions in private, because this is how we would like to be treated ourselves. Other examples of principles include: 'be true to your word'; 'be proactive'; 'know thyself'; and 'seek first to understand, before being understood'.

In the digital age, principles are more important than ever before. Our culture is fluid and constantly changing. Rules are too rigid, and 'following your heart' is too loose. If we are to make space in the clutter of life, we will need to embrace principles that are both directional and flexible, and that guide us towards reality.

THE SPACE FRAMEWORK

In this part, we will explore the principles of spacemaking – five 'true north' principles upon which we can build our applications and practices:

S et Limits

P lan Patterns

A ssign Rest

C ultivate Community

E mbrace Silence

This framework is backed by research and is ripe for rediscovery in the digital age. They are not rules but timeless principles essential for human flourishing.[3]

Over the next few chapters, we will explore what it means to be a Spacemaker, by setting limits on our time; planning patterns in our schedule; assigning rest before work; cultivating face-to-face relationships; and embracing silence.

Are you ready to make some SPACE?

CHAPTER 7

SET LIMITS

In 1949, Bennett Cerf, one of the founders of Random House publishing, waged a fifty-dollar bet with upstart author Theodor Seuss Geisel, commonly known as Dr Seuss. It was a simple challenge – write a children's book using fifty or less child-friendly words.

This was harder than it sounded. *The Cat in the Hat*, Seuss's most popular book at that time, contained 236 distinct words and had taken nine months to pen because of the need to use simple, readable words for young children. Not one to give up on a challenge, Seuss dug deeper and produced his bestselling work, *Green Eggs and Ham*, containing exactly fifty distinct words.[1] This wonderful book has sold more than eight million copies and is one of the most popular children's books of all time.[2]

Limitations, as Dr Seuss discovered, force us to eliminate clutter. They increase our focus, enhance our creativity and help us to get the right things done.

THE VALUE OF LIMITS

When I started a consulting company, it was off the side of my desk. I had a family, a mortgage and was not ready to dive into a risky start-up without testing the water first. My 'real' job was managing a government health service, four days a week, allowing minimal time to launch our enterprise. My business partner, Tim Hynes, was in a similar situation. It was frustrating juggling two careers at the same time – a stressful tug of war that continued for nearly two years. Even still, looking back, this extreme limitation of time delivered unexpected benefits. We were forced to ruthlessly choose what to do, and not do, and this shaped the design and culture of our company. We narrowed our niche. We outsourced work and delegated much faster than we would have otherwise done. We automated communications. We systematised our processes. We expanded our training by uploading our content to e-learning platforms. Rather than Tim and I becoming a bottleneck for growth, which is common in consulting, our severe time constraints forced us to build a scalable business model from the beginning. As a result, we were able to sell part of our company to a third party, and now have more time and space to pursue other things.

This chapter is about setting limits. As explored in the paradigm, setting limits is a way of taming power. It is also a strategy to live in deliberate opposition to the freedom and choice narratives that compel us to chase more. As Spacemakers, we embrace the logic of limits by saying no to some things in order to say yes to better things. We willingly set limits in the pursuit of longer-term goals. We consider constraints across work and life, such as saving for a holiday, maintaining a healthy waistline, or shifting the amount of time we spend on a screen.

PATHOLOGICAL GAMER

Taipei, the capital of Taiwan, can be dreary in winter. Grey clouds cover the sky, and people head indoors to avoid smog. On 6 January 2015, a Taiwanese man named Chen walked into his favourite internet café to brighten up his day.[3] Tragically, he never walked out again.

Chen was a pathological gamer. He was addicted to the role-playing video game *Diablo 3* and spent hours slashing monsters in the underworld to escape reality. Chen was an ordinary thirty-two-year-old man with a typical life, but online he became a supernatural monk with divine powers. In real life, Chen sat cramped in an internet café, eating junk food, avoiding sleep, only leaving his computer sporadically to visit the toilet. In the role-playing fantasy world, he had the ability to cast spells, climb walls, collect gold and defeat the Lord of Terror, Diablo.

In *Diablo 3* you can die and respawn many times over, irrespective of how violently you are killed. Unfortunately for Chen, the real world wasn't as forgiving. After three days of non-stop gaming, and almost no sleep, Chen collapsed over his keyboard, foamed at the mouth and died. According to paramedics, his heart failure was the direct result of inactivity and physical exhaustion, caused by internet addiction.[4]

This is a sad and tragic story on many levels, yet it is by no means an isolated incident. In the last ten years, internet gaming deaths have been recorded throughout China and South-East Asia, as well as occasionally in the United States and Great Britain.[5] In 2008, according to *The American Journal of Psychiatry*, the average South Korean high school student spent 23 hours a week gaming. As a result, more than 210,000 children aged six to nineteen required medication or even hospitalisation, causing the South Korean government to label internet addiction as 'one of its most serious public health issues'. A decade later, almost 20 per cent of South Korea's population – nearly ten million people – are now at risk of internet addiction.[6] In China, 13.7 per cent of adolescent internet users meet the internet addiction diagnostic criteria – about ten million teenagers in total.[7] In the United States, as with Australia, aberrant behaviour is often undiagnosed because addicts access games from home, rather than from internet cafés. Therapists in such countries are not specifically trained to assess for internet addiction as they are in Asian clinics, and preventative measures are not widely implemented across the school curriculum.[8]

Concerns about the prevalence and impact of internet addiction are rapidly growing in the West. Recently, the American Psychiatric Association included Internet Gaming Disorder (IGD) in Section III of the DSM-5 (the mental health handbook) as a 'condition warranting further study'.[9] Specialised internet-addiction treatment programs and inpatient rehab centres are also appearing, such as The

Cabin in Sydney[10] and reSTART near Seattle.[11] Gaming may not be a full-blown health epidemic in the West, yet gaming deaths provide a warning to us all – unlimited online activity is bad for our health. Full stop.

HOW MUCH IS TOO MUCH?

Chen's story raises a number of questions for us to consider. When it comes to engaging in the online world, how much is too much? To avoid food, sleep and toileting is ridiculous to the extreme, yet when does 'healthy' end and 'unhealthy' begin? If I spend five hours a day online, is that too much? What about ten hours? Or fifteen?

Most research to date has focused on children. An Australian Government National Guideline, informed by the America Academy of Pediatrics, recommends that children under two years of age avoid all screen activities, including television, electronic media and DVDs. Between two to five years old, less than one hour per day is acceptable, extending to a maximum of two hours a day for young people aged five to seventeen years. This guideline is for entertainment-related screen activities, as opposed to computer-based study. The main message is clear. If you want your child to remain emotionally, physically and mentally healthy as they grow up, teach them to self-monitor the way they use screens.[12]

For adults, the message is more complex and nuanced. When examining trends, experts consider variables such as personality, age, occupation, media type and media habits. As explored previously, the average American adult spends 12 hours a day in front of a screen, which extrapolated, is the equivalent of thirty-four years of life.[13] This is a significant investment of time and energy and will inevitably impact our ability to invest in other activities, such as relationship building, physical exercise, practising a craft or engaging in deep thought. We are all different. Some of us will need more time online than others. Just don't be like Chen. Don't be limitless.

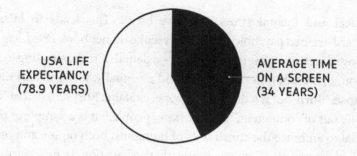

USA LIFE
EXPECTANCY
(78.9 YEARS)

AVERAGE TIME
ON A SCREEN
(34 YEARS)

KNOWING OUR LIMITS AS LEADERS

Recently, I re-watched the DC Comic blockbuster, *Wonder Woman*, set in the trenches of the First World War. In a battle scene, Diana (aka Wonder Woman) makes a dash through no man's land, dodging hundreds of rounds of machine-gun fire using only her gold armbands and a tiny shield. Diana overcomes her enemies in a glorious display of athleticism and is, of course, victorious.[14]

As entertaining as this movie might be, it is not real life.

In real life, humans fall down when shot point-blank. To be human is to live with limitations, to humbly accept our mortality and to embrace constraints. Now of course, intellectually we know this to be true, but in practice, we often pretend to be superhuman. Sure, we may not jump off buildings or wear underpants on the outside, yet when we strive to achieve near impossible standards, at any cost, we deny our humanity.

Leaders, in particular, struggle to slow down. We are hungry and self-motivated. We work hard and take risks. We stretch ourselves to the limit. These are positive attributes, unless we push ourselves too far, damaging ourselves and our teams in the process. We may be leaders, but we are not machines. We are vulnerable, fallible and prone to fatigue. We need sleep and downtime. We need fun and food. We need to stop and smell the roses from time to time. Whether we like it or not, none of us are limitless.

Life is more than work, and more than the things we can achieve. In the myopic pursuit of success, some of us ignore niggling signs of physical and mental stress, until we break. This leads to burnout. Harvard-trained psychologist Dr Borysenko, in her book *Fried*, suggests that overwork is a symptom of denial – a denial of reality leading to frustration, cynicism, inner emptiness and eventually, physical and mental collapse. 'Burn-out is a disorder of hope', explains Borysenko, that 'sucks the life out of competent, hard-working people'.[15] It is a symptom of our refusal to embrace the constraints of humanity, both online and offline. Hear me correctly. I'm not saying that exhaustion is necessarily our doing. We live in a demanding world with extremely challenging roles. Aiming high is admirable. Long hours are often necessary. What I am saying is that sometimes, as leaders, we lose perspective in our pursuit of success. We push ourselves harder than we need to, driven by pride, insecurity or fear, and avoid logical limits to our detriment.

In contrast, Spacemakers don't try to be superhuman. We acknowledge our weaknesses and appreciate our limitations. We take notice when our bodies are asking us to 'slow down', or our minds whisper 'enough'. By taking the long-view, we make space to rest and refresh, even when pursuing demanding goals. This is about accepting our frailty as human beings rather than striving to be what we are not. Grace Marshall puts it this way: 'I believe absolutely passionately in being human. Being superhuman is a lie that robs us of life and there is beauty in imperfection.'[16] I couldn't agree more. As we celebrate our limitations, our shortcomings and weaknesses, we can align our expectations with reality. We are human. Nothing more, nothing less. The world doesn't need you or me to be a superhero. Human is enough.

AUDIT YOUR DIGITAL HABITS

So how do we make a start? How do we embrace life-giving limits that help us make space in the clutter of digital life? A good place to begin, in my experience, is a self-awareness activity called the 'digital habit audit'.

A digital habit audit is a simple and practical way to better understand your baseline digital behaviours. The goal is to help you establish life-giving digital and non-digital patterns, and limits, in line with your values. By objectively reflecting on what you habitually do, you can increase your capacity to critique and therefore modify your rhythms. Keep a notebook by your side, and make a list of everything you do throughout the day, paying particular attention to your digital habits.

Here's an example of what the first step of your audit might look like, as a list of regular morning routines:

- Wake up to phone alarm
- Check social media newsfeed and scan inbox for new messages
- Scan political news on phone
- Go to the toilet (while scanning the news)
- Have a shower
- Review day by checking the calendar over breakfast
- Brush teeth
- Get on pushbike and ride to the office

After identifying your habits, spend time reflecting on your list. You may find it helpful to highlight positive habits in green and negative ones in red, visually representing practices that need to change. What habits are helpful? What habits are unhelpful? What habits align with your values? What habits will stop you from achieving your goals?

Armed with this feedback, you now have the information you need to re-establish better routines. Let's say, for example, that you are uncomfortable about how much time you spend scrolling the news, and instead, want to start each day in a more positive frame of mind.

Here is how your routine might change:

- Wake up to an 'old-fashioned' alarm clock (charge the phone outside of bedroom)
- Lie in bed and meditate on three grateful things
- Go to the toilet and think about how to tackle the day (no phone)
- Have a shower
- Make breakfast and turn on phone to check calendar, messages and email

- Brush teeth
- Get on pushbike and ride to the office

This is a hypothetical scenario. There is no right or wrong pattern for everyone. Your ideal routines will be shaped by your values, relationships, personal goals and stage of life. The aim is to become self-aware and intentional about when, where and how often you use your digital tools.

A DIFFERENT TYPE OF LOGIC

Rather than avoiding boundaries, Spacemakers celebrate the logic of limits. We unplug to avoid addiction. We audit our digital habits. We take time out to simply be. Making space involves shifting our mindset, not just our actions, as limits are healthy and boundaries life-giving. Dr Seuss discovered this when he wrote a book using just fifty words. Chen neglected this reality by gaming non-stop in an internet café. As leaders, we can celebrate our humanity by acknowledging our weaknesses. By saying no to some digital activities, we get to say yes to a range of other meaningful pursuits. We get to narrow our focus, establish parameters and implement predictable patterns in line with our values – which is the focus of our next principle.

IN SUM

- Limits are important for human flourishing. They help us to focus, create and set priorities. (Remember Dr Seuss and the strict word limit that led to a bestseller.)

- Our society has established screen-time recommendations for our children, and yet unlimited online activity is also damaging for adults. (Remember the story of Chen and his gaming binge in Taipei.)

- There is a tendency among leaders to push themselves too hard and burn out. Burnout is a symptom of a deeper denial, a denial to accept the fragility of our humanity. (Remember Wonder Woman and her arm bracelets.)

- Self-awareness can be increased by undertaking a digital audit. Keep a notebook by your side, and make a list of everything you habitually do each day, paying particular attention to your digital habits.

- We can embrace the logic of limits in all areas of life, including our use of screens. By saying no to some things, we build capacity in our lives to say yes to other things.

SOMETHING TO THINK ABOUT

Is there a digital habit that takes up a considerable amount of your time? What practical actions might be helpful to limit it?

CHAPTER 8

PLAN PATTERNS

It was the early Middle Ages. The Roman Empire had crumbled and with it, stability, order and discipline. The once glorious capital of Rome had been ransacked by barbarians, plundered and set on fire. Goths, Huns and other Germanic tribes were flooding the land. Roman society was in disarray.

The empire had provided safe conditions for trade and agriculture, education and infrastructure, but now everything was in flux. People were fleeing to the countryside. Roads and aqueducts were in ruins. Food was in short supply. The military had collapsed, and state borders were no longer defined. On top of this, the great Athenian schools of philosophy had closed after a thousand years of existence, and people were forgetting how to read and write. Nothing could be taken for granted, including family, state and vocation. Everyone did what they could to survive.[1]

Into this cultural storm entered a young man named Benedict.

Benedict of Nursia was born in Italy around AD 480. Born of wealth, he was disillusioned by the moral and social decay of Roman society and left the capital in search of a better future. Like many spiritual seekers of his day, Benedict became a hermit, living for three years in a cave at Subiaco, south-east of Rome. During this time, he matured in character and disposition, gaining the respect of those around him. He learnt to fast and pray. He studied famous works and developed a compelling vision for a new society. Benedict left his cave, gathered numerous followers and formed a monastic society on a hilltop called Monte Cassino. Eventually this group became the Order of Saint Benedict.

It is here, in this refuge, that Benedict wrote one of the most influential texts of the Middle Ages, simply known as *the Rule*. Inspired by the motto *ora et labora*, Latin for *pray and work*, monks devoted themselves to eight hours of prayer, eight hours of sleep and eight hours of manual work, sacred readings and works of charity. They shared everything in common and built habits and rhythms that reflected their values – making space for the things that mattered. Pray, work, sleep, repeat. This simple but reproducible pattern granted security for all who embraced the cloistered life. The *predictability* of the pattern created stability. Over time, many followed their example, and thousands of communities formed across Europe, creating order and prosperity in the wake of a fallen empire.[2]

From a historical viewpoint, Benedict did far more than revitalise Catholicism. According to historian Dwight Longenecker, 'by fleeing civilisation Benedict saved it, for it was the monasteries of Benedict that eventually preserved the culture of the ancient world'.[3] Monasteries are one of the primary reasons we have literacy, philosophy and poetry today.[4] With libraries vanishing, it was the monks who preserved and copied our ancient Greek and Latin manuscripts, thereby guarding Western culture. On top of this, they developed sophisticated business methodologies to stimulate and reboot the economies of Europe.[5] Monks baked bread, crafted beer, sold cheese, raised livestock and hosted guests, much like an ancient Airbnb. According to sociologist Rodney Stark, it was from the monasticism of the ninth, tenth and eleventh centuries that capitalism was first developed.[6] Monks were so productive and inventive that by the 1500s, a third of all the land in England was owned by monastic movements. Not bad for a simple pattern of work and prayer (with some savvy business dealing on the side).[7]

WHAT ARE PREDICTABLE PATTERNS?

Predictable patterns are repetitive actions and behaviours that shape who we are and who we are becoming. Our patterns reinforce our beliefs and codify our values. When we make our bed, catch a bus to work or scan notifications continuously, we are, in a sense, becoming our future selves. Because of neuroplasticity, our patterns influence our thoughts and emotions at a biological level, shaping our identity.

According to Pulitzer-prize-winning reporter Charles Duhigg, 'more than 40 percent of the actions people perform each day aren't actual decisions, but habits'.[8] This is particularly relevant when considering our technological behaviours. Although some of our digital patterns are helpful, others are unintended. We fall into digital routines without meaning to do so, propelled by the addictive design of the apps we use. The more we repeat these patterns, the stronger they become, absorbing even more of our time. If we are to rethink and recalibrate these habits, we will need to be intentional. The more we understand about our personal patterns – how they develop, and how they can shift – the more we are able to make space for the things that matter most to us.

Many books have been written about habit formation and the science of changing one's habits.* It is not my intention to dive deeply into this subject, or the psychology of changing behaviour. Instead, my aim is to provide foundational information to help us understand the importance of patterns in our quest for making space.

PATTERNS AND IDENTITY

According to habit expert, James Clear, 'every action is a vote for the type of person you wish to become'.[9] Our patterns shape our thinking, our actions and, ultimately, the life we live. This has been true in my experience ... reflected in my choice of beverage.

Few people enjoy coffee the first time they taste it. I remember giving my six-year-old son his first sip of coffee. His response was predictable, 'Oh, Dad, that's disgusting!' Coffee is an acquired taste. It is bitter, strong and has a unique flavour. Truth be told, when it comes to

---

* For a deeper dive into personal habit formation, both theory and practice, I suggest reading *The Power of Habit* by Charles Duhigg, and *Atomic Habits* by James Clear.

drinking coffee, I'm a late adopter. I didn't enjoy it much until I took up consulting as a career, which necessitated meeting numerous clients in cafés.

Now, I know that caffeine isn't particularly good for me. It makes my heart race, is bad for digestion, disrupts my sleep and is not particularly kind on the wallet. I didn't set out to create a rhythm of drinking coffee each day – it was accidental. I ordered my first coffee because others were drinking it. The more I consumed, the more I learnt to enjoy coffee. The predictable pattern of drinking coffee on a regular basis altered my perception of coffee. In a relatively short amount of time, I went from accepting coffee, to liking coffee, to loving coffee, to *needing* coffee. As my tastes changed, so did my identity. I went from being a person who occasionally drank a cup of coffee, to identifying myself as a 'coffee drinker'.[10]

Patterns form our personhood in a variety of ways. The more we eat sugar, the more we desire sugar. The more we exercise, the more we crave the feeling of exercising (well, some of us do, anyhow). The more we swipe our phone, the more we need our phone. The very act of doing something on a regular basis, as a consistent pattern, influences our desires, and the orientation of our heart. This is neither good or bad, right or wrong. It just is. The trick for anyone wishing to make space in a directional way, is to be intentional.

FORMING INTENTIONAL PATTERNS

The most productive leaders I coach are intentional in how they live and work. They are conscious about their priorities and values, and organise their lives around predictable patterns. Typically, they bookend each day with a wake-up and wind-down routine. They prioritise space for physical activity and deep thinking. They consider their digital behaviours when designing their routines.

Take Alan for example, the chief executive officer of a global retail company operating from Melbourne.[11] During a consultation, I asked Alan about his personal productivity habits and was struck by the clarity of his answers. As the head of a multinational company, Alan's career consumes most of his time, demanding extremely long hours. Whether we agree with his priorities, Alan is incredibly deliberate in how he sets about achieving his goals. He habitually makes space for the things that are important to him.

Alan begins his day at 5 a.m., pouring a cup of coffee before answering emails that arrive in his inbox during the night from America, South America and Europe. He eats breakfast with his children, engaging in conversation without his phone. Next, comes the train commute, where he clears all remaining emails, reviews his schedule and writes a mini-plan for the day using a dedicated to-do list app.

Once in the office, Alan completes urgent actions and delegates tasks to his personal assistant, before processing his inbox to zero again at 11 a.m. (now that Asia and Australia have come online). At 12.30 p.m., Alan heads out for a run to manage his stress and maintain fitness. This activity doubles as mental processing time to clear his head and focus.

Each week, Alan has a pattern to meet with each of his direct reports for an hour online. He values these relationships and prioritises time in his busy schedule to build rapport and unblock problems with his executive team.

Meeting rhythms are also intentional. Mondays, Tuesdays and Thursday are back-to-back with meetings. Alan only accepts an appointment if it is scheduled for fifty minutes rather than an hour. This allows him a ten-minute window between meetings to scan his email, document thoughts and delegate next actions. In contrast, Wednesday and Friday afternoons are protected from other people's agendas. Alan sets these times aside for higher-order thinking or to tackle projects that require concentrated effort.

Alan is an exceptional leader, with an extremely complex role and demanding portfolio. To stay on top of his game, he requires more discipline than most. What matters here is not his capacity but his intentionality. Alan's rhythms are designed, not accidental, and his success is reflected in his patterns.

Spacemakers are intentional in how we form patterns across our work and life. By examining our behaviours, both online and offline, and making course corrections, we can align our patterns with our priorities in a consistent and deliberate way. In doing so, we make space for the things that really matter. If we have completed a digital audit, we may already be aware of the patterns that we wish to alter. We can think about how to initiate these changes in a predictable, rhythmical way. There will also be a chance to explore a series of predictable patterns to unplug and unwind when we get to the 'practices' part of the book.

PATTERNS IN THE WORKPLACE

Predictable patterns are not only beneficial for individuals, but also companies, businesses and non-profit organisations. In any human system, values are caught more than taught, meaning that our repetitive actions speak louder than our words. If a team of people eat together every lunch time, they communicate different values than if they eat alone in front of a screen. Organisational culture, defined as 'what we do around here', is influenced more by conversations, meeting rhythms and social patterns, than by programs and policies.[12]

As a consultant, I work alongside organisations that are both creative and intentional in how they embed their values as collective patterns. For example, a skin-care company, inspired by Japanese culture, shape their office norms around the value of 'politeness'. New staff members are taught how to pour tea and organise their workspace in a minimalist way. They are instructed to reset meeting rooms using three bowls and a water jug, and are encouraged to talk quietly at lunch time. These may be unconventional practices, but collectively they create a peaceful, respectful, harmonious culture, in line with the founder's vision.

Netflix, according to co-founder and CEO Reed Hastings, also use corporate patterns to codify their values. Hastings attributes the success of Netflix to its culture of *candid feedback*, where honesty is so important that to disagree and not speak up 'is tantamount to being disloyal to the company'.[13] Staff are encouraged to say what they really think, even if it means confronting their boss in front of others.

Managers routinely seek feedback on their own performance during team meetings. Written 360-degree surveys (without anonymity) are required for all creative staff.* Live 360-degree feedback (where teams spend hours challenging one another over dinner) is routine. By recruiting top performers and expecting everyone to speak up, Netflix is maximising its ability to adapt quickly in a competitive industry, by leveraging the value of candour.

These are just two examples of predictable patterns at work, where organisations are intentionally shaping culture in line with their stated values.

PATTERNS IN FAMILIES

Predictable patterns are also a powerful way to strengthen families of various shapes and sizes. According to research, children who grow up with patterns are happier, healthier and more resilient,[14] as 'routines provide children with consistency, confidence, security, trust, and a sense of safety'.[15] Although too much rigidity can be counter-productive, routines such as eating together, doing the dishes, reading out loud and cleaning one's bedroom provide a secure foundation for healthy development. In the words of authors Mike and Sally Breen, 'predictable patterns are what love looks like in a family'.[16] If this is true, then establishing healthy patterns – including healthy *digital* patterns – can be an expression of love.

The digital and non-digital routines that we establish with our children, and model ourselves, will invariably shape our family's culture. Family patterns can either make space, or take space away from our lives, so Spacemakers reflect on how we relate and connect as a family,

---

* The 360-degree tool is a way of providing employees with performance feedback from different perspectives, including managers, peers, direct reports and customers. Feedback is traditionally written and anonymous, allowing others to say what they really think. A disadvantage of anonymity is that criticism is hard to process, especially when nameless. Mature, brave and honest conversations are often needed to resolve issues.

and build better patterns to communicate and reinforce the values that are important to us.

PATTERNS TO TRANSFORM A COMMUNITY

As we have explored, individuals, teams, families (and even monasteries) thrive when formed around predictable patterns. The same principle can be applied to almost any community of people.

We are all familiar with the African proverb, 'It takes a village to raise a child.' One of the challenges of living in a consumer culture is that we are busy, time-poor and self-contained. Many of us live alone. If we are to experience village life in a deeper way, we may need to be intentional about the rhythms and patterns we create in order to connect regularly with one another.

A number of years ago, my wife and I became aware of our need for a 'village'. We had moved cities to pursue our careers and found ourselves isolated with no grandparents or extended family support. We realised that we would need to make space in our busy routines to create a friendship network. Thankfully, we had a connection with our immediate neighbours – a professional couple with two young children – and decided to eat together every Wednesday evening at 6 p.m. We reasoned that each of us had to cook and feed our children either way, so why not do this together?

One week our neighbours cooked. The next week, we cooked. We took turns in opening our homes, keeping things as simple as possible. Wednesday night was not a dinner party, but a rough and ready meal that we happened to share with friends. We drank soup, or shared pasta, and cleaned up mess. Some weeks were short and sharp. Others were long and raucous. Over time, we became like family. We then invited other neighbours, who invited their neighbours, and our gathering grew.

A decade on (and more than five hundred meals later) this simple weekly ritual has become a defining event in our street. We consistently eat with twenty to twenty-five people from our neighbourhood, rotating houses week by week. One person cooks, another brings cheese, another bread, another ice cream, and of course, a few bottles of Shiraz. We share a table with international students, asylum seekers, unemployed singles, white-collar professionals, toddlers and teenagers – a rag-tag community of neighbours and friends experiencing life together. Truth be told, 'big dinner' takes a lot more energy than it used to, but it is highly rewarding. We needed a village, and in the end, this is what eventuated.

Looking back, it all started with a simple pattern of eating together once a week. Since this time, other communities have been inspired by our story, with 'big dinners' popping up in a number of places around our city. People meet, eat and leave somehow renewed. It's a simple and transformative rhythm that works.

POSITIVE DIGITAL PEER PRESSURE

One of the unexpected benefits of being part of a village has been the positive culture experienced around screen use – or, rather, *lack* of screen use.

For those of us who are parents, we are acutely aware of the complexities of raising our children in a digitally saturated society. When speaking about technology in schools, parents tell me how uncomfortable they feel about screens 'taking over' – but they also feel pressure to give their children what others have. You see, when 'everyone' has a phone in primary school, it is hard not to follow suit. When 'everyone' is faking their date of birth to access social media, it feels prudish to take the moral high ground. We love our children and feel torn between doing what they want, what people say they need and what they *really* need – and this struggle can be exhausting.

Big dinner, and the community surrounding our weekly meal, has become a supportive network to help us navigate these challenges. During community meals, we don't use our phones, because we decided early on to avoid screens at our table. It wasn't a strict rule but a community norm. When others began to join us, they unconsciously imitated our practices, and a culture formed. We're not super strict about this, and when new friends arrive, we err on the side of hospitality rather than dictate digital terms. But if they become regular participants, and start to change our culture, we explain our heart for a distraction-free space, and people seem to understand.

By starting a consistent pattern, we have unwittingly created a community of people who share a digital parenting philosophy. Not everyone has the same rules, but we do support each other. Several families now eat without screens at home. They share what they're thankful for and talk about real issues around their table. Rather than being 'the only ones' who don't have a phone, our children now have peers with similar house rules. There are 'aunties' and 'uncles' who they know and trust and who help us out when we make mistakes. And we do make plenty of these, as we struggle together to raise a community of digitally aware and emotionally healthy young adults.

By creating a simple but consistent pattern that others could enter, we have made space for community and connection, which in turn is helping us to live out our own values.

START SMALL

If we want to shift our habits and make space in the hustle and bustle of life, we will need to develop predictable patterns in line with what matters to us. To achieve this, individually or collectively, we need a strategy. And more often than not, it's better to start small. This enables us to achieve projects we might otherwise have found overwhelming. When we started meeting with our neighbours, eating a weekly meal together was realistic. Cooking a 'big dinner' for an entire street, to begin with, was not.

Minor, regular shifts in behaviour, repeated over time, can bring about astounding results. One small win results in another small win, which in turn, produces exponential gains.

There are numerous ways to apply this principle in practice:

- If you want to get stronger, start with five push-ups a day, and build on it.

- If you want to read more often, start with three pages a day, and build on it.
- If you want to strengthen a relationship, text someone a compliment each week, and build on it.
- If you want to improve team relationships, ask one team member how they're doing each week, and build on it.
- If you want to grow your business, phone three clients each day, and build on it.

The same principle applies for eliminating digital activity from your schedule, using planned patterns.*

- If you want to spend less time on email, close-down your email program for an hour a day, and build on it.
- If you want to get more sleep, set an alarm to be screen free from 9 p.m. on Sunday evenings, and build on it.
- If you want to improve your focus, read a book without your phone nearby, and build on it.
- If you want to model better digital habits in front of your children, put away your devices at breakfast, and build on it.
- If you want to clear your mind at work, go to lunch without a screen, once a week, and build on it.

Irrespective of whether you are seeking to shift your digital habits, shape organisational culture or build a supportive community of friends, the power of patterns is available to all.

Start small. Be intentional. Plan a pattern for yourself and others, in line with your values, to make space in a repetitive way.

---

* Further detail about how to redesign daily digital habits can be found in a later chapter – the *daily pause*.

IN SUM

- Predictable patterns are repetitive actions and behaviours that shape who we are, and who we are becoming. Because of neuroplasticity, our patterns influence our thoughts and emotions at a biological level, shaping our identity. (Remember coffee as an acquired taste.)

- As Spacemakers, we can be deliberate in how we live and work. We can codify our values and priorities as intentional patterns. (Remember Alan and his exceptional rhythms.)

- Shared patterns are a strategy to shape culture in workplaces, families and communities. By developing collective rhythms, we can create like-minded communities around what we think is most important. (Remember Benedict and his Rule, and the 'big dinner' community on my street.)

- If you want to shift your habits, individually or collectively, be realistic and start small. Small wins accumulate over time and result in larger wins.

SOMETHING TO THINK ABOUT

What is one pattern that you can adopt across work or life, to create space for the things that matter? Are you able to break this down into a plan and make a start this week?

CHAPTER 9

ASSIGN REST

I typically dread the week before a family holiday. Timelines tighten, and everything becomes urgent. After delegating tasks and clearing my to-do list, I set an 'out of office' reply and close my laptop. Then holiday preparations begin. We create a shopping list, pack board games and bikes, along with sketch pads to entertain our children. We scribble down last-minute items, such as toothbrushes and phone chargers. It's a flurry of activity.

My special job is to pack the car. Space is tight in the back of our five-door hatchback, making packing an adventure. We strap five bikes to the roof and squeeze shopping bags below our feet. Whether or not everything will fit is always touch and go – with the exception of our last trip, where I achieved the unachievable in record time. Our belongings fitted snugly. Weight was evenly distributed. There was even space for my children to stretch out their legs. Not to be smug, but I was extremely pleased with myself.

This feeling didn't last long.

I entered our house and, to my dismay, found two suitcases waiting to be packed as well.

I learnt two important life-lessons that day, secrets I wish to share with you here. First, cussing loudly in front of your children does not strengthen family harmony. Second, it is materially impossible to 'squeeze' two suitcases into a jam-packed car. Even still, I gave it a go. I rearranged our car boot in myriad ways, shuffling bike helmets, pillows, kites and shoes, yet nothing worked. It was hopeless. There was no way to retrofit these large items. The solution to my packing dilemma was to unpack the entire car and reorganise it from scratch, starting with the largest items first.

I began with suitcases, followed by tennis rackets, finishing with shoes, pillows and books. After rearranging the car afresh, everything had a place. It took a bit of creativity (sorry kids, no leg-room again) but everything fitted. As we drove to our destination, I reflected on my packing ordeal. The lesson was obvious – pack big stuff before packing small stuff. If we start with the most important items first, the leftovers flow naturally. This is a principle for packing, but it's also a lesson for life. How often do we order our time and priorities in this way?

IT IS HARD TO MAKE SPACE FOR REST

Rest is important. We need to rest on a regular basis to be healthy, happy and productive. But in the digital age, physical and mental rest is hard to come by. Many of us are forgetting how to rest.

I once asked an exhausted client a question: 'How do you rest?' Her response was revealing:

> I'm not sure that I know what rest is? I don't know if I ever really rest. I get up early and work hard all week. On the weekend, I become a taxi mum and drive my kids to hockey, dancing or to various birthday parties. We always seem to have something on. The best thing is when I get to crash on the couch with my husband and watch Netflix, when we're not working or studying that is. Holidays are good, but even these are tiring. Don't get me wrong – they're lots of fun – but last time we came back from a family adventure, I needed a holiday from my holiday! Sad, isn't it [with a tentative laugh] ... is everyone this frantic?

As a productivity consultant, I constantly meet people who are rushed and pressed for time. There is social pressure to be busy and little space to slow down. People fill their downtime with constant activity, almost by accident. There are errands to do, home improvements to complete, episodes to catch up on. These activities are enjoyable but not always restorative. Come Monday morning, our minds are not rested nor our bodies restored. Why are weekends so tiring? Why are quiet times so noisy? Could it be that we are working longer and harder than ever before, or is something else going on to make our space less restful?

THE PRODUCTIVITY OF REST

At the beginning of the twentieth century, Henry Ford undertook numerous in-house studies to determine the optimal working conditions for maximised manufacturing output and profitability. Ford's discovery, now legendary, was that 40 hours a week provided the best environment for long-term profitability because healthy workers were productive workers. When Ford's employees worked more than the ideal amount of hours, let's say, 55 or 60 hours a week, mistakes and absenteeism increased, with little or no gains to overall productivity (thereby reducing company profits). In response to his findings, a five-day week was implemented across the Ford Motor Company in 1926, resulting in increased profitability and reduced labour unrest. By 1940, backed by similar experiences in other sectors, the Fair Labour Standards Act was amended by congress, enshrining a 40-hour work week throughout America.[1] Other countries soon followed, including my own country, Australia, which adopted the 40-hour work week on 8 September 1947.[2]

A lot has changed since Ford revolutionised the manufacturing industry. Wars have been fought and recessions overcome. Automation and the internet have created an army of knowledge workers, more likely to work at home than on a production line. Few of us clock on and off in the traditional sense, and the intersection between work and life is permeable. Attitudes around work and overwork are also shifting, with fewer people working just an eight-hour day. In spite of all these changes, one thing remains: we are biologically human, with a need to eat, sleep, procreate and exercise. In spite of our advances, the human body is fundamentally the same. We are no more capable of working 60 hours a week, at an optimal level, than we were in Henry Ford's day. This is not conjecture but science.

Research studies continue to reinforce Henry Ford's discovery, that working extremely long hours is bad for our health, our relationships and long-term productivity. In a recent study, Boston University academic Erin Reid noted that 'managers could not tell the difference between [the productivity of] employees who actually worked 80 hours a week and those who just pretended to'.[3] Although longer hours might increase kudos in today's competitive workplace, there is little or no evidence to suggest that overworked employees actually accomplish more.

In a similar vein, game developer Daniel Cook describes the process by which long hours reduce productivity over time. Based on several flexible-hours research studies, he determined that a programmer working 60 hours a week for a prolonged period of time, reduces their output to below that of a person working a steady 40 hours a week.[4] In the short-term, working 60 hours a week will boost our productivity and increase our performance, but if we sustain this for more than a few weeks, performance always collapses.[5]

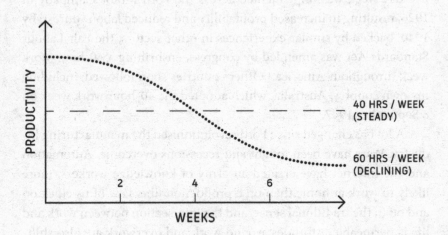

This finding has been repeated in numerous sectors, including the construction and manufacturing industries.[6] In the end, more is not better. If you crunch too many hours, you end up achieving less.

One reason for this dramatic decline in performance is sleep deprivation. People who work extremely long hours on a regular basis, typically do so at the expense of a good night's sleep. Sleep debt, according to research, 'has a neurobiological cost which accumulates over time'.[7] Sleep studies show that when a person loses just two hours of sleep a night for one week, their mental and physical performance declines. Mistakes go up, and concentration goes down, as if they had stayed awake for 48 hours straight! Here's the interesting part. When study participants were asked to rate their own performance, they *inaccurately* reported being more productive than they really were. They significantly underestimated the extent of their tiredness. Sleeplessness can therefore become a form of self-deception. Chronically tired workers lose their capacity to accurately judge their own performance, creating a temptation to push on in spite of diminishing outputs.

THE ORDER AND PRIORITY OF REST

The late Stephen Covey famously stated that proactive people make 'the main thing the main thing'.[8] They identify their priorities and organise their rhythms accordingly. For Covey, the 'main thing' included life-giving activities, such as writing, planning, building, exploring, relating and creating. In the digital age, I would also include activities of attention, such as thinking, focusing, reflecting and resting.

Rest can be harder to achieve than work, so if we are to include rest in the 'main thing', we will need to be proactive. Like my packing misadventure, if we start with work and 'squeeze' in rest, we will always feel busy. Emails, tasks, notifications and meetings shout for our attention. The only way to experience deep and restorative rest is to assign it as a priority, giving it attention and allowing our work to flow around it. As a Spacemaker, assigning rest comes first in our thinking and scheduling, before we plan our work. I am not suggesting we spend the majority of our time lying in a hammock sipping champagne (as nice as this sounds). Work is valuable and rightly takes up the majority of our time. Assigning rest is less about quantity and more about priority. Start with rest and end with work. As you reorder your rhythms, 'working from rest rather than resting from work', you will be healthier, happier and, ultimately, more productive.[9]

If you feel busy and overwhelmed in work and life, give more attention to how you rest. This may sound counter-intuitive, but it is surprisingly effective.

HOW DO YOU REST BEST?

Before we can invest more deeply in this practice, we must first understand how we rest best. Cal Newport, in his book *Digital Minimalism*, distinguishes between two modes of rest – high- and low-value rest.[10] High-quality leisure activities are active and deliberate. They include hobbies, such as playing music, learning a martial art or crafting timber. They can be physically active, such as playing sport; or socially active, for example, a commitment to a Rotary club. They can involve quiet pursuits, such as journaling; or noisy ones, such as board games with children. Although these activities require effort and self-mastery, they are deeply rewarding. They have a way of filling the heart, mind and soul. In contrast, low-quality leisure activities are passive and consumptive in nature. They are easy to do and typically involve a screen. We can use up an entire evening pursuing low-quality leisure activities, without trying. We can look at our watch and wonder where the time has gone, but we also don't feel restored.

In Newport's thinking, 'low-quality digital distractions play a more important role in people's lives than they imagine. In recent years, as the boundary between work and life blends, jobs become more demanding, and community traditions degrade, more and more people are failing to cultivate the high-quality leisure lives that … [are] crucial for human happiness.'[11] As time poverty increases, we are gravitating, en masse, towards passive forms of entertainment. What if we were to do the opposite, embracing active and intentional forms of rest instead? This might involve knitting a jumper, reading a novel, baking a cake or riding a bike. These pursuits require more planning, but they are often more fulfilling in the long run. I am not suggesting we should avoid zoning out when brain-dead or bored.

ASSIGN REST | 121

But we can be aware about how much time we are spending on such activities. Knowing ourselves deeply and investing in those activities that leave us feeling energised, refreshed and renewed over time, will lead us towards better rest.

THE DIFFICULT CHOICE TO BE UNBUSY

Minimalist blogger Joshua Becker writes, 'Busy is a choice. It is a decision we make. We are never forced into a lifestyle of busyness. The first and most important step to becoming less busy is to simply realise that our schedules are determined by us. We do have a choice in the matter. We don't have to live busy lives.'[12] I understand that not everyone has complete control of their calendar, but I do agree with the sentiment behind Becker's statement. He is implying that almost all of us have a say in how we use our time, and in most cases, we have more control than we choose to acknowledge. If busy is a choice, then unbusy is also a choice. Rather than go with the flow, we have an option to set our priorities, determine our own schedule, say no, or not yet, and improve our lives.

Even still, I appreciate how hard it is to assign rest in our fast-paced world. It takes maturity to invest in rest and to master it over time. Many of us have demanding jobs. Tiredness and exhaustion are part of the deal. I understand what it feels like to be trapped in a habitual cycle of busyness, committed to too many good things. I know what it feels like to run dry and to draw credit from my emotional, physical and relational bank accounts. And I know how long it can take to recover after crunching too many hours to meet deadlines.

The pursuit of space is not for the faint-hearted – there are tough choices to be made in our quest to be unbusy. In theory, we all want to experience a more restful lifestyle, but in practice, it can be costly. Day by day, there are small sacrifices – little decisions to prioritise rest over work. We may not get our inbox to zero, or finish our report, or win that extra client. These choices can be emotional, and they add up. On the macro level, if chronic exhaustion is damaging your health, happiness or dearest relationships, a substantial lifestyle adjustment may be necessary.* Some people downshift – whether that be a less demanding job, renting a smaller house, driving a cheaper car or moving to a slower city – in order to free up time, money and energy. Others establish stronger boundaries, saying no to a promotion, new kitchen, extra qualification or a credit card upgrade. These choices can be hard, but Spacemakers keep in mind the larger aim – to make space in line with our deeper values. Unbusy is life-giving. Deep rest is worth fighting for. A few sacrificial decisions, in the pursuit of a slower, more meaningful existence, are often worth the cost.

Deep rest, the type of rest that renews a person over time, is more than a day off. It is more than time away from the office 'not working'. It is active, not passive, and requires a certain level of energy and participation. Like any skill, restorative rest does not happen by accident, but is acquired through practice.

For Spacemakers, rest is not an afterthought but a way of life. We assign rest before work, making the 'main thing the main thing'. We are aware of how we rest best, pursuing high-quality leisure activities over low-quality ones. We prioritise time for self-care, physical activity, craftsmanship and mental renewal. We also book our holidays in advance, making sure, in all circumstances, we pack our suitcases first.

---

* According to work-life researcher, Barbara Pocock, 70 per cent of people working fifty hours or more would like to cut back to gain a better work-life balance, even at the expense of their pay cheque, but the nature of their role makes it nearly impossible. In my experience, coaching global corporate executives, some positions are fundamentally unsustainable. No matter how smart we work, 'balance' is unachievable. If pursuing a role like this, be honest about the long-term costs on your health, relationships and social life.

IN SUM

SOMETHING TO THINK ABOUT

- Rest is essential for personal productivity. When people work more than forty hours a week on a regular basis, their output declines. Chronically tired workers lose their capacity to accurately judge their own performance because of sleep debt. (Remember Henry Ford and his discoveries.)

- In the digital age, we are losing the art of deep rest. Deep rest is more than a day off and more than time away from the office. Like any skill, rest requires practice, effort and self-mastery. (Remember my client's comment: 'I'm not sure that I know what rest is.')

- Be aware of how you rest best. Maximise the quality of your time off by pursuing high-quality leisure activities, such as crafts, physical activities and social hobbies.

- The pursuit of space is not for the faint-hearted – there are tough choices to be made in our quest to be unbusy. We may need to sacrifice something from our lives, to experience a more restful lifestyle. (Remember 'busy is a choice'.)

- Assigning rest is a way of ordering your world. Start with rest and end with work, as a rhythm. As you prioritise rest as the 'main thing', work will naturally sort itself out. (Remember that suitcases must be packed first.)

CHAPTER 10

CULTIVATE COMMUNITY

It was 2003. A second-year psychology student from Harvard University sat in his dorm room late at night, typing code into a computer. Having recently hacked into Harvard's online archives, he was downloading hundreds of student photographs to create an interactive 'hot or not' website, featuring real-life college students.

FaceMash, as it was called, placed two randomly selected female student images side by side and asked the user to rate which one was more attractive. It was a boyish experiment that went viral. Within four hours of going live, FaceMash attracted 450 visitors and 22,000 photo-views, a huge amount of traffic for its day. The site was quickly shut down by campus administrators, yet it became a critical milestone in the history of social networking.

At the time, the internet was still developing. Google was competing with Yahoo in the search-engine wars. Myspace had not yet been released. Flip phones were popular, and Hotmail was a thing. People logged on to the internet to gather information but not to connect socially with one another. The FaceMash experiment was formative because it showed that students wanted to connect online with peers. They were curious about each other and keen to interact dynamically. FaceMash may not have been the most tasteful website, yet it spurred its founder to pursue a more mature social experiment. Just one year later, this sophomore reproduced 'the entire social experience of college and put it online'.[1] His name? Mark Zuckerberg.

Facebook is one of the most influential companies in the new millennia, with nearly three billion active users. This social network promises to 'help you connect and share with the people in your life' and to do so for free ('it's free and always will be').[2] This is a very compelling promise. It speaks directly to our humanity, to our longing for belonging. We can connect with hundreds of friends at the same time. We can share experiences from a distance, sending photographs and emojis from the comfort of our living rooms. That's amazing.

If Facebook can connect us with the people in our lives in a rich and meaningful way, do we still need to see each other in person? Should we bother investing in the complexities of face-to-face friendship?

Of course we should.

We know intuitively that life is better together, and that online networking is not a replacement for in-person relationships. Our experience of Zoom-fatigue during COVID-19 testifies to the value of warm-bodied friendship. Even still, when it comes to social interaction, our collective habits are changing. We are spending more time online and less time building concrete, in-person relationships. Even when we are together, we are often engaged with our devices.

These realities raise a number of questions. What is the relationship between face-to-face community and online social networking? Is it symbiotic, one complementing the other, or is it competitive? If we are to 'connect and share with the people in our life' in a deep and meaningful way, how might this best be done? Are we heading in a positive direction with this, or do we need to recalibrate?

PHO SOUP?

Last year, a new café opened up right next to my office. Like most places in the city, it was beautifully designed and immaculately presented, both inside and out. Everything was organic and ethical, from its locally sourced radishes to its Papua New Guinean twice roasted coffee beans. The waitresses wore fair-trade T-shirts, embossed with a minimalist logo. Even the chef looked the part, with his manicured hipster beard no doubt fashioned using argan oil from Morocco. Needless to say, I had to check this place out. So I organised to meet up with a friend for breakfast.

It was a fun experience. The service was great and the menu eclectic. We had interesting conversations and fabulous coffee. After scanning the menu, I ordered a bowl of pho: a warm, hearty beef noodle soup. Pho, for those unfamiliar with the term, is a Vietnamese street meal, traditionally served with strips of raw beef (that melt in your mouth), aromatic bean shoots and fresh basil. The deep, smoky flavours are created by roasting beef bones in an oven, before boiling them to create a healthy stock. Influenced by my Asian background (my father being Chinese), pho has become one of my favourite meals, even for breakfast.

When the soup arrived, it was steaming hot and beautifully presented, yet I soon realised that something was different. The soup was tasty, but not in the way I expected. It had a pho-like flavour – a hint of fresh ginger, a touch of star anise – yet something was missing, something essential. Then it dawned on me. Everything on the menu was vegan or vegetarian. This was a vegetarian café, and I had ordered beef noodle soup! On closer inspection, I was eating a mushroom-based, organic vegetarian pho, with no beef. I had been duped. Rather than real pho, I had been served faux pho!

In the same way, it can be hard to identify faux community from an authentic expression, particularly in the digital age. Social networking may look and feel similar to in-person community, but it is not the same. Like Vietnamese pho, face-to-face community is deep and flavoursome. It warms the heart and energises the spirit, in a meaty and messy way. People who commit to the long, slow burn of sharing life together reap enormous benefits – increased health, happiness and a deep sense of belonging. They experience something that looks and feels very different to a broadly connected, loosely knit online network.

In this chapter, we will explore the advantages of cultivating face-to-face community, and why it's an important principle for Spacemakers. It can be tempting to replace time-consuming relationships with digital ones, yet this may not always be as beneficial as might first appear. In fact, emerging research is revealing some surprising discoveries.

SOCIAL CONTACT AND HUMAN BIOLOGY

For millennia, human beings have lived in tribes, relying on one another for warmth, protection and companionship. We have raised children in villages, working, hunting and surviving in close proximity to one another. If we ever found ourselves in isolation from the tribe, it was usually for negative reasons – we were sick, in danger or had been deliberately shunned by the elders for breaking a sacred norm. Until recently, humans have always shared life together in extended families. We desire physical connection, community acceptance and warm-bodied relationship. We are biologically wired this way. It's coded in our DNA. Social media may provide a sense of community, but the conditions are very different to the face-to-face environments that have shaped our brain and biology since prehistoric times.

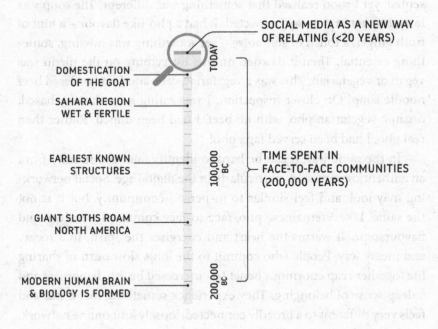

Our genetic disposition for community is demonstrated by the considerable body of evidence linking social connectedness with health and well-being.[3] Susan Pinker, a neuroscientist on the cutting edge of social research, has investigated the impact of personal interaction on our hormones and neural circuits. Remarkably, close relationships alter our genes at a cellular level. For example, women with breast cancer who are socially connected are four times more likely to survive than those who are socially isolated. Tests revealed that when breast cancer patients spend time in the presence of loved ones, it has a biological impact on the immune system, which in turn reduces tumour growth. In addition, positive social interactions have been shown to stimulate the release of endogenous opiates, which act as local painkillers. They reduce the secretion of hormones such as adrenaline, noradrenaline and cortico-steroids, which in turn reduces the impact of disease on our tissues.[4]

Other studies show similarly astounding results, linking an increase in social interaction with a corresponding increase in life expectancy. Socially connected people have fewer heart attacks and recover faster from their injuries. They are less likely to die when they are young and less likely to experience dementia when they age. Susan Pinker concludes: 'Neglecting to keep in close contact with people who are important to you is at least as dangerous to your health as a pack-a-day cigarette habit, hypertension, or obesity.'[5] This graph represents activities that most reduce our chances of dying.[6]

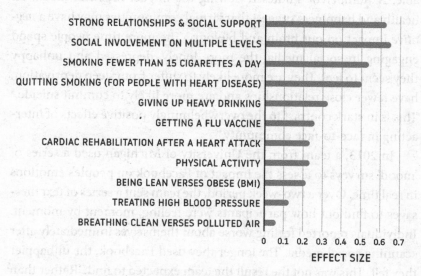

Reproduced from Julianne Holt-Lunstad et al. *(PLoS Medicine)*

The research clearly shows that people who build strong relational networks are happier, healthier and more satisfied with their lives. By maintaining close and regular contact with a diverse range of people, they are mentally stronger, more resilient, and suffer fewer addictions. But there is a catch. Almost all social research, literally thousands of studies, champion the benefits of warm-bodied, in-person relationships, unmediated by a screen.

DO ONLINE COMMUNITIES MAKE US HAPPIER?

Social networking platforms such as Facebook and Instagram seek to reproduce the experience of community online. They promote togetherness and belonging. On the surface, these networks look, act and feel like community. As we share photos, emoticons and banter online, we experience a certain degree of relational affinity. Yet questions remain. If social interaction is good for our health, do online communities match up? Do they make us stronger and happier, or are they a faux version of the real thing?

Though research is still emerging, the initial results are not favourable. A number of studies reviewing the impact of social media on health and happiness suggest that virtual communities may have a *negative* impact on our brain and biology.[7] The more time people spend engaging in social media, the more lonely, depressed and unhappy they seem to feel. They are more likely to suffer from sleep deprivation, have fewer close relationships and are more likely to commit suicide.[8] This is in stark contrast to the overwhelmingly positive effects of interacting in face-to-face community.

In 2013, a team from the University of Michigan used a series of 'mood' surveys to assess the impact of Facebook on people's emotions in real time. Over a two-week period, the team sent a series of text messages to find out how participants were feeling, moment by moment. Individuals reported feeling worse about themselves immediately after scanning social media. The longer they used Facebook, the unhappier they felt. This was not the result the team expected to find. 'Rather than enhance well-being', they concluded, 'Facebook may undermine it'.[9]

In a later study, Danish researchers set out to investigate an already-validated link between Facebook and unhappiness. They wanted to discover whether it was Facebook that made users unhappy or if unhappy people gravitated towards Facebook. Five hundred regular Facebook users were asked to give up Facebook for a week and to delete the application from their smartphones. At the end of the study, Facebook 'quitters' felt happier, less lonely and less envious than a control group (who continued as usual).[10]

Interestingly, neurochemistry may provide further clues to explain why connecting online is less enriching than in person. An ancient molecule, oxytocin, acts as a neurotransmitter in the brain to support the development of close bonds. Physical contact, such as a warm hug or a pat on the back, stimulates the release of oxytocin, thereby strengthening trust and affinity in a group. This 'bonding' chemical is released whenever we spend time together or talk on the phone with a loved one. It is not released when we send a text message or an emoji or when we comment on a post. At a biological level, it seems that social media does not reproduce the heart-warming experience of being together in person. Sending and sharing messages digitally may have its place, but it is a faux replacement for verbal and physical interaction.[11]

DOES IT MATTER HOW WE USE SOCIAL MEDIA?

As we have explored previously, teenagers are particularly vulnerable to excessive digital activity. Social media overuse is associated with a loss of happiness, self-control and emotional regulation. In adults, the message is nuanced: social media *can* be beneficial and life-enhancing – in *some* circumstances. We can connect online with people who matter most to us. We can communicate with loved ones and support friends in crisis. We can look out for each other and provide encouragement to socially isolated individuals. In theory, the benefits of social media are unlimited – adding value to existing relationships. But in reality, it's a little more complex.

Infrequent social media users have a lower risk of developing mental health problems than more prolific social media users. Active usage (posting updates and commenting on posts) is more positive than passive usage (scrolling newsfeeds and mindlessly viewing videos). Individual personality traits also affect the impact of social media on an individual. Those who have a tendency towards obsession or to comparing themselves with others are more likely to be adversely affected. (Comparison almost always makes people feel less happy, irrespective of whether they compare themselves positively or negatively.)[12] Social media, when used deliberately and in moderation, is a value-adding technology, so long as it doesn't take up too much space. How we use our tools and how often we use them makes all the difference.

SPACE TO PURSUE SOMETHING CONCRETE

Though the research suggests there is some value in connecting with our friends online, digital communities are not concrete communities, and never will be. There is no quality scientific evidence to suggest that digital forums can or will improve our health, in the way face-to-face communities can.[13] Social networking does not reduce our anxiety. It does not build our resilience to fight disease. It does not increase our chances of living a long and happy life. Facebook and other social media apps will never be able to 'reproduce the entire social experience of college and put it online'. In some circumstances they add value. But they also remove space from our lives. We must therefore be considered in how deeply and how often we turn to our screens for human interaction – for digital communities are a faux version of the real deal.

TRADING DOWN

In economic terms, everyone knows the value of trading up. We buy shares when they are low and sell when they are high. We discover a 'bargain' when we purchase something for less than it is worth. It would be foolish to intentionally exchange an item of higher value for one of lower worth. This is common wisdom.

Time is no different. Our time, being finite, is one of our most precious capitals. And every hour we spend scrolling our newsfeed is one less hour for something else. This may be one less coffee with a colleague, one less book read with our child, one less over-the-fence interaction with our neighbour. According to a Stanford time-diary study, this is precisely what is happening across all social demographics: 'People who spend more than five hours a week of their personal time online have less face-to-face contact with their strong ties.'[14] In other words, we're exchanging time away from concrete relationships (which are wonderful for our health) for time spent on social media (which is neutral at best, and potentially damaging to our health). This begs a simple question. Is this a well-considered trade?

I am not suggesting that every hour spent online is a misuse of our time. In business circles, for example, there is a large cohort of people who don't actually use social media to socialise with friends anymore. They network, encourage and support one another as entrepreneurs, using groups to build knowledge and strengthen client relationships. As a company director, I am a member of a number of industry groups that provide updates, share practical ideas and create client leads. Again, social media can be a valuable tool, so long as it doesn't divert too much time away from warm-bodied relationships.

REAL FRIENDS ARE HARD TO FIND

It may be tough to admit, but it is not easy to make real friends. We live in cities, separated by distance. We fence our houses to divide our patch from our neighbours. We think individually, not collectively. And we are time poor. Our modern lifestyles are no longer conducive to hanging out in person, which is why it is so attractive to connect online. Virtual communities are readily available. They are safe, uncomplicated and fit around our lifestyle. They take no energy to join and demand little in return. And this is why they are faux communities.

Participating in a warm-bodied community, in contrast, is demanding. It asks something of you. It involves cooking, cleaning, doing the dishes and spending money. It requires that you turn up and participate, even when you feel tired. Real community is messy and noisy. It requires you to forgive others and say sorry for your mistakes.

Sometimes you share laughter. Sometimes you pass on germs. Real community involves time and commitment, and it is good for the soul.

Friendship – committed friendship – is the bedrock of community. Close friends support us in good and bad times. They laugh at our jokes and challenge us when we act foolishly. They are loyal and honest and fun to be around. We may sometimes annoy each other, but we always have each other's back.

In a society obsessed by immediacy, many of us are forgetting what it means to be a truly good friend. As computer scientist and writer Jaron Lanier points out, if 'we have accumulated thousands of friends on Facebook ... this can only be true if the idea of friendship is reduced'.[15]

At the end of your life, when you look back and reflect on the good times, chances are that your most memorable moments will not be in front of a screen. When people are at death's door, it is times of friendship that they tend to remember most fondly – the painful, joyful, hard-won sacrifices of a life shared together. *This* is why we disconnect. *This* is why we make space for concrete community. The easier path is not always better for us. Vegetables are healthier than sweets. And a few loyal friends are more valuable than a thousand faux followers.

TAKE THE FIRST STEPS

For all these reasons, Spacemakers choose to invest in face-to-face community. Our aim is not to avoid social media altogether, but to use it discerningly. As explored in the paradigm, there is value in being a considered adopter of technology. We can make decisions about how we build social capital, investing in warm-bodied relationships rather than accidental and addictive modes of social networking.

If you are open to reconsidering your lifestyle, and want to peg back some time to invest in deeper relationships, here are some tips.

STEP 1: SET LIMITS

For most of us, the first step is to reduce the amount of time we spend scrolling our social media newsfeeds. This is particularly important for moderate to heavy users of social media. (Light users are on social media less than an hour a day, all platforms combined.) Perhaps start by implementing one or two of the following practical solutions:

- Reduce the number of apps you use. As the famous saying goes, 'Less is more.'[16] This is most certainly true for social media. Can you consolidate to one or two accounts?
- Select specific times in your week when you choose to check your social media feeds. There are no hard and fast rules here. You are the best judge on how much time you wish to spend online. Remember, every hour spent on Instagram is an hour lost elsewhere.
- Delete all social media apps from your smartphone. These apps are designed to take up as much of your attention as possible, encouraging you to snack on digital content throughout the day. You can keep your apps open and available on your laptop or tablet. Just don't have them constantly by your side.
- When using social media, be active not passive. Don't mindlessly scroll for hours like a zombie, but participate creatively – upload photographs, type comments, engage in conversations, encourage others. Research says that it's better for your mental health when you engage in this way.[17]
- Where possible, be honest and authentic. Try not to fabricate an 'amazing' life by manicuring photos or overselling your image. This makes people envious and encourages unhappiness. Just be yourself.
- Review the number of 'friends' you keep. Be ruthless and unfriend connections you have no close affinity with. This way, you can use your time to build stronger connections with fewer people rather than calling everyone a friend.
- If you aim to use social media for business, rather than personal reasons, you may want to install the News Feed Eradicator.[18] This Chrome plugin allows you to replace your newsfeed with a static quotation, allowing you to access Facebook groups without getting caught in the infinity scroll.

- Lastly, remember your 'why' by asking yourself these questions. Does this technology strengthen or detract from my closest relationships? How do my digital habits align with my values? And how might I better prioritise space in my life to be with the people who are important to me?

STEP 2: PLAN PREDICTABLE PATTERNS

Having freed up time in your schedule, you can now reinvest in face-to-face relationships. Start by identifying people who really matter to you. Write down their names and describe why you want to reconnect. If you get stuck for ideas, scroll through your list of social media contacts. Could you invite one of these 'friends' for coffee?

Next comes the application. How will you reconnect?

To deepen your friendships, develop predictable patterns. Don't exhaust yourself but take the long view. You might start by eating lunch with a friend each fortnight or head to the cinema once a month. Think about the patterns you currently have in your life and build on them. Can you invite a friend to go running or talk as you buy groceries together? If you can't meet in person, might a phone call be a way to start? Whatever you choose to do, keep it lightweight and low maintenance. It is amazing how quickly friendships can deepen by creating a simple rhythm.

Lastly, if you're up for the challenge, move beyond individual friendships and build meaningful community. In a previous chapter, I described how my family created a welcoming community using predictable patterns that others could join. Head to the same pub at the same time every week. Invite your friends. Invite friends of friends. The same strategy can work for both social and service-based activities. Open your house for board games every Friday night. Meet at your local park and kick a ball about. Open a soup kitchen. Volunteer at a nursing home. Whatever culture you decide to create, make it consistent, sustainable and welcoming. Over time your social capital will grow.

People are hungry for real community. They are looking for something warm and meaty. They are waiting for us to log off and reconnect as friends.

IN SUM

SOMETHING TO THINK ABOUT

- People who build relational networks are happier, healthier and live more satisfying lives. But there's a catch. According to research, this must be face-to-face.

- The benefits of cultivating relationships are not just emotional but biological. When we connect with loved ones (in person), our genes alter at a cellular level, allowing us to recover faster from disease. (Remember that neglecting to keep in close contact with people in our life is as dangerous as a pack-a-day cigarette habit.)

- Social media, a relatively new medium, promises to help us connect and share with the people in our life. The implicit promise is that virtual communities will reproduce the benefits of face-to-face relationships. This claim is not supported by evidence. (Remember my faux pho soup.)

- Social media, despite its many benefits, may negatively impact our health and happiness. As a society, we are trading in-person relationships (something enormously valuable) for time spent on social media (something of lesser value). Is this a considered trade?

- Warm-bodied relationships are messy, time-consuming and demand something of us. They are more costly than virtual relationships but enrich our lives more deeply.

- To strengthen concrete community: i) set limits on time spent on social media, and ii) plan patterns to invest in face-to-face social bonds.

SOMETHING TO THINK ABOUT

Who would you like to spend time with this month? And
how might you connect with them on a regular basis?

CHAPTER 11

EMBRACE SILENCE

In early 2020, the world began to shake. A new and highly virulent virus known as COVID-19 spread rapidly from Wuhan in China, infecting people everywhere. With exponential rates of contagion causing panic across the globe, countries implemented a variety of measures to contain the spread. In my country, Australia, we implemented a six-week lockdown, closing borders and shutting schools and non-essential services. Millions of people were forced into self-isolation to contain the first wave of the virus. Jobs became obsolete. Social commitments stopped. Collectively we entered a liminal moment, experiencing something we all crave: more space. For many, coronavirus gave us the space we needed to bake sourdough bread, tend the garden, take up painting, or start a podcast. We changed our routines. We spent quality time with our children. We learnt new skills. Even for those who did not slow down, working from home with children by their side, lockdown offered a break from normality. It allowed us to withdraw from commitments, re-examine our priorities and reflect on life's meaning.*

Disruptive silence has a way of unhinging us. I have been surprised by the number of people in my social circles who have made

---

* I recognise that many people experienced a longer, more painful lockdown than where I live in Australia. Many lost jobs, regular social connections and lived in highly stressful family environments – even violent ones – without reprise. Rather than silence, many of my friends in Europe and North America have experienced lockdown as a gruelling and exhausting marathon. Time will tell what learnings will emerge from this experience.

radical life-changing decisions as a result of this time of shaking. My graphic designer friend, Tom, for example, closed his firm to join the construction industry. Tanya, a long-term client, left a decade of medical practice to dabble in permaculture. A friend and church minister, Dave, took the plunge to become a registered nurse. And although it was risky to change careers in a recession, for each of them, their decisions emerged from the enforced silence. In the words of novelist Sarah Dessen, 'Silence is so freaking loud!'[1] And silence *can* be loud, if we choose to listen. When we listen deeply, we almost always change.

There is power in being alone with our thoughts, with less to do. For many in Australia, lockdown reminded us of the value of simplicity and withdrawal. One of my coaching clients, Mae, expressed her desire to remember what she had lost: 'I miss the stillness [of self-isolation]. I'm back at work and study, and I'm driving my children everywhere. I want to learn from this experience. I want to structure in times of silence again.' What if, instead of waiting for another global pandemic, we could embrace the practice of silence.*

WHAT IS SILENCE?

Silence is quiet. It is time away from distraction. It is time alone with ourselves. To be silent is not merely an absence of speaking, but the calming of our mind to listen deeply. Alone, we can decompress from the non-stop stimulation of modern society. We can still our thoughts and contemplate. Silence is both a posture and a practice, a willingness to withdraw and reflect. This habit can take many forms, from

---

* The COVID-19 pandemic functioned as a collective rite-of-passage event for a many in our society, with self-isolation triggering a shared liminal experience. We 'left' the safe and secure society that we once knew, experienced a time of wilderness (with elements of risk and disorientation), and re-entered as different people. In line with rite-of-passage events, this cohort had an opportunity to mature individually and collectively – reflecting on where we had come from, what we were experiencing, and who we wanted to become. A critical component of this liminality included silence.

meditation to mountain bike riding, yet it almost always requires a withdrawal from everyday life, to enter a state where our mind is free from the input of other minds.[2]

Silence and solitude, as historical practices, are often described together. Solitude is time away from others and silence is time away from noise. For simplicity, I have chosen to use these terms interchangeably because they are connected. Silence is an expression of solitude and vice versa. We must retreat from others to be silent, and without silence, there is little value in being alone.

In her 2012 TED talk, Susan Cain said, 'We have known for centuries about the transcendent power of solitude. It's only recently that we've strangely begun to forget it.'[3] Embracing silence on a regular basis is easy enough to comprehend but much harder to implement. Many of us avoid silence because it makes us feel uneasy, particularly those of us who are extroverted by nature. Alone, we experience thoughts and emotions that we might otherwise run from, so instead we listen to music, check messages, play games – anything to avoid the uncomfortable silence of the soul. It doesn't have to be this way. Wayne Oates, a professor of behavioural science, suggests:

> Silence is not native to my world. Silence, more than likely, is
> a stranger to your world, too. If you and I ever have silence in
> our noisy hearts, we are going to have to grow it. ... You can
> nurture silence in your noisy heart if you value it, cherish it,
> and are eager to nourish it.[4]

In other words, silence is rarely developed by accident and must be embraced intentionally. Like a muscle that strengthens with activity, stillness can be mastered with practice. With perseverance and time, silence can become our closest friend – quiet in the storm of life, unhurried and unhindered by circumstance.

There are three important reasons why Spacemakers embrace silence. By stilling our mind and steadying our emotions, we can build self-awareness, strengthen our personal convictions, and pay attention to the whisper of our soul.

SILENCE AND SELF-AWARENESS

A number of years ago, I gave my mobile phone number to an internet service provider, who published my details on the web. Within days, I received a maelstrom of unsolicited phone calls from overseas telemarketing companies, seeking to elicit business. These interruptions were frustrating and fractured my attention throughout the day.

At one point, I was working on a presentation that required deep concentration, amid a barrage of 'No Caller ID' interruptions. After the fourth call, I lost my cool and decided to blast whoever was on the other end of the line. As suspected, there was a click and lag, before a male voice launched into a scripted introduction.

Ignoring social niceties, I snapped angrily and shouted through the phone line: 'Who are you? Why are you calling? Are you a company?'

There was a pause, and then, in a sheepish voice, the unnamed telemarketer replied: 'No sir, I am not a company. I am a person.'

I must admit, this response took me by surprise and made me smile. The salesman, struggling to grasp the English language, had taken my question literally and decided to reassure me of the bleatingly obvious – that he was not a machine but a person! I subsequently told him never to use my number again and hung up the phone.

This interaction took less than a minute, and I returned to my document without a second thought. The next morning, however, in my habitual time of silence, this heated conversation came to mind. Something about this call made me feel uneasy. Had I been too angry or abrupt? Quite possibly – although I was surely justified in doing so! Excuses aside, I took out my journal and reflected on my experience, in silence. As I stilled my mind, I realised just how profound this man's comment had been. I had not been speaking to a machine, or to a company, or even addressing a 'No Caller ID'. I had verbally chastised a *person*. I was rightly angry at the company that spammed my phone, yet I regretted being so aggressive towards a human. My conscience reminded me that, in fact, I too had once been a telemarketer at university, making unsolicited phone calls to sell vouchers that no one needed. I found it to be a soul-destroying job, but I needed the money to pay my rent. Now with the shoe on the other foot, I was the aggressive recipient, treating an unnamed, unknown person as an object to vent my own frustrations.

This inglorious moment, detected in my time of silence, revealed my tendency towards self-deception. I am an organised and task-oriented person, but the shadow side is that I sometimes bypass relationships to get things done. How often, I wondered, had I traded kindness and empathy for speed? How often had I failed to recognise my own team members as people? Armed with these questions, I took notice of other situations where I was abrupt and unkind – the time when I snapped at my son without reason, criticised a barista for slow service, half-listened to a colleague, lacked empathy for my injured wife. These may seem like small moments, acceptable irritabilities, but they add up. They represented a pattern and trajectory that I needed to change if I was to live according to my values. For the next few months, as I interacted with various people, I decided to pay more attention to their humanity. I started to observe my team and consider their feelings. I smiled in the street, and 'wasted' time in banter. Some days have been more successful than others. There are times when I am still too busy to care. But with practice, my self-awareness has been increasing, as well as my capacity to respond patiently and kindly to adverse situations.

This is not a grand or amazing story, yet I hope it is a useful one. It is a small example of the type of insight that can be gained when we take time out to examine our actions. Silence is a powerful enabler of self-reflection, thinking about our own thoughts in a considered way. In education, this is called metacognition – the ability to critically analyse our own thinking. When we reflect in silence, we can learn to articulate our feelings, motivations and actions more clearly. We can critique our perspectives and attitudes. We can improve our ability to learn.[5]

Deep silence leads to deep thought – a precursor, as we have explored, to shifting our paradigm. In silence, we remember to say no to the trappings of unlimited choice, to tame our power and to examine our deeper loves. In silence we can make space in our mind and our heart, to see the world differently. In fact, Holocaust survivor Viktor

Frankl famously suggested that we detect, rather than invent, our life's calling.[6] In silence, we can learn to detect meaning in seemingly unimportant moments – a random comment here, an unusual event there, a dream, an experience, an ill-defined feeling. Over time, these moments add up, providing us with guidance and direction, *if* we pay attention to them. We can ignore our inner thoughts, repress our feelings and 'power on', but there are consequences. At best, we take longer to detect when change is afoot. At worst, we end up living a shadow of the life we're meant to live.

Cal Newport has suggested that when you avoid silence, 'you miss out on the positive things it brings you: the ability to clarify hard problems, to regulate your emotions, to build moral courage, and to strengthen relationships. If you suffer from chronic solitude deprivation, the quality of your life degrades.'[7] In this sense, the practice of silence is essential for spacemaking. Alone, we make space to think about our thinking. Alone, we build self-awareness by eliminating noise and distraction. Alone, we remain quiet enough to detect life's meaning.

SILENCE AND PERSONAL CONVICTION

There is a concept in the New Testament scriptures known as *erēmos* (pronounced *er'-ay-mos*). The English translation of this ancient Greek adjective is *wilderness* or *desolate place*.[8] *Erēmos* refers to a physical environment, such as a barren desert or lonely road, but is also metaphorical, describing our struggle with silence. In *erēmos*, we withdraw from the world. In *erēmos*, we quiet our mind. In *erēmos*, we find peace in desolate places. This idea is counter-intuitive in modern culture. Our pleasure-seeking society tends to avoid pain and hardship rather than embrace it. Solitude is dangerous. Silence is a curse. But if the ancient Scriptures offer us wisdom, there is strength and certainty to be found in *erēmos*.

Jesus of Nazareth was no stranger to the wilderness. In the Gospel of Luke, we read: 'The news about him spread all the more, so that crowds of people came to hear him and to be healed of their illnesses.

But Jesus often withdrew to lonely places (*erēmos*) and prayed.'[9] It seems, from this account, that Jesus was popular ... super popular. After performing a number of miracles, everyone wanted an autograph from this upstart Rabbi. Sick people came flocking to Jesus in the hope that they might touch his clothes.[10] Crowds were becoming unruly, forcing Jesus to escape by boat to avoid being crushed.[11] Yet, in spite of danger and exhaustion, Jesus remained calm.[12] He listened to questions. He fed the masses. He showed kindness and compassion in unexpected ways.[13] How was this possible without burnout? In the face of adversity, how was composure maintained? To understand Jesus' serenity, we can look for clues in *erēmos* – in the practice of habitually withdrawing to lonely places to be still. Unlike modern-day executives, the more popular Jesus became, the more he seemed to retreat. In the wilderness, in prayer-filled silence, he found his strength – a source of identity, conviction and courage in the chaos of life.

One of the most unusual accounts of the life of Jesus was his showdown with Satan.* This took place in a wild and uninhabited place. 'Jesus, full of the Holy Spirit, left the Jordan and was led by the Spirit into the wilderness (*erēmos*), where for forty days he was tempted by the devil.'[14] There is debate about the nature of *erēmos* in this passage – it is clearly a location, the Judaean desert, but also a place of solitude. At a cursory read, the message is simple. Evil is encountered when we are at our lowest, in this case, isolated, vulnerable and in need of physical sustenance. On the other hand, when we examine the pattern of Jesus' leadership, we discover an alternative explanation that has relevance to us all. What if the wilderness was never a place of weakness for Jesus but a place of strength? What if *erēmos* was a familiar place, a source of courage? Satan may have wanted to take advantage of Jesus' fragility when choosing the desert as a battleground, yet perhaps this place of silence was to Jesus' advantage?

---

* The Greek word for Satan is *satanas*, meaning adversary or hostile opponent. Another Greek word, *diabolos* (or devil), means slanderous and malicious one. Both words describe the personification of evil. This is a different idea than our cultural stereotype of a red man with horns and a pitchfork.

As we examine the life of Jesus, a pattern emerges – one of silence *before* activity. Jesus did not act until he had engaged in a time of reflective silence. He withdrew to a lonely mountain before choosing the apostles.[15] He withdrew to a quiet garden to pray before facing the cross.[16] Contemplation leads to courageous action – we see this pattern in the saints who followed Jesus' example. Patrick escaped from Ireland, then returned after receiving a vision in solitude. Martin Luther King Jr heard an inner voice when alone in his room ('Stand up for justice. Stand up for truth').[17] Mother Teresa sustained her energy for the poor through daily habits of withdrawal ('we need silence to be able to touch souls').[18] And although the Christian understanding of silence is particular, great people from all religious and philosophical traditions have befriended silence: Lao Tzu, Marcus Aurelius, W. A. Mozart, Henry Thoreau, Franz Kafka, Thomas Edison, Mahatma Gandhi, Albert Einstein, even Yoda (I couldn't resist.)[19]

The concept of *erēmos* can also be understood psychologically. The capacity of humans to act unethically is a reality we must all face. According to psychology professor and popular author Jordan Peterson, Jesus' battle in the wilderness carries metaphorical meaning for Western culture. It is the archetypal encounter between good and evil. Christ was 'willing to confront evil – consciously, fully and voluntarily' – which we must all be prepared to do, if we are to 'take responsibility' for our own 'destructiveness'.[20] In Peterson's mind, evil is not something that we fight 'out there' but a reality we must confront in ourselves. In a similar vein, seventeenth-century French philosopher and mathematician Blaise Pascal suggested: 'All of humanity's problems stem from man's inability to sit quietly in a room alone.'[21]

It is easy to point out the flaws in others but much harder to examine our own, unseen areas. This is not a cheerful premise but a necessary one. In silence, we can learn to question our own self-talk. In silence, we can see the world from different perspectives. In silence, we can gain the moral fortitude to confront our failures and conquer our fears. We avoid war with others by confronting ourselves, in silence.

Life is fraught with difficulty. There are hard choices to be made and barriers to overcome – both internally and externally. If we are never silent, we may struggle to clarify our values, wrestle our demons and commit to the wisest (rather than the easiest) course of action. We may also struggle to remember the good in ourselves. Silence can help us recollect just how brave, generous and committed we can be. Wilderness is unpredictable, and almost never comfortable, which is why we need to practise it. The *erēmos* builds character and conviction, by forcing us to face ourselves. We must not be afraid of being alone. There is much to learn from the wilderness.

SILENCE AND THE SOUL

According to Parker Palmer, the soul

> is like a wild animal – tough, resilient, resourceful, savvy. It knows how to survive in hard places. But it is also shy. Just like a wild animal, it seeks safety in the dense underbrush. If we want to see a wild animal, we know that the last thing we should do is go crashing through the woods yelling for it to come out.[22]

I love this definition of the soul. It is consistent with my experience of discovering myself in quiet places. When I refer to the soul, I mean the essence of a person; who we are beyond any role or possessions that we may hold; who we are apart from our successes or failures, beyond relationships. It is what the mystics call the inner-self – not so much an anatomical reality but a felt experience of human existence. Whether or not you are comfortable with the word *soul*, we all understand the necessity to meet with, and engage in, the deeper aspects of ourselves; our inner-longings, our core identity, the fragile parts of our histories that make us who we are today.

Like a wild animal, at home in the undergrowth, the deepest parts of a person are delicate, revealing themselves only when atmospheric conditions are right. Our soul needs time and permission to open up, which only happens in places of peace, not hurry. In digitally saturated environments, how often are the surroundings conducive to this? How often are conditions truly quiet? It seems that many of us work too hard and are too digitally interconnected to give our souls a chance to speak. In the words of theologian Ronald Rolheiser, in a society that is constantly connected, 'we are distracting ourselves into spiritual oblivion'.[23]

Silence, in contrast, provides a mechanism to explore our spiritual selves. In *Strengthening the Soul of Your Leadership*, author Ruth Haley Barton argues that in solitude 'we stop believing our own press. We discover that we are not as good as we thought but we are also more than we thought.'[24] This is the paradox of those who mine the depth of their soul, in search of the gold. The spiritual person is brave enough to confront their darker moments – their disappointments, selfish actions, deep shame – and at the same time, appreciate themselves all the more richly. Hiding from our soul is not the answer. There is joy and wonder in learning to be alone in silence.

SILENCE AND UNPLUGGING

If silence is about slowing down, unwinding and thinking clearly, then we need environments free of noise – including digital noise. Unplugging from technology is a logical prerequisite to silence.

In my experience, and many others I've coached, the quality of our silent times is substantially different when a digital device is by our side. An innocent text message or notification is usually enough to break our attention. When tending to our soul in silence becomes too much for us, it is all too tempting to pick up our phone and distract ourselves with something whimsical.

So if we are to practise silence – deep silence – we will need to put our devices aside. We will need to regularly unplug and focus our attention on our current surroundings.

HOW TO BEGIN THE PRACTICE OF SILENCE

If your world is like mine, you may find it hard to embrace the habit of silence. After a long period of neglect, it may take effort to warm up your 'silence muscles' – but take heart – being alone with your thoughts can work for anyone, irrespective of technique. As Ruth Haley Barton testifies:

> Solitude does its work whether we have any cognitive under-standing of it or not. Just as the physical law of gravity ensures that sediment swirling in a jar of muddy river water will even-tually settle and the water will become clear, so the spiritual law of gravity ensures that the chaos of the human soul will settle if it sits still long enough.[25]

The secret to experiencing silence, therefore, is not to try harder but to wait longer. It is less about technique and more about persistence.

When it comes to application, there are many ways to embrace silence.* For me, it begins first thing in the morning. Each day, I lie on my bed, dozy but awake, and spend ten to fifteen minutes reflecting on the day ahead. I say the Lord's Prayer, give thanks for the goodness of my life and ask for help for the day ahead. It is a wonderful way to prepare my mind for a new day. There are other simple practices that enrich my life like this. When at the gym, I run on a treadmill without listening to podcasts, which for me, is a form of silence. From time to time, I light a candle and pay attention to the flicker of the light. I drink coffee on my outdoor sofa without distraction. I escape to the Australian bush and listen to my thoughts as I walk. Silence is not re-strictive but creative. You do not have to be religious like me to make a start. Find an expression that works for you.

When it comes to application, there are myriad rituals you can explore, depending on your personal story. Silence, as a spiritual prac-tice, is embraced by all major religions and spiritual philosophies. In Judaism, God speaks in the silence. In Buddhism, a 'noble silence' leads to knowledge. In Christianity, contemplation compels stillness. In Islam, silence is the path to wisdom. So when it comes to choosing a

---

* In a later chapter, the *daily refresh*, we will explore how to practically unplug and refresh, twenty minutes at a time, as an expression of silence.

method of contemplative silence, feel free to research more fully, based on your own beliefs.

As with any new habit, the smartest way to start is slowly. If silence is a stranger, is it possible to put away your phone for a few minutes and breathe in and out? If waiting for a bus to arrive, can you spend ten minutes observing your surroundings? Or when sitting on a park bench, pay attention to the sights and smells without distraction? As Spacemakers, we can train our brains to slow down by starting small and then building up slowly. Over time, with practice and perseverance, we can discover patterns of silence that work for us.

Silence is simple but never painless. It can feel costly to put our phones away and on silent. It can be hard to think about our thoughts, when our thoughts are tender and revealing. Be patient. Be still. Be silent.

IN SUM

SOMETHING TO THINK ABOUT

- Silence is quiet. It is time away from distraction. It is time alone with ourselves, away from the input of other minds.

- Silence is disruptive. It has a way of unhinging us. When we force ourselves to be still, we can be drawn to reconsider our direction in life. (Remember COVID-19 and the experience of being in lockdown.)

- Silence builds self-awareness, allowing us to detect meaning in the seemingly insignificant moments of life. We can learn to think about our own thoughts. (Remember my abusive call-centre outburst and metacognition.)

- Silence strengthens our personal conviction by forcing us to face ourselves. We build moral courage, wrestle demons and make hard decisions in the wilderness. (Remember the showdown between good and evil in the *erēmos*.)

- Silence is necessary to make peace with the soul. Like a wild animal, at home in the undergrowth, the right atmospheric conditions are needed to encounter our spiritual selves (inner longings, core identities, meaning). By paying attention to the whisper of our soul, we can learn to appreciate ourselves at a deeper level, warts and all.

- The practice of silence is not complicated. The secret is not to try harder but to wait longer. You may wish to explore a number of different practices, but the essence is to regularly set time aside to be quiet and alone, without digital distraction.

SOMETHING TO THINK ABOUT

Do you enjoy silence? What might it look like for you to practise a period of silence each day?

DISCOVER THE PRINCIPLES

In this part, we delved into five 'true north' principles to help us make space in the digital age. As a refresher, here's the framework:

S et Limits

P lan Patterns

A ssign Rest

C ultivate Community

E mbrace Silence

Like all principles, the SPACE framework is timeless and unchanging, anchored in human experience. These ideas have always been important, but even more so in an age of digital distraction. We *set limits* because life is not limitless. By saying no to some things, we can say yes to what matters most. We *plan patterns* to establish individual and shared norms. By *assigning rest*, we slow down and sustain our productivity. We *cultivate community* to invest in face-to-face relationships, becoming more resilient. And we engage with the inner work of *embracing silence,* to think our own thoughts, away from other minds.

Combined, these five principles help us make space in the clutter of digital life – space to rest, reflect and relate to others in meaningful ways.

PRINCIPLES
ON A PAGE

We all need principles on which we base our lives. By choosing to orientate our digital practices around these SPACE principles, we are setting ourselves up for positive change.

Set Limits: Limits help us to focus, create and set priorities. Rather than trying to be superhuman, we can embrace the logic of limits in all areas of life, including our use of screens.

Plan Patterns: Patterns are repetitive actions and behaviours that shape who we are, and who we are becoming. They enable us to codify our values and our priorities, individually and collectively.

Assign Rest: Assigning rest is a way of ordering our world; starting with rest and ending with work as a rhythm. By making rest the 'main thing', we can sustain our personal productivity over the long haul.

Cultivate Community: We can make space for healthy, in-person relationships by setting limits on social media, and planning patterns to strengthen social bonds.

Embrace Silence: By stilling our thoughts, and steadying our emotions, we can build self-awareness, strengthen our personal convictions and pay attention to the whisper of our soul.

MAKE IT
HAPPEN

Below are three questions to help you stop, reflect and gain the most from what you have explored.

What *3 significant insights* have arisen from what you have read so far?

What *2 practical actions* will you commit to doing soon?

What *1 big question* do you still have?

PART IV

THE
PRACTICES

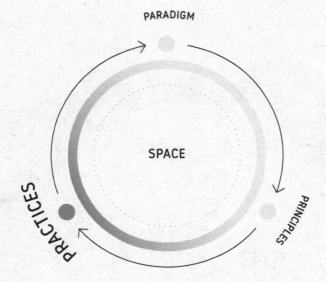

PARADIGM

SPACE

PRINCIPLES

PRACTICES

*Almost everything will work again
if you unplug it for a few minutes,
including you.*

ANNE LAMOTT

Some people enjoy discussing ideas but struggle to apply them in practice. I often encounter this challenge when training groups of professionals. A particularly outspoken participant might raise a question or offer critique to stimulate discussion. Ideas flow. Debate is robust. I enjoy such candid conversations because they keep me sharp, but if others in the group start losing interest, I close the conversation by asking a simple, personal question: 'You are obviously passionate about this idea. How do you plan to *apply* this in your own life?' Here's what typically happens. The questioner goes silent or deflects the question. They lose their gumption, and we move on. My intention isn't to be unkind or unfair. It is simply to insist that all ideas are translated into practice. If we are committed to our beliefs, we must also be willing to test them in reality. At some point, our personal convictions must make their way onto our to-do list.

THE MAGIC QUESTION

As a productivity consultant, I am obsessed with a particular question. I ask this question in every meeting, every coaching session, and with every group I facilitate. It is an incredibly useful question, which assists clients in translating ideas into practice.

'*What is the next action?*'

I first stumbled upon this gem when reading *Getting Things Done* by David Allen.[1] This question works for two reasons. First, it's *personal*, encouraging us to take responsibility and ownership for our ideas. Talk is easy, but action is difficult. By asking this simple but profound question, we force ourselves to choose a next step, and by implication, commit to own an action. It forces us to *do* something about the things we discuss.

Second, 'What is the next action?' is a *practical* question. When faced with a complex or difficult problem, it is easy to become overwhelmed or confused. This question encourages us to break down large and complex projects into small, manageable steps. 'Change career' moves forward with the simple next action of updating a curriculum vitae. In the personal sphere, 'moving house' might feel overwhelming, but it starts by completing a property application or by finding packing boxes. If you find yourself bogged down by complexity, or stuck in long-winded meetings with lots of talk and minimal action, try asking the question, 'What is the next action?' It works a treat for both individuals and teams who are habitually stuck.

ANNUAL, WEEKLY AND DAILY PRACTICES

Up to this point, we have explored the paradigm and principles of spacemaking, building a conceptual framework necessary for digital habit change. Ideas are important and frameworks necessary, but it's now time for specific and practical action.

In this final part, I will outline a series of habits and rhythms to help us make space in a culture of distraction. These practices are organised around annual, weekly and daily patterns. The annual (or seasonal) patterns allow us to prioritise longer periods of space away from digital noise. The practice of a technology-free day, once a week, is a circuit breaker to help us rest deeply. The daily practices allow us to refresh our mind and make the most out of the small opportunities, or digital pauses, that present themselves each day.

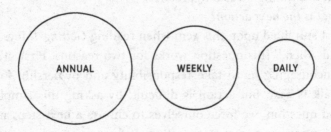

There is a debate among productivity experts regarding how to align our habits with our priorities. Some say that we should organise ourselves top-down (annual, weekly, daily) and others bottom-up (daily, weekly, annual). Stephen Covey, using a top-down methodology, suggests we develop a personal mission statement ('begin with the end in mind') before shaping our weekly and daily practices.[2] David Allen, in contrast, believes it more effective to tackle our immediate concerns first, capturing tasks and organising projects to make room for higher-order thinking. This ideology is reflected in the words of John Kotter: 'When alligators are nipping at your heels, you need to deal with the alligators.'[3] In my experience, both philosophies have merit and are effective when applied with skill. I personally gravitate towards top-down thinking – annual, weekly, daily practices. That said, once you have read and considered each chapter, feel free to implement practices in any order – top-down or bottom-up – depending on what is logical to you.

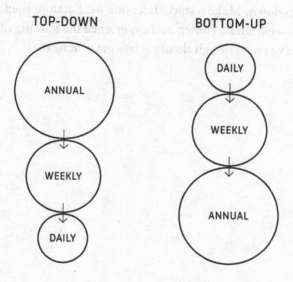

In a similar way, each of us will approach spacemaking through different lenses, influenced by our background, learning styles and life-stages. What energises an extrovert will likely be draining for an introvert. Spacemaking for a businesswoman with a mortgage will differ from a stay-at-home university student, or indeed, a single mother with toddlers. Income, ethnicity, gender and education all shape the way we experience space. So does our stage of life – leaving school, learning a trade, buying a house, changing careers, remarrying, moving cities, planning for retirement (and everything in between). In writing this book, I acknowledge that my circumstances – as a married professional with three children – may be different than yours. The stories I share are not templates to copy but examples to consider, as you creatively adapt each practice to your own situation.

As you read these pages, I encourage you to pause and apply what you are learning. Ask and answer the magic question – 'What is the next action?' Between chapters, there is an opportunity for you to consider two simple questions: 'What is one thing that stands out to you?' and 'What is the next action?' If at any stage you feel overwhelmed, be kind on yourself: spacemaking is a process. Consider your situation. Break things down. Make a start. Take one next action, then another, and another – eliminate clutter, and experience the making of space.

OK, you've read enough theory – let's get practical.

CHAPTER 12

START WITH
HOLIDAYS

A number of years ago, I undertook a team health consultation for a government agency. We were invited to spend time with a senior leadership team who were unhappy and dysfunctional. Our remit was to assess the dynamics of the team, diagnose pain points and make recommendations. After gathering information from surveys and interviews, we came to the uncomfortable conclusion that the team's problems stemmed from the hyperactivity of the senior leader. (Let's call him James.)[1]

James was intelligent, passionate and worked incredibly hard in his role. No one questioned his dedication to the job. He consistently worked sixty to seventy hours a week and had not taken a significant break in two years. This, in part, was the problem. James was almost always tired and drained. He was frantically busy and focused on the wrong things. Rather than providing clear direction, his instructions were haphazard and changeable. In his exhaustion, James struggled to make decisions and was becoming a bottleneck to progress. He complained of being overloaded but insisted on being involved in everything. The team were frustrated and hurt.

Our conclusion? James was exhausted, and everyone knew it, except for him. This was a sensitive issue, but in the end, we made our recommendations. James was no longer performing at his best. His colleagues were concerned about his health. He needed a proper holiday to catch up on sleep and reflect on his habits. Unsurprisingly, when we shared our observations with James, we hit a wall of resistance. He acknowledged that he was tired and slowing the team down but responded by saying, 'Work is really busy right now. When things slow down, *then* I'll take a holiday.' Guess what? Slowing down never happened. James is still running on empty, and meanwhile his team still suffers. The last time we checked in, tensions were rising. The unit was underperforming. Capable staff were leaving. All of this, because James was not willing to stop, unwind and care for himself.

TOO BUSY TO STOP

According to Australian work-life research, 40 per cent of people who work more than forty-five hours a week say they are too busy to take a holiday. The reason they give is they are 'just too busy to stop'.[2] This is a dilemma, because the busiest people in society are the ones most in need of a break.

As a small-business owner, I understand this tension. It is hard to take time off. My income reduces when I stop invoicing. And my team have to cover my work when I am away. If I am to experience regular, meaningful rest, it needs to be intentionally planned in advance. This is why my family have developed a pattern of rest throughout the year. Typically, we rest for a week in April, a week in September and a longer period of time around Christmas. My wife and I also head away for a romantic weekend without our children, in the middle of winter. These breaks are scheduled in our diary in advance before any work commitment, speaking engagement or conference is considered. Rest is a priority, and we know our pattern. Our holidays are not necessarily expensive, but they are non-negotiable.

Here is what my pre-booked patterns of annual leave look like.

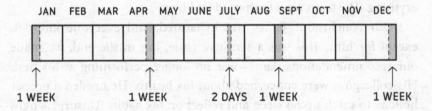

I recognise that not everyone receives holiday leave. You will need to adapt this principle to your own situation. In Australia, workers are entitled to four weeks of annual leave by law. This is the same across Europe (although nations such as Spain, France and the United Kingdom have even more generous leave entitlements). The United States, in stark contrast, is the only industrialised nation not to legally require employers to provide paid annual leave. One in four North Americans have no paid leave (23 per cent), and the average worker in the private sector receives only ten days annual leave a year.[3] For those living in the United States, I appreciate it is harder to 'start with holidays' because you receive so few. It is therefore even more important to maximise the time you do have, and to lean heavily on the weekly and daily practices to prioritise rest as a rhythm.

Taking this into consideration, planned holidays are tremendously important to set up the year well. As Spacemakers, we can remain fresh and productive by making it a priority to assign rest before work. Spacemakers pre-book holidays before locking in work commitments. We make the most of our precious time off by aligning our breaks with seasonal work pressures. As we have explored previously, rest is a skill that you practice. Can you lock in your annual leave in advance? Are your holidays fit for purpose? Are they shaped around a logical pattern?

PATTERN, PURPOSE AND PAY

When planning your annual leave, consider the *pattern* and timing of your holidays in response to historical or anticipated seasons of stress. In my role, the start of the year is typically frantic, making April a great time to decompress. Late July and August are often low points for my family, following a long, cold Tasmanian winter. We are tired and irritable after four months of darkness and need a decent break. As such, we book a week-long holiday in early September to give us something to look forward to. There are other ways to plan your pattern, beyond typical pressure points. You might look ahead and predict the need to rest before or after a particular life event, such as a product launch, house move or birth of a baby. There's no right or wrong pattern. Organise your holidays around seasons of stress to optimise your energy.

Purpose is a factor when planning your annual leave. Consider the specific outcome or benefit you want to achieve. Why are you taking a break, and will it meet your needs? For our family, April and September holidays are about slowing down and reconnecting as a family. We stay in a log cabin, read books and play board games. January, in contrast, is for activity and adventure. We get outdoors, socialise with friends, spend money and experience new things. Not every holiday is the same. Not every holiday will achieve the same outcome. Are you aiming to slow down or see the world? Are you seeking to socialise or spend time in solitude? Are you planning to get fit or laze on a beach? Consider what you really need, individually and as a family, and structure your holidays accordingly.

Lastly, consider *pay*. If finances are a barrier, get creative – a restful holiday does not need to cost the earth. Some of our most memorable breaks as a family have been spent camping with friends. This is both inexpensive and enjoyable. Time in nature, sleeping under the stars, is an amazing way to clear the mind and energise the soul. So is sitting around an outdoor fire, listening to crickets chirp. That said, another option is to stay at home, which is the preferred way of resting for many cultures. In Indian society, for example, people work hard so they can rest at home. They think it foolish to do otherwise. Indian entrepreneur Jossy Chacko describes his first experience of an Australian holiday in this way:

In India we never went away for holidays. Our home was our resting place. My Aussie friends worked overtime to pay for their dream houses, with air conditioning, heating, carpets, mattresses, pillows, doonas, indoor plumbing … all of which was left locked up two hours away. Instead we slept on the grass and froze in the rain, like people in the Indian slums, just to get some rest and recover from the rat race. … I couldn't understand it.[4]

Seen from this perspective, it does seem unusual that we leave our comfortable houses to head away on holidays. If you are deliberate and structured in how you plan your staycation, relaxing locally can be a life-giving way to break routines.

A SIMPLE LIFEHACK THAT WORKS

Start with holidays and plan the year in advance. This foundational lifehack is enormously helpful to begin each year well. Even if you have little control in when you can take annual leave, you can still be considered. Don't go skiing in Japan just because others are doing it. Instead, choose a holiday that will achieve your desired outcomes, within budget, in response to your identified seasons of stress. It only takes a short amount of time to lock in your leave, and it guarantees a bit of space throughout the year. If you don't have your next holiday booked, what are you waiting for? Open your calendar, choose dates and start planning.

IN SUM

- Plan your holidays in advance before scheduling work commitments. Don't let busyness be an excuse for not taking annual leave. (Remember James and his comment: 'When things slow down, then I'll take a holiday.')

- Consider the pattern and timing of your holidays in response to historical and anticipated seasons of stress.

- Think about the purpose of your time off. Make sure your holidays address your actual needs and achieve desired outcomes.

- If finances are a barrier, get creative. A restful holiday does not need to cost the earth. (Remember an Indian man's perspective on leaving home to rest.)

SOMETHING TO THINK ABOUT

What is one thing that stands out to you from this chapter? What is the next action?

CHAPTER 13

A DAY TO THINK

I have a friend called Gil, who is a mentor in my life. Gil is an executive director in a fast-paced company. One morning, he was leaning back in his chair with a coffee in hand, gazing out of a window. A colleague walked past, looked in and gave a cutting comment, 'I see you're working real hard, Gil.' With a confident grin, Gil turned around and responded, 'Yes actually, I am. I'm doing my *most important work*.' Then he put his feet back up and continued enjoying the sunshine.

Here's the thing that struck me about this interaction. Gil was not being sarcastic or defensive. He was confidently stating truth. As a thought leader, product developer, people manager and strategist, Gil is paid to think, not just act. He is responsible for leading his company wisely, unlocking problems and setting direction. This requires well-thought-out decision-making. For Gil, staring out of a window to ponder his role, his people and projects is genuine work. It is an internal discipline that enables his teams to avoid the reactive busy work so common in workplaces that refuse to think.

Our second practice helps us to be more like Gil, making time for strategic thinking on a seasonal basis. Many of us desire time for deep thought but feel guilty about downing our tools to think deeply. To overcome this resistance, we need to shift not only our calendars but our mindset. There are, of course, 'acceptable' ways to engage in strategic thinking, which usually look more like frantic activity. Ad hoc strategic meetings, long-term planning sessions and off-site retreats are common practices to help us forecast the future with colleagues. But as a Spacemaker, we can do more than this, making time to lead ourselves in addition to these corporate rhythms. It's important to make space to review our direction, both personally and professionally, and take time out every few months to think deeply.

HOW TO ESTABLISH A SEASONAL SILENT RETREAT

As a husband, father, business owner and community leader, I take thinking very seriously. One of the most helpful practices I have discovered is to establish a seasonal silent retreat – a day away from the office, once a quarter, to brew on big ideas.

In summer, autumn, winter and spring, I dedicate an entire day to ruminate. I head to the beach, turn off my phone and spend eight hours alone with a journal and pen. I look back and reflect on my past season, and project forward to the future. I rarely enter these days with an agenda but instead allow my mind to focus on whatever currently has my attention. One time, I reconsidered our marketing strategy for an upcoming product launch. Another occasion, I reflected on my upcoming anniversary and the card I wanted to write to my wife.* There are no rules to this retreat, except for seasonally making space for the mind to think. Not only are these days refreshing for me but they also deliver amazing outcomes. Many of my best ideas, which have guided my personal and professional future, have resulted from these times of deep reflection.

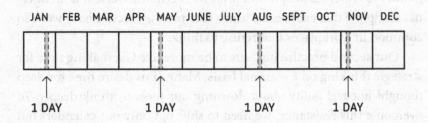

---

* Most of us think about work when we are at home, so it seems legitimate to think about personal issues, within reason, during working hours. Creative ideas occur when we give our attention to what we need to give our attention to, resulting in better outcomes in all spheres of life.

Many of us as professionals agree that a retreat is a good idea, but we find it hard to adopt in practice. We don't consider thinking to be *real* work. We can feel guilty leaving the office to ponder our role in paid hours. This is illogical, particularly if we manage people, run projects or set direction for others. If strategy is part of our job description, then to *not* prioritise thinking time is to neglect part of our role. But we struggle to reason like this. We are not supported to take time out for deep thinking, but this must be challenged. How many ill-conceived projects get off the ground to then fade out half-finished? How many hours are wasted in recurring meetings with no outcomes? How many systemic issues or team disputes could be avoided with a well-thought-out intervention? Imagine how differently our organisations would function if we, as leaders, gave ourselves permission to think.

Spacemakers have a different mindset. We work hard, but we also consider what we are doing, and why we are doing it. A seasonal silent retreat is not particularly time-intensive – just four days spread over a year – but it can save us months of lost productivity.

If you own your own business, pre-book thinking retreats at the same time you plan your holidays. If you work for others, and are concerned about how your manager might react, be brave and communicate clearly. Explain why you are motivated to implement this practice, how it fits in your job description and what you aim to achieve as a result. Call it a 'trial' – just four days a year to think about your work – and attribute any 'aha' moments to this practice when they occur. To support your request, you may even want to cite Gallup researcher Marcus Buckingham, who said, 'The best leaders I've studied all discipline themselves to take time out of their working lives to think.'[1] Alternatively, if you are the manager of a team, you have an opportunity to empower others to think deeply. Invite your direct reports to 'pilot' this practice with you. Organise your staff to cover each other's work, or hire temporary help, or accept skeleton staffing to enable your leaders to leave the office for a day. By working together and establishing a 'thinking culture' within your unit, you can reduce stress, unblock problems and avoid reactive work.

THE HABITS OF SET AND RESET

Productivity guru, David Allen, famously suggested, 'If you don't pay attention to what has your attention, it will take more of your attention than it deserves.'[2] There is value in focusing your mind on whatever issues are most pressing at the time, whether these are 'big' or 'small' things. Different seasons require different levels of self-examination. If you were to lose your job, for example, it would be appropriate to spend your time giving attention to longer-term concerns: Why did I lose my job? Am I in the right career? Do I need to move cities? If, on the other hand, you feel snowed under by emails and are struggling to achieve a pressing deadline, big questions are a distraction, and it's better to focus your attention on immediate and pressing matters: When will I complete my presentation? Can I stay late at the office tonight? How will my children eat dinner? In other words, sometimes we need to give attention to higher-order problems, and at other times, near-term issues. This is not only true in daily experience, but across the landscape of our life.

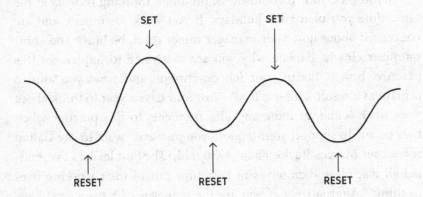

If we step back and examine our life over decades, we are likely to observe a series of peaks and troughs, which I describe as *set* and *reset*. These twists and turns reflect seasons when our need for *nearer-term* or *higher-order* cognition was greater. As Spacemakers, we can recognise our current season of life and adjust our habits of thinking accordingly.

Reset periods of our life, represented by the trough, are times of uncertainty. We feel confused about our situation and our direction. We are unclear about our longer-term goals and personal priorities. We feel unbalanced, like a train heading in the wrong direction. In the trough, it is reasonable to question our values, our purpose and life trajectory. It is reasonable to focus our attention on big things. Times of reset are commonly triggered by life events, such as a redundancy, relocation, sickness, death or divorce. It is, however, possible to reset in 'good' times, when our routines become so stale that we long for something new. In times of reset, it is wise to avoid jumping to a solution too quickly. Instead, unplug, slow down and wrestle deeply with the problem. Don't be in a hurry to escape a season of reset. Allow yourself the space and time to ruminate on uncomfortable ideas.

In contrast, over the course of a lifetime, we also experience peak seasons of *set*. During these times, we know what we want to achieve and are clear about how to get there. When in set, we need to get moving. This is not a time for philosophy but action. We plan projects, schedule appointments, book meetings and balance budgets. We progress our goals, no matter how difficult they may be. Set seasons are not mindless seasons. They too require deep thinking and meaningful examination, but the nature of our questioning is different. When in set, for example, I try to focus my attention on near-term issues rather than abstract ones. I avoid double-guessing goals, and focus on how to progress milestones instead.

Truth be told, as a mover and shaker, I prefer seasons of set to reset. Reset is a time of transition, of liminality, of fog. It is directionless. It is not knowing. Despite these difficulties, reset is tremendously valuable and essential for maturity. These seasons build character and develop resilience. They open possibilities. They keep us fresh. Having experienced a number of these transitions myself, I have learnt the tools to navigate my way through. I review my life goals. I read books to expand my thinking. I reach out for wise counsel. Reset is active and difficult. Rather than achieve operational tasks, it requires that we consider possibilities, change perspectives and overcome fear. Eventually, by avoiding easy answers, clarity almost always emerges. Goals become clearer. Options open, or close. We transition again from reset to set, from a trough to a peak, and start to tick-off tasks from our to-do list once again.

CREATE A POST-IT NOTE TIMELINE

A practical way to consider our future direction, in times of reset, is to develop a personal timeline, for as the saying goes, 'To move forward we must look back.' By reflecting on our past experiences, we can discover insights to guide our future. Terry Walling from Leader Breakthru, and researcher Dr Robert Clinton, have pioneered a fantastic tool called the *Post-it note timeline* to help us discover patterns and lessons from the past. The following instructions are a simplified adaption of Walling's method.[3]

If you are in a season of reset and struggling to know what to do next, map out your personal timeline using the instructions below.

STEP 1: BRAINSTORM YOUR JOURNEY

Think about the last season of your life, which may be five, ten or fifteen years in length. Get a pad of yellow sticky notes to record experiences, both good and bad, from your last season. If you want to get creative, use pink Post-it notes to represent difficult or painful memories – we learn a lot from these experiences. In no particular order, write down meaningful events, noteworthy experiences and significant people who have influenced your journey. Use one Post-it note per idea. Once your brain is empty, place these notes on a table, a large board or a really long wall (if you have a lot of notes).

STEP 2: ORGANISE YOUR TIMELINE

The next step is to organise your Post-it notes in chronological order, starting with the oldest moments on the left, moving to your current situation on the right. It may be helpful to organise these notes into 'chapters', representing significant periods of your life. However, if containing your reflections to a recent season (as opposed to your entire life), a chronological layout works fine. When finished, you will have a chronological line of yellow and pink sticky notes, representing better and harder times.

STEP 3: CONSIDER KEY INSIGHTS AND LIFE LESSONS

Now that your timeline is complete, put some effort into considering what it all means. What key insights or life lessons have you have learnt from your last season? Where are the transition points that represent a significant change or milestone? What can you learn about your passions and core convictions? How have your painful experiences shaped you? How have your successes impacted you? The aim of this activity is to gather information about your past, in order to provide clues for your future. Try to distil your insights into a handful of life lessons that shape who you are in a deeper way. You may choose to write these down as a list.

STEP 4: DREAM ABOUT YOUR FUTURE

After taking a break to clear your mind, grab a fresh pad of Post-it notes and begin to describe your future. I'm not talking about a strategic plan but an articulation of what your next season might look like, let's say, in one to three years. Use a separate sticky note for each idea, dream or project. Be creative. This is an opportunity to imagine your future in a fresh way. Do you want to write a book, travel to Paris, start a business, downshift to part-time work, get a promotion, pay off your house or start a community garden?

This activity may be done as an individual, or with a partner, depending on your desired outcome. The aim is to imagine a future informed by your past, guided by your emerging life lessons.

Once completed, take time to look at what you have written down. What projects or activities stir your heart the most? What motivates you? What might be possible? What aspects could you not live without?

STEP 5: COMMIT TO NEXT ACTIONS

Finally, after another small break, return to your timeline and take action. You want to get practical and commit to next actions. What are three tangible, meaningful actions that you can do this month to start moving? Are there projects you wish to start or stop? Are there people to talk with? Are there decisions to make? And of course, ask and answer the magic question: what is the next action? Share your plans with people you know and trust – a partner, friend or coach. It can be hard to transition through a time of reset, and support and accountability is vital.

The intention of this final component is not to map out your next twelve months in detail. That is unrealistic and creates too much pressure. Instead, it is a chance to select a handful of next steps, opening up possibilities for the future. You can always repeat this activity at another time, during your next thinking retreat or digital detox (more about this in the next chapter), to help you navigate the next bend in your season of reset.

ACT ACCORDING TO YOUR SEASON

There are times in life when action is needed, and other times when deep thinking is the best action. Know your season, and shape your habits accordingly. In times of reset, a day-long silent retreat can provide you with the space you need to ponder big questions. You may want to utilise a structure of some sort, such as a personal timeline, or keep it unstructured to ruminate on whatever has your attention. At other times, during seasons of set, thinking is more immediate. Be willing to focus your attention on unblocking goals and solving pressing issues. In every season, the question should not be, 'Do I need to think?', but 'How will I make the space to think?' Will you set aside a day, quarterly, in your calendar, to think deeply and achieve your very best work? Where will you spend this day? When will you make it a reality?

IN SUM

- Thinking is real work, but most leaders are reluctant to prioritise time for deep thought. (Remember Gil and his comment, 'I'm doing my most important work.')

- A quarterly silent retreat is valuable to 'give attention to what has your attention' (David Allen).

- Leaders and managers should not shy away from organising a day away from the office to think deeply. We may need to be creative in how we communicate this activity with others in our workplaces.

- Over a lifetime, we will all experience seasons of *set* and *reset*. A Post-it note timeline is a useful method to help you discover patterns from your past to guide your future.

- Different seasons require different patterns of thinking. As Spacemakers we can recognise our current season of life and act accordingly.

SOMETHING TO THINK ABOUT

What is one thing that stands out to you from this chapter?
What is the next action?

CHAPTER 14

DIGITAL DETOX

Some places are more sacred than others. They are revered places where memories are easily made. Piccaninny, my family's favourite holiday retreat on the east coast of Tasmania, is one such place. It is a home away from home, a place of rest and retreat away from technology.

Piccaninny is not a fancy place, which is why we love it. It is rustic and remote, with a wood fire, outdoor toilet and at least one resident huntsman spider. Surrounded by native Australian shrubs and trees and connected to bore water, it has both a remoteness and homeliness that is hard to find in the city. It's cosy, comfortable and disconnected from the outside world. We love this log cabin, with its small herb garden growing in an old sink and a quirky outdoor bath, but it's not for everyone. There's lots to do, but only if you slow down.

On a typical day, my wife and I wake to the sound of a rooster crowing, then doze in bed for an hour. At least that's how we started pre-children. Nowadays, we wake to bickering about who has the warmest blanket, and pretend to sleep while our youngest jumps on our bed for a *Kung Fu Panda*-style pillow fight. But we do get to stay in our pyjamas for most of the morning and eat whenever we feel hungry. We read books, play board games, observe the local birdlife, fly kites, make sandcastles and feed cows. By leaving our phones in the car and devices at home, our options are reduced, and we make our own fun. One time, my children and I spent an entire day exploring the beach. We splashed in the sea, found a lost penguin and made up stories about a 'dragon egg' shaped rock. With the scent of seaweed permeating the chilly air, we searched for cockles and eventually made our way back to the cabin, blue-lipped and ready to enjoy an outdoor bath. Feeling both tired and refreshed, from having done a lot and a little in the same day, we curled up for the evening in front of a blazing open fire. It was fabulous.

Winnie-the-Pooh famously says: 'Don't underestimate the value of doing nothing, of just going along, listening to all the things you can't hear, and not bothering.'[1] I tend to agree. We talk about disconnecting from digital technology as if it is a chore or a burden. Yet I remember that one day at the beach more vividly than the hundreds of hours spent online before and after. Simple things, experienced in the moment, leave the deepest impressions. I love digital technology and the opportunities of our age, but life is also rich and meaningful when shared together offline, uncomplicated by a screen.

As the years continue, and my children get older, they have started to complain about the thought of having to disconnect from digital technology (sometimes ad nauseam). Their world, like mine, is becoming screen-centric. But each time we immerse ourselves in a slower schedule, devoid of digital distraction, my children soak up the experience and long to return again. It is like muscle memory. We need time out to remember how to 'listen to all the things we can't hear'. This is the value of an extended digital detox. For a time, we may forget how to do nothing, but we soon remember again.

WHAT IS A DIGITAL DETOX?

A digital detox is the practice of fasting from digital technology for a significant period of time as an annual holiday or seasonal retreat. It can be a valuable circuit breaker for anyone who feels addicted to their devices, providing objective distance to test our heart, renew our mind and recalibrate our habits. A typical digital detox requires disconnection from all devices for five or more days. This extended period of time is a helpful reset, or reboot, allowing us to test our motivations and renew our thinking.

HOW CAN THIS WORK IN PRACTICE?

Practically, there are different ways to achieve a digital detox. Most commonly, people head away on a holiday to unplug and slow down. Camping trips or retreats in the wilderness work well, especially if you discover a Wi-Fi and mobile phone reception black spot. That said, internet-free zones are increasingly rare nowadays, so you may need to institute some old-fashioned self-discipline. Leave your devices at home or lock your phone in your car for the duration of your fast. That way, you can still call for help in the event of an alien invasion. There are, of course, structured digital detox retreats, organised by tourism and event management companies, catering for people who wish to slow down. Yoga on the beach, followed by massage and meditation, sounds wonderful but is often expensive. A digital detox does not have to be exotic or cost the earth.

There can also be flexibility in how we design our retreats, influenced by our household structure. If footloose and fancy-free (yes, no children), there is value in disconnecting from all digital media … because you can. Be a purist. Go cold turkey. Experience both the difficulty and beauty of a longer period of silence. If, however, you're heading away with children, compromise may be needed. As parents, we understand how valuable quiet time can be when our children are enjoying a screen. This is particularly true for single parents who are more constantly in demand. In our family, as our children grow older, our digital detox holidays are becoming less rigid. Our children don't go screen free anymore, but they do significantly reduce their media consumption. When away, we now enjoy family movie nights together, eating chocolate chip cookies, huddled around a laptop. Although it is harder to find a movie that everyone is willing to watch, being together feels better than viewing alone. As family dynamics change, communication and negotiation may be needed. Consider why you are fasting from digital technology, set limits that work for everyone and enjoy the camaraderie of a quieter retreat without constant media.

Finally, if you cannot find a place to travel away from home, staying put is an option.[2] Take your digital devices and lock them in a storage box. Better still, give them to a neighbour to avoid tempta-tion altogether. If necessary, tell your employer, colleagues, friends and family what you are intending to do in advance – think of this as a conversation starter ('you're doing *what*?!') – then actively pursue so-cial and recreational activities that do not require a screen. That said, I don't recommend the 'stay at home' approach unless you truly have no alternative. It is less fun and requires more discipline. By remaining in your normal environment, your habit triggers remain unchanged: *It's time to get out of bed – I'd better check my phone – oh no!* It is also harder, logistically, to get by without a phone in your normal environ-ment. This is not to say that a home digital detox cannot be done. It simply requires greater commitment.

PLAN YOUR DIGITAL DETOX

For several years, I have taken a digital detox at least once a year. At first it was out of desperation – I was exhausted, anxious and at risk of burnout – but not anymore. Nowadays, I cherish my digital detox as a way of enriching my life. It is a reboot and restart.

If you are interested in taking the plunge, here are some pointers to help you get going:

- Book a time in your calendar to disconnect for an extended period of time, ideally five or more days in a row. If you don't plan this in advance, it won't happen. Lock it in today.
- Set an 'out of office' reply and update your newsfeed if you want to communicate your reason for being offline.
- On the day of departure, disconnect from all devices. Physically remove your phone and smartwatch from your side. Leave other devices at home. Pack a journal, books, games and other essential items to enjoy instead.
- Don't over-schedule your time. This is not a Disneyland ad-venture. It may be helpful to shop for groceries and prepare meals in advance, but apart from the essentials, go with the flow. Don't fear boredom. Make space and slow down.

- When you arrive at your destination, replace online activities with concrete experiences. Play the ukulele. Read books. Sleep in. Make love. Do fun stuff that does not involve a screen.
- Don't be surprised if this retreat is difficult to begin with. You may feel uncomfortable or even agitated at times during your detox. Your brain will crave input from the outside world. Your mind will search for distraction. This is normal. Resist the urge to reconnect too soon.
- At the end of your digital detox, before re-entering 'real life', reflect on what you have learnt. Was it difficult? When did you crave your devices, and what specifically did you crave? What positive experiences have emerged from your time offline? What have you learnt about yourself – your heart, your head or your habits? Are there any long-term changes you wish to make to your patterns as a result of these discoveries?
- Lastly, appreciate your time away from digital distraction – cherish and enjoy the space. Some of it will be enjoyable and some of it hard, but there's treasure in the silence. Don't leave without the gold!

If you are like me, keeping a digital fast may be a hard thing to do. After years of practice, I still take a few days to readjust to this new routine. Like other addictions, my hunger for information comes in waves – first thing in the morning, before dinner, in the evening. This tension is good for me; indeed, it's the purpose of a digital detox. By uncoupling myself from the outside world, I gain the opportunity to listen to my mind rather than the minds of others. I am reminded of who I am and what I value, beyond the noise. We like to think of space in positive terms, but space, as we explored in the chapter on embracing silence, is also uncomfortable. It is revealing. Take the lessons that you learn from this time of withdrawal and re-enter 'real life' in a less compulsive, more considered way.

When and where will you book your digital detox?

IN SUM

- A digital detox is the practice of fasting from digital technology for a significant period of time, as an annual holiday or seasonal retreat. It can be a valuable circuit breaker for anyone who feels addicted to their devices.

- A typical digital detox requires unplugging from all devices for five or more days. This extended period of time allows us to test our motivations, renew our thinking and recalibrate our routines.

- Practically, there are different ways to achieve a digital detox. Most commonly, people head away on a holiday to unplug and slow down. If you are heading away with children, communication and compromise may be needed. With a bit of creativity, everyone can enjoy the camaraderie of a quiet retreat without constant media.

- An extended period of time without devices can help you review and reboot your habits. These habits can be maintained and re-enforced by adopting the weekly and daily digital practices outlined in the following chapters.

SOMETHING TO THINK ABOUT

What is one thing that stands out to you from this chapter?
What is the next action?

CHAPTER 15

WEEKLY DAY OF REST

A day off each week to rest and replenish the soul isn't a new idea. It's a very old idea that's worth recycling. In 1951, a New York rabbi named Abraham Heschel, published a seminal work called *The Sabbath*, about the Jewish custom of resting from work (and work-related technologies) a day each week. He wrote that Sabbath is a day 'of independence of external obligation' where 'the solution to mankind's most vexing problems are not found in renouncing technical civilisation, but in attaining some degree of independence from it'.[1] Written long before the internet, Heschel predicted a future where technological devices would master us, unless we maintained a day, once a week, of independence.

Although Heschel's advice was not widely heeded, the idea of a structured day of rest is experiencing a renaissance in our age. Authors of all persuasions are critiquing the state of rest in the West and seeking solutions from our past. 'There is ample evidence that our relationship to work is out of whack', writes *The New York Times* columnist Judith Shulevitz. 'The Sabbath is to the week what the line break is to poetic language. It is the silence that forces you to return to what came before to find its meaning.'[2] A widely published journalist, author and editor, Shulevitz is not advocating a return to religion, per se, but an adoption of ritualised rest as a way of slowing down and remembering life's meaning. She is one of many contemporary voices calling us to bring back the Sabbath.

WHAT IS A WEEKLY DAY OF REST?

A *weekly day of rest* is a ritualised day without work, once a week, to consciously make space and slow down. It typically involves unplugging from some or all of our digital devices in order to eliminate distraction. This day is more deliberate than a 'weekend' and more restful than 'time away from the office'. It is a structured weekly ritual with the ability to restore our mental health, fuel our productivity and renew our closest relationships.

A ritualised day of rest may be a simple idea, but it is surprisingly hard to implement. Of all the practices in this book, I suggest that it is both the hardest to establish and the most life-giving when maintained. Such a day is only possible with design and discipline, built on a comprehensive belief system that supports the making of space. It is one thing to turn off your phone for a day, but another to reorientate your schedule and sustain this pattern over time, in opposition to the forces that compel us to do otherwise.

Looking far and wide for a weekly practice related to spacemaking, I have found no better tradition than the Jewish Sabbath to draw upon. No practice in any area of society comes close to the design and purposefulness of the Sabbath. I therefore suggest we turn to the originators of the Sabbath for inspiration and guidance, to help us overcome the tyrannical forces of hurry.

WHAT IS SABBATH?

The Sabbath emerged as an ancient Jewish practice when Moses led the people of Israel out of Egypt. As a nation of slaves under the oppressive building-regime of Pharaoh, the Jews had never known anything but work. They had laboured without rest for generations. Their children had known nothing but toil. So when Moses led his community out of Egypt and through the wilderness, it was a challenge to re-educate them to stop and rest deeply. Listed above 'don't murder' and 'don't steal' is a curious command to 'take a day off'.[3] In Judeo-Christian creation accounts, God created the world in six days and rested on the seventh, and if the Jewish nation were to be truly free, they needed to do the same. The fourth of Ten Commandments, 'remember the Sabbath day, to keep it holy', is not just an instruction to rest but an invitation to embrace the freedom that rest represents. The commandment is not just about rest but about culture and identity – slaves work seven days a week, but free people take a day off.[4]

In application, Jews celebrate the Sabbath together to remember their freedom. The Sabbath begins before sunset on a Friday evening and concludes an hour after sunset on Saturday evening.* All work is discontinued, rest is ritualised, and in some traditions, mandated. Rituals vary from group to group but most involve proscriptions and prescriptions. Proscriptions have to do with not working, whereas prescriptions encourage festivity, worship and other collective expressions of spirituality.[5]

A *weekly day of rest* enables all of us to embrace some of the benefits of the Sabbath. As suggested by Shulevitz, 'If the Sabbath you choose to observe isn't a religious one, you should nonetheless be religiously disciplined in your approach to it, observing it every week, not just when it's convenient.'[6] Like the Jewish Sabbath, a weekly day of rest requires planning and preparation. There is a start and an end. There are proscriptions and prescriptions. There are shared practices. There is a commitment to unplug from technology. To be sustained over time, these practices must also be grounded in a compelling freedom story – values and beliefs that underpin a commitment to making space in a sacrificial way. Spacemakers value space. This is why we have spent time unpacking the principles and practices in this book. If we are to unplug, unwind and think clearly in our slavishly demanding culture, we will need an alternative story – one strong enough to inspire and sustain digital-habit change.

---

* For adherents of Christianity, Sabbatarian rituals are more eclectic and diverse. Congregations typically adhere to 'the Lord's Day' – a 24-hour period on a Sunday to particularly focus on loving God, loving one another, to read Scripture and replenish the soul.

TWO PILLARS OF REST AND REFLECTION

When the sun sets on a Friday evening, Jewish people from around the world light candles, drink wine, sing songs and initiate the Shabbat (or Sabbath). There is meaning in every aspect of this tradition, both theological and cultural. Although I am not Jewish, I am inspired by the beauty of these rituals, particularly the lighting of two candles, representing the central themes of the Sabbath, which are *rest* and *worship*.*

For a weekly day of rest, I also propose two pillars – *rest* and *reflection* – represented diagrammatically by two candles.

REST   **REFLECTION**

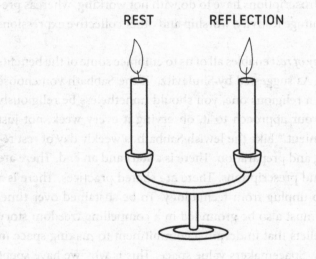

Rest is the commitment to not work. It involves defining what work is, what it is not, and shaping our day around truly restful activities. We will explore these questions in more detail later in the chapter.

---

* In borrowing Sabbatarian principles and practices, my intention is to honour the wisdom found within Jewish and Christian traditions. These are treasures worth restoring, even if interpreted in an unconventional way. I am not suggesting that the 'weekly day of rest' is the Sabbath – which is why I have chosen a different term to describe this practice. The Sabbath is based on a different story, inseparable from the worship of God.

Reflection is about lifting one's mind beyond the mundane, spending time thinking about life's meaning, remembering who you are, what you value and why you exist. This can be done either individually or with others. This may involve contemplative activities, such as meditating, writing in a journal, digging a garden or sitting in silence. It could involve creative pursuits, such as painting, drawing, playing music or crafting wood. For some, reflection includes self-development, such as reading books, visiting museums or listening to podcasts. For others, there's a spiritual component, such as attending church services, singing in groups or praying with others.

Even though a weekly day of rest is structured, it is never rigid. This is a day of joy and celebration, a chance to soak in the beauty of life without a device in your hand. What does rest look like for you and your family? What does reflection require of you? If an activity involves deep rest or personal reflection, go for it. Select activities you enjoy and that contribute to your well-being.

With the two foci of rest and reflection in mind, we are now ready to plan our weekly day of rest, using what I call *the Five Ds*. That is, we need to select a *day*, prepare *dinner*, select *dos* and *don'ts*, and, of course, formulate a plan to *disconnect* from our devices.

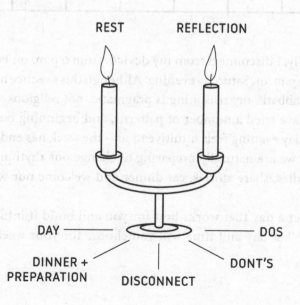

HOW TO DESIGN A WEEKLY DAY OF REST

Before you read on, grab a pen and paper. As you review each of the *Ds* outlined below, write down notes to plan your weekly day of rest. Do this activity individually, or with a partner, and if applicable, include older children. This list will become a framework to guide you as you practise your weekly day of rest.

STEP 1: SELECT A DAY

The first decision you need to make is what day you will rest each week. It can be surprisingly hard to set a pattern. For those who work during the week, some choose a Saturday, others a Sunday. Shift workers and people with changing schedules will need to be creative. The secret is to design a regular and consistent day off until it becomes habitual.

MON	TUE	WED	THU	FRI	SAT	SUN

Personally, I disconnect from my devices from 6 p.m. on Friday evening to 6 p.m. on Saturday evening. Although this practice mimics the Jewish Sabbath, my reasoning is pragmatic, not religious. As a family, we have tried a number of patterns, and beginning our Sabbath on a Friday evening feels intuitive to us – the week has ended, and as a family we are naturally preparing to change our rhythm. We light two candles, share stories, eat dinner and welcome our weekly day of rest.

Select a day that works best for you and build it into your calendar. What day and time will you choose for your weekly day of rest?

STEP 2: FACTOR IN DINNER AND PREPARATION

Like any special event, preparation is essential if you are to lean into rest. For us, this means preparing dinner and tidying the house in advance. Again, we borrow from our Jewish custodians, who consider preparation for the Sabbath as important as the holy day itself.[7] Many Jews buy groceries, cook meals and clean the house to avoid working on the Sabbath. Some might go further, taking out the light globe from the fridge to avoid 'lighting a fire' on the Sabbath. How you prepare, of course, is a matter of personality and preference. If you are happy to hang out in a messy house, with a pile of dishes, and eat takeaway food for a day, then strictly speaking, no preparation is required. But for most of us, a tidy house is synonymous with psychological rest. Some level of forethought is needed.

Each person's routine will vary according to the level of flexibility their work allows and their own unique life circumstances. The idea is to prioritise a weekly day of rest that best serves you and your family. To give an idea of what this can look like in practice, here's our family routine. On a Friday afternoon at 4 p.m., when the alarm on my phone goes off, I finish what I am working on and return home. This is an intentionally early finish to allow me time for preparation. My wife, who works part-time, is typically home by 3 p.m. Around 4.45 p.m., when I enter the house, there is a buzz of activity. Our children contribute alongside us – vacuuming the carpet, putting away the dishes, bringing in firewood, folding clothes and sweeping the kitchen floor. The aim isn't to make the house spotless but liveable. At our best, we also prepare an extra-large serving of food to avoid meal preparation the following day.

This preparation ritual has inherent value, beyond resetting our home for the weekend. For me, it is a mental activity that enables me to transition between work and rest. On Friday afternoon, vacuuming is meditative and cleaning re-energising, because it signifies that my weekly day of rest is about to start. Cleaning is a holy ritual, a preparation for something new. As I put out bins and shake the doormat, I mentally leave work at the door and enter a mindset of rest.

In a similar way, there is great value in developing a *ritual* to kick-start our weekly day of rest. This is the second component of preparation. There are myriad options for how to create a ritual, with plenty of room for creativity. To initiate our family's weekly day of rest, we light two candles, pour drinks, serve food and say a thanksgiving prayer. We ask our children about the meaning of both candles. We talk about rest and reflection as a value. We discuss how we might rest and reflect in the time ahead. The secret is to create a ritual that is personal, interesting and enjoyable. This ritual creates a sense of anticipation and allows our family to transition from work to rest more easily.

STEP 3: DISCONNECT

Making space for deep rest almost always requires a technology rethink.

In practice, here's what I do to unplug on my weekly day of rest:

- I turn off my laptop and iPad and put them away – out of sight, out of mind.
- I turn off my smartphone, keeping it on charge but switched off.
- I don't check my calendar, to-do lists, email, social media or scan the internet.
- I rarely watch television (unless I'm with other people, in which case it feels social and contributes to cultivating community).

Without a doubt, the most radical of these activities is removing my phone from my side each week. For many of us, this is unthinkable. Over the years, I have tried a number of less extreme strategies – immobilising apps, turning off Wi-Fi, relying on self-discipline to avoid checking email – and none have been as successful as keeping my phone out of sight. When my phone is in my pocket, my mind thinks about how I might use it. Effort is required to avoid scanning the news, checking my email, texting friends or adding items to my to-do list. That said, I'm fairly flexible in my own 'rules'. Sometimes on a Saturday,

I'll scan my phone in the middle of the day, in case there's an important text message. If I'm heading out socially, I keep my phone in my pocket, switched off, in case we need to change plans. But most weeks, my aim is to totally unplug as a habit.

If disconnecting from your phone is a deal-breaker, think creatively and find a workable solution. Some people buy an additional 'dumb' phone to use on the weekend (allowing them to turn off their smartphone and eliminate intruding client calls). Others download anti-distraction apps or disable key features, thereby limiting internet functionality on their devices. Then of course there's self-discipline. Simply avoid using the internet. Whatever your preference, be consistent. Make a plan and stick to it for at least four weeks.

STEP 4: DEFINE YOUR DON'TS

To experience a richer rest, we must produce a list of proscriptions, or activities to avoid on our weekly day of rest. These are not rules, but norms, guiding us in what we *don't* want to do. In order to create such a list, we must first explore what 'work' means for us.

Imagine you are a professional gardener. Every day is physically active – you mow lawns, trim hedges, pull out weeds and spray blackberries. Work is done outdoors, exposed to the elements. You are rarely in the office and almost never in front of a screen. If this is work, then what does 'not working' mean for you? To start with, it is unlikely to involve gardening. In addition, you may want to avoid activities that replicate work, such as outdoor activities and manual jobs around the house. These tasks are similar to your paid profession. Rest, in contrast, will look and feel different. It might involve reading a book, eating at a café, or watching a movie. This is, of course, a generalisation – it is wholly possible that building a fence or riding a mountain bike may be your thing – yet those who are physically active in their salaried work often enjoy inactive forms of rest.

In contrast, a white-collar professional who spends all day online will need to consider a different set of dos and don'ts. Think about a manager who has back-to-back meetings, hundreds of emails and is constantly connected to a device. Their job is sedentary and heavily information based. They are available day and night. What does it mean for this person to 'stop working'? What does a day of restorative rest look like for them? For such a leader, deep rest will almost always involve a digital fast. Rather than relaxing in front of a screen, it may be healthier to get outdoors and start gardening.

For those who are employed for their high-level knowledge, productivity is no longer primarily defined by physical activity.[8] Most of their work involves the mind. As such, when defining what work means to a knowledge worker, it's important to consider internal machinations, as well as external activities. Again, we can borrow from Jewish theology, this time the concept of *melachah,* or *mindful-work.* *Melachah* refers to the intention behind the work we do – the thoughts and internal motivations shaping our actions.[9] Work is both internal and external, involving action and intention. This is worth considering when designing our rhythms of rest.* For me, reading the news or checking the stock market are expressions of 'mind work'. Scanning social media groups or reading leadership books are also work-like. When defining your don'ts, it is important to consider those activities that trigger *melachah.* Avoid activities that consistently trigger your brain to focus on your work.

So to define your don'ts, write a list of activities that look and feel like work to you. Start with obvious behaviours like 'going to the office', progressing to work-like activities, such as 'typing on a keyboard'. Next, stretch yourself to identify activities that make you think about work in a tiring way. Combined, these activities will form your list of don'ts. On your weekly day of rest, your aim is to reduce or eliminate time spent on these pursuits.

For me, I avoid emailing, scanning the internet, texting, writing or ticking things off a list. I avoid hard conversations. I minimise social activities. I avoid talking about global events. For my wife, a registered

---

* Of interest, the concept of *melachah* is not unique to Judaism. In Australian law, we understand the difference between murder and manslaughter to be the intent to harm. The intention behind our actions is worth considering.

nurse and mum of three, work is anything that involves caring for people. That means her don'ts include cooking, cleaning, shopping or dealing with family issues (outside of immediate and unavoidable outbursts). For my three children, moving into their early teens, the story is nuanced. We allow a certain amount of screen time in the morning, because it gives them joy, but access to their devices is limited. Homework and piano practice are not required. 'Eating vegetables', despite their objections, does not qualify as work.

What is work for you? What does it mean for you to 'not work'? Start your list.

STEP 5: DEFINE YOUR DOS

Having defined your work, it is important to discover how you rest best. This is the fun part, and involves finding invigorating activities that add value to your life. Again, we need some theory, before defining our list of *dos*.

Rest is an individual phenomenon. We all rest in different ways. Some of us are introverts and others extroverts. Some rest actively and others inactively. Singles, couples, parents with young children, parents with older children, empty nesters and retirees all have different opportunities and challenges when it comes to rest.

One of the most important factors to consider when determining how you rest is your *personality type*. Are you an extrovert or an introvert? Extroverts gain energy when around people and are prone to boredom when left alone with their thoughts. They enjoy human interaction and take pleasure in social activities. Stereotypically, extroverts enjoy talking, networking and socialising. They leave a party feeling more alive than when they arrived. Introverts, on the other hand, recharge by spending time alone. They are de-energised by crowds and by people they don't know well. They enjoy solo activities, such as reading, playing music, hiking and fishing, which involve space to think and process internally.

Studies show that one third to one half of us are introverts.[10] Statistically, if you spend your weekly day of rest with another person, it is likely that you will share it with someone of the opposite personality type. If extroverts want to be around people, and introverts prefer time alone, how do we navigate these differences? Is it possible, as an extrovert, to socialise for part of the day with friends, allowing your introverted partner to read a book? As an introvert, can you schedule a few hours of solo time before or after you head to lunch with your partner's friends? With communication, compromise and creativity, it is wholly possible for everyone to rest in the way they need, so long as each person is willing to serve the other.

A second factor to consider when determining what work means for us, is whether we re-energise *actively* or *inactively*. Rest does not have to involve a sofa. It can occur on a bike. In the words of productivity author Alex Soojung-Kim Pang, 'physical activity is more restful than we expect, and mental rest is more active than we realise'.[11] Because of the sedentary nature of my work, I enjoy being active during my day off. I am not busy or productive, but I do use my body. Sometimes I walk, or ride, use a brush-cutter or chainsaw wood – all cathartic activities that help me to clear my mind and enjoy fresh air.

This isn't a complex concept – rest can be physically active – yet it differs significantly from Jewish and Puritan traditions where manual labour and strenuous activities were almost always prohibited on the Sabbath. In my mind, given our modern-day sedentary context, activity is a legitimate form of rest when pursued with restful intentions. Don't use 'activity' as an excuse to produce more, compete more or drive yourself to achieve something that is really work. If you must complete a home improvement or achieve a manual task by a particular deadline, it may be better to leave it for another day. Examine your heart, asking if rest and reflection are your primary motivations. If yes, enjoy the physical alertness that comes from being active.

Lastly, it is important to consider how we rest with other people in *different life seasons*. One person's work is another's recreation. If you live with others, navigating rest collectively can be complicated. It can also be deeply rewarding when you get it right. As a family, we do our best to keep Saturdays clear of structured commitments because we cherish a day with no plans. We don't have to be somewhere or go out in the car. We don't feel pressured to rush from one thing to the next. This allows us to be flexible and adaptive. After a shared breakfast, we plan our day as a family. As an introvert, I often mountain bike ride in the morning to clear my head, giving me energy to socialise with my extrovert wife and our friends in the afternoon. Around midday I make sandwiches and spend time with my children, giving my wife space to relax at home without responsibilities, or journal without distraction. Sometimes life throws a curve ball, and our day becomes less restful than is otherwise ideal. But most times, through a commitment to rest and reflect, our collective 'day off' is a deeply rewarding experience for all.

Different seasons of life bring different challenges. When we had young children, moments of rest were harder to come by, especially during the day. Now that our children are growing up, my wife and I have less time alone in the evening but more time to sleep-in. Everyone has a different situation, requiring creativity and the willingness to adjust patterns when needed. Right now, our challenge is navigating the social pressure on families to participate in school sport. It is good for our children to run about in winter, so we have agreed to spend Saturday mornings on a soccer oval, cheering together as a family. For the rest of the year, we say a firm no to Saturday sport so we can slow down and enjoy unstructured rest.

In every stage of life, even when stretched, you can enjoy a life-giving weekly day of rest by knowing what you are doing and why you are doing it. This is the reason a *dos and don'ts* list is so valuable. It provides a structured framework to help you maximise the quality of your rest, in line with your season of life. If you need help in creating your own plan, refer to the worksheet in Appendix 1 and the summary of my family's personal framework in Appendix 2.

CONSIDER WHAT YOU WILL GAIN

A weekly day of rest is a game changer but can be hard to get off the ground. I truly acknowledge how difficult it can be to reorganise your schedule and your patterns around the values of space and rest. Most people are attracted to the idea of a day without set commitments, consumer purchases, home renovations and digital distractions but struggle to make the leap when it comes to implementation. It is challenging to work against the tyranny of the urgent, especially when trying to make changes alone. Can you share this practice with a few like-minded people, set a challenge and do this together? Can you ask others to support and cheer you on?

When contemplating this practice, one of the hardest barriers to overcome is our attachment to our phone. As we have explored, we love and admire what our phones can do for us. But as Heschel suggested in the 1950s, if we are unable to gain back 'independence' from our technologies, over time they will surely control us. When considering this, it is natural for us to focus on what we might *miss out* on – weather updates, text messages, news reports – and how this will negatively impact our lives.

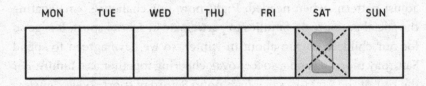

But, as Spacemakers we need to flip our thinking and focus on what we have to *gain*. For one glorious day each week, we get to enjoy an entire day of creative white space.

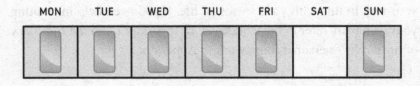

A ritualised day of rest, once a week, is worth fighting for. Such a pattern will transform your life by transforming your ability to rest. According to American scholar Walter Brueggemann, 'people who keep Sabbath live all seven days differently'.[12] As I've engaged with a weekly day of rest, this has certainly been my experience, as well as others who have engaged with this. We can be independent from our devices if we choose to unplug. Rather than live in metaphorical Egypt, with its tyrannical schedule of never-ending work, we can set aside a special day each week to be unbusy and unplanned. Turn off your devices as a habit, even if it feels hard to do. Slow down and reflect on life's meaning. Share a day of rest with people you most love, and experience a healthier, more productive, more satisfying week.

IN SUM

● A weekly day of rest is a ritualised and intentional day, once a week, to unbusy yourself. It involves unplugging from digital devices to make space and slow down.

● This practice is informed by Jewish and Christian traditions of Sabbath, yet some of the benefits can be experienced by all.

● The two pillars of a weekly day of rest are rest and reflection. *Rest* is more than 'not working'. It involves the pursuit of life-giving activities. *Reflection* is time spent thinking about meaningful things that nourish the soul.

● To plan a weekly day of rest, develop an action plan using *the five Ds*: select a *day*, factor in *dinner* and preparations, *disconnect* from your devices and define your *dos* and *don'ts*. The aim is not to create a set of rules but a flexible structure to guide your day.

● When implementing your plan, don't focus on what you might miss out on but recognise what you have to gain. Enjoy a glorious day, each week, of creative white space.

SOMETHING TO THINK ABOUT

What is one thing that stands out to you from this chapter? What is the next action?

CHAPTER 16

DAILY REFRESH

There is a brown, leather recliner chair in my father's dental surgery, which has been in our family ever since I can remember. It is a special chair – tattered, scratched and faded from decades of use. As children, we used to launch ourselves off this recliner, jumping into a mound of pillows. Now in my father's office, it has a quieter life, providing comfort for a daily siesta. Rather than a bedraggled chair, it is a space-making armchair, giving my dad the energy he needs to work each day.

My father, you see, has what I would call a superpower – the ability to nap almost anywhere, on demand. Over the years, his napping has become legendary. Every lunch, after a busy morning of scaling, filling or extracting teeth, my father will put away his gown, enter a room in the back of his dental surgery, recline in his brown chair and nap. In a short forty-minute lunch break, my father will nap for twenty minutes. He swears by this routine. Over the years it has helped him to relax, refresh and re-enter the day with a sense of vigour. It is a surprisingly effective way to make space.*

Now, I realise that most of us don't have the luxury to sleep at work, even if we are self-employed like my father. No one wants to get fired for 'napping on the job'. However, my father's power-nap routine is an expression of what I believe we all need in our day – a time to pause

---

* Sad to say, I did not inherit my father's napping gene. On rare occasions when I attempt to sleep during the day, it takes me at least forty-five minutes to fall asleep, and I feel drowsy and lethargic afterwards. Some people get all the luck.

and a place to stop – to routinely refresh our mind and body, without digital distraction. I call it the *daily refresh*.

WHAT IS THE DAILY REFRESH?

The daily refresh is about taking time out, every day, to pursue energising activities away from a screen. This can include a vast array of life-giving pursuits, such as journaling, meditating, painting, praying or running. These activities do not require a lot of time – twenty minutes is often enough – but they must occur regularly. As a mini-break, the daily refresh is a practice that almost anyone can implement as part of their spacemaking journey.

Up until now, we have explored the importance of establishing annual and weekly patterns to unplug and unwind, all of which have been systematic and structured. These practices provide an overarching foundation to help us enter the day with confidence. However, the battle for space is also fought in the trenches of everyday life, under the crossfire of text messages, work meetings, hungry children, utility bills and home maintenance. It is here, where our battle for space is most fierce, that *daily rhythms* kick in. A small break from frantic activity, repeated each day, can make the difference between a distracted, exhausted life and a life well lived.

When it comes to selecting a twenty-minute daily ritual, there is an enormous array of options to choose from. What works for one person will not translate to another. What worked in one season, may not work in the next. In this way, the daily refresh is the most flexible of all the spacemaking practices. We need to experiment until we find a daily pattern that sticks, constantly adapting to maintain space on the front line of life.

I personally have a number of practices that work in different seasons, such as reading, praying, journaling, riding, swimming and walking. I may not always use the *same* twenty-minute rituals, but I always have *some* form of twenty-minute ritual to refresh my mind. Most often, these bookend the day – morning and night – to help me start and end with mental relaxation and centredness. Whenever my routines get stale or I feel unmotivated, there is freedom to switch routines. This is the beauty of the daily perspective – it is dynamic and responsive to our situation. We can change things up in response to the ebb and flow of life.

If you feel wired and tired, you may not have the endurance to keep a full day of silence, but almost all of us can find twenty minutes in our day. Better to start small and build up our reps over time. Like building muscle or cardiovascular fitness, there is no rush to create too much space, too soon. Climb incrementally. You might begin with five minutes of breathing or one gratitude statement or ten minutes of journaling once a week. Be kind on yourself as you build up space-making muscle. Make a quick start and refine as you go.

THE GEEKY-MEN'S BOOK CLUB

For the last decade, I have been part of a leadership book club. Four times a year, a group of working professionals get together and discuss books about productivity, leadership, management and personal growth. It is a way to stretch our thinking and spur each other on ... and a fine excuse to drink whisky as friends. Our partners make fun of this group and the serious books we read. They call it the 'geeky-men's book club'.

One of the reasons I like this group is the mixture of members. We come from a diverse range of professional backgrounds (including architecture, viticulture, social work, real estate and financial advising) and hold different cultural and spiritual beliefs. Everyone is a leader in their field, so the conversations are insightful. But despite our differences, we all have one thing in common: we are all stretched for time and need more space.

So when it came to writing this chapter, I decided to draw on this group of capable leaders to discover how they make space each day. How do they refresh and recharge? How do their habits reflect their values, their stage of life and personalities? And in what ways do they unplug? I recorded snippets of our conversations, covering a variety of interesting practices to help us discover solutions of our own. There are myriad ways to include time-out rituals in your daily schedule. Be creative and find one that works for you.

To start with, Tim, a project manager, discussed the benefit of walking around the city:

> If I'm at work and get the slumps, and can't stop yawning, the best thing I can do is go for a walk. I silence my phone and walk around the block a few times. It gets the blood pumping and helps me to stay alert. It's like having an afternoon coffee and recharges me for the rest of the day.

David, a digital marketer, also shared his reflections about walking:

> I work from home most of the time and have a lot of flexibility. There's a walking path at the end of my street, with trees on both sides. When I need a break, I put on my trainers and walk to the end of the path, then jog back again. It's not about the exercise, as it's not a long track. It's about clearing my head and helping me think. This walking path has been a life-saver for me. I pace it two or three times a day.

David continued with reflections about keeping a gratitude journal:

> My house is pretty small, and it can be hard to find a quiet place when the kids are around. But I have a couch on our front deck, and it's where I stop and think. I don't always succeed, but most mornings I throw on some layers and spend a few minutes looking at the trees. I listen to birdsong. I write down three things I am thankful for. I also journal my thoughts for the day. It helps me to prepare and get my head right.

Gabi, a communications business analyst, discussed his practices of meditation and mindfulness:

> I listen to a guided meditation every night for twenty minutes,

using an app on my phone. I know it's not technically unplugging, but it works as part of my wind-down routine. It slows down my brain before I go to sleep. So I lie on the floor and listen to a person talk me in and out of a meditation. There is music in the background, but after a while, I don't notice it – I tune out, and it's very relaxing. It helps me to be in the moment.

Haji, an entrepreneur with multiple businesses, described being at the gym as a way of making space:

My daily refresh takes place at the gym. I go there in the morning, and it's my time. I don't bring the phone. Instead, I talk to friends. I work out really hard and feel like I've achieved something – and it feels good mentally and physically. Afterwards, I'm energised, invigorated and my endorphins are going. It sets me up well, and I feel like I've won the day.

On the practice of prayer, Haji gave further advice:

As a Muslim, I pray five times a day. It's what we do. On New Year's Eve, one of my friends made me laugh by saying that his 'resolution' was to get all his prayers done in one go. He was being funny because prayer doesn't work like that. There's something valuable about stopping five times a day, as a ritual. I sometimes pray with others, which is community building. And it helps me to think about bigger things.

Michael, an architect, enjoys playing music as a way of making space:

Music is my thing. When I have a guitar in my hand, my fingers start moving and my mind relaxes. There's something about playing an instrument that is different to anything else I do. It connects me to others and to the world around me. It's easy to play for an hour and lose track of time.

And my father's napping habit also resonates with Tim:

> I like to nap. It refreshes my whole day. When I was studying
> at university, I used to nap a lot. I even napped during my lec-
> tures – my brain was still taking stuff in, but I was sleeping. I'm
> sure that my lecturers noticed that I was napping ... although
> my writing hand kept moving!

HOW MIGHT YOU REFRESH YOUR DAY?

As we have explored, there are different ways to refresh our mind, body
and soul, as a daily habit. We can all build twenty-minute spaces into
our schedule to reflect, relax and unwind.

To plan your daily refresh routine, consider a place, a pattern and
a plan:

- Find a *place* to unwind – like a brown leather chair, an outdoor
  couch or a local walking path.
- Create a *pattern* to be consistent – like a regular gym routine, a
  morning gratitude journal or an evening meditation.
- Make a *plan* with enough detail to trigger the habit – like buying a journal, meeting up with friends or keeping running
  shoes by your desk.

For most people, it only takes fifteen minutes to come up with a solid
plan. Grab a pen and paper. Brainstorm at least five options. Talk about
it with a partner or friend, if you need to process externally. Consider
the patterns that have worked for you in the past. Reflect on your current habits – what is working now, and what's not working? With past
and present in mind, you have enough information to adopt or adapt a
new routine. You can carve out five to twenty minutes a day to refresh
your mind, without devices. Stop and breathe, and then read on.

IN SUM

- The daily refresh involves taking time out, every day, to pursue energising activities away from a screen. They can include a vast array of life-giving pursuits, to refresh our mind, body and soul. These activities do not require a lot of time – just twenty minutes is enough – but regularity is important.

- The battle for space is fought in the trenches of everyday life, which is why we need intentional habits throughout the day. Experimentation and adaption can help us find patterns that work in different seasons of life.

- Like physical training, there is no rush to build spacemaking muscle too quickly. Better to start small and build up our reps over time. Brainstorm options and make a plan. Consider ideas, such as reading, journaling, playing an instrument, meditating, praying, walking, jogging, riding, swimming, painting, drawing, napping – the list goes on.

- To help us design our daily refresh routine, consider these three things: a *place* (where we can refresh), a *pattern* (as a consistent time each day), and a *plan* (the things we need to do to carve out space each day).

SOMETHING TO THINK ABOUT

What is one thing that stands out to you from this chapter?
What is the next action?

CHAPTER 17

DAILY PAUSE

Given the choice, would you prefer to spend a few minutes alone with your own thoughts or receive painful electric shocks? As ridiculous as this sounds, this option was given to a cohort of participants in a series of eleven studies examining how we think.

Timothy Wilson, a psychology professor at the University of Virginia, recruited more than seven hundred volunteers to investigate how we respond to being alone with nothing to do.[1] Participants were asked to sit in a sparsely furnished room without phones or social media, for six to fifteen minutes and entertain themselves with their thoughts. Most people did not enjoy this experience. Even when repeated in their own home, volunteers reported the lack of external stimulation to be 'unpleasant'. Like 83 per cent of American adults who report spending 'no time whatsoever' relaxing or thinking, these participants found it painful to just sit and think.[2]

It is one thing not to enjoy thinking but another to prefer painful or unpleasant activities over doing nothing. In a further experiment, an electric shock was given to volunteers before they entered the room. So uncomfortable was this experience, that participants stated they were willing to pay money to avoid another jolt. These same volunteers were asked to sit in a room to think, but this time, had the option of pressing a button to self-administer another electric shock. They were discouraged from doing so, but the option was available. To Wilson's surprise, 67 per cent of men and 25 per cent of women chose to shock themselves, rather than ideate:

Typically people did not enjoy spending 6 to 15 minutes in a room by themselves with nothing to do but think. They enjoyed doing mundane activities much more, and many preferred to administer electric shocks to themselves instead of being left alone with their thoughts. Most people seem to prefer to be doing something rather than nothing, even if that something is negative.[3]

These results are troubling and lead us to our next spacemaking practice – the *daily pause*.

WHAT IS THE DAILY PAUSE?

In digitally enriched environments, it is tempting to fill every waking moment with external stimuli. Like participants in Wilson's study, we have trained ourselves to crave continuous input, reaching for our devices as a habit, even when doing so is counterproductive. In contrast, the daily pause is about knowing when to access and not access our digital tools each day. Remember the inverted-U curve? If we overuse our digital technologies, cascading down the right-hand side of the graph, we lose the benefits we previously gained. Multitasking, distraction, anxiety, fatigue and a loss of focus are all symptomatic of digital overuse, indicating the need to pause, breathe and think deeply.

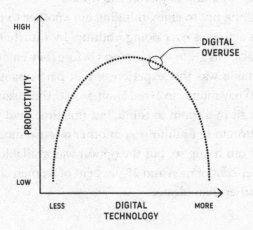

There are dozens of opportunities to pause throughout our day and experience the benefits of unmediated time. The daily pause is not a single practice but a series of small decisions to maximise the space available to us each day. In the remaining chapter, we will explore how to sleep, eat, exercise, conduct meetings and build community without distraction. Research suggests that in each of these areas, less technology can be beneficial. I would advise against trying to implement every idea at once but instead identify the most valuable for your situation. Select one or two practices to start, and enjoy a distraction-free pause in your day.

DISTRACTION-FREE SLEEP

Sleep deprivation is a major problem in the digital age. Most of us are aware that using a screen late at night impairs our capacity to fall asleep. Blue wavelength light emanating from our screens affects our sleep-wake cycle, reducing the timely release of melatonin, a sleep hormone released by our pineal gland.[4] If we sleep near our phone, merely having it vibrate or emit light can reduce the depth and quality of our sleep.[5] There are many complex factors impacting insomnia and sleep deprivation – genetics, stimulants and medical conditions to name a few – but these basic digital tips can help you to get a good night's rest:

- At least an hour before you head to bed, wean yourself from screens and create a power-down routine. Set an alarm on your phone to remind you to switch off your devices. Take a hot shower. Read a book. Listen to music. Reduce the amount of ambient light in your environment to stimulate the release of melatonin in your blood stream.[6]
- Charge your phone outside of your bedroom. This is the easiest way to improve your sleep. Without a phone by your side, you will fall asleep more easily. You will be less likely to scan your phone in the middle of the night. You are more likely to wake refreshed.

- When you do wake up, avoid checking your phone too quickly. Don't start with the news, which is often depressing. Don't check email or scan social media. Instead pause. Take a few minutes to open your eyes, think about your day and process your own thoughts.

- If you need an alarm to wake up, use an alarm clock. They still exist. Alternatively, use a Fitbit or smartwatch with an alarm function. Don't let the 'I need an alarm' excuse stop you from building better habits.

- If you have a television in your bedroom, consider moving it elsewhere. Dedicate your bedroom as a space for sleeping rather than screen-based entertainment.

- For children and teenagers, consider prohibiting screens from the bedroom. This is not just about sleep but mental health and happiness. There's plenty of evidence to indicate that harm is reduced when screens are removed from bedrooms, reducing exposure to hardcore pornography, online grooming and cyberbullying.[7] Depending on the age of your children and their existing habits, this may require respectful conversations and negotiation. Start by modelling healthy digital habits in your own life before asking your children to change their behaviours.

Sleep is ground zero for personal productivity, improving mental alertness, resilience and reducing obesity. Enjoy a daily pause late at night and early in the morning. Don't let your screens or devices stop you from having a decent night's sleep.

DISTRACTION-FREE MEALS

Dinner is more than eating. According to multiple research studies, the simple habit of eating together without a screen is one of the most important behaviours you can foster as a family.[8] According to bestselling author Charles Duhigg, eating together is a 'keystone habit' because it unlocks benefits in multiple domains of your life:

Families who habitually eat dinner together seem to raise children with better homework skills, higher grades, greater emotional control, and more confidence. ... It's not that a family meal ... *causes* better grades. ... But somehow those initial shifts start chain reactions that help other good habits take hold.[9]

Interestingly, studies show that the quality of food we eat is irrelevant – pizza works just as well as organic broccoli when it comes to language development and social cohesiveness.[10] The benefits of a family meal are about social time and conversation, unmediated by a screen.

Here are some tips to unlock this keystone habit in your own life:

- Sanction the dinner table as a digital-free zone. When you sit down to eat a meal together, silence your devices and store them out of reach. Model the behaviours you want others to imitate, particularly around teenagers. You may want to adopt these memorable 'commandments' from media journalist, Susan Maushart: 'Thou shalt bring no media to thy dinner', and 'Thou shalt bring no dinner to thy media.'[11]

- Don't answer a home phone (if you still have one) or check text messages during the meal. This may sound harsh, but in reality, small interruptions shift your focus away from those sitting across the table from you.

- Provide structure and definition by marking the start and end of your evening meal with a simple ritual. For us, we wash our hands before sitting down and saying grace. For others, it may work to say what you are thankful for. To finish the meal, we pack away our dishes. If someone needs to leave early, they ask for permission to leave the table. I recognise that these are middle-class practices that relate to my culture. The aim is not to be prescriptive but deliberate. Give definition to your meal, and avoid using a screen during this time.

- Let conversation flow without a device in your hand. Here are some fantastic questions to stimulate family discussions:

- What are you thankful for today? (A way of practising gratitude.)
- What is your high-low-buffalo? (A highlight, a low point and a random fact or funny incident from your day.)
- What did you try hard at today? (A growth mindset question from social psychologist Carol Dweck.)[12]
- Have you experienced any wonderful failures or challenges this week, and what did they teach you? (Inspired by Malcolm Gladwell's desirable difficulty theory.)[13]
- What is one thing that you appreciate about [insert the name of a family member] and why?

• If you are in a season of life where you often eat dinner alone, you might try to eat with a group of friends or family once a fortnight, to enjoy these benefits yourself. Many people will readily share their table with you if you commit to a regular time, help with set up and pack up, and contribute meaningfully to the costs.

Eating together without digital distraction is a simple but transformative habit – a daily pause, improving literacy, mental health and family cohesiveness. What is one change you can make to implement a digital-free meal?

DISTRACTION-FREE EXERCISE

Digital technology is helpful and can encourage physical activity. Fitness apps assist habit formation by tracking our progress, and music makes exercise enjoyable. The downside to exercising with external input in our ears is that it changes our ability to think our own thoughts when our mind is most alert.

Physical activity is also a keystone habit. More than just improving our physical strength, regular exercise improves sleep, mental health and cognitive performance. By increasing blood flow to the brain and releasing feel-good chemicals, such as endorphins and serotonin, exercise places our mind in an optimal state of alertness, ideal for deep thought.[14] As such, some of the best leaders I know deliberately turn off their devices when engaging in physical exercise, to encourage ideation and problem-solving. Even though they enjoy listening to music, podcasts and audiobooks, they also see the benefits of making space to walk, run or ride without digital input.

Here are some ideas about how this can work:

- If you run, ride or swim – or do any other solo physical activity – consider making a time in your week to do so without headphones. Allow your mind to think about whatever issues or opportunities are pressing at the time. If you come up with an 'aha' moment, write it down at the end of your session and capture any actions on your to-do list.
- Walking is a great way to think – a way to both stretch your legs and clear your mind. Find a physical environment that enables you to think fresh thoughts. Pay attention to the sights and sounds and allow your mind to wander as you walk.
- If you listen to a lot of podcasts and audiobooks when exercising, it may be worth making one of your workouts 'digital free'. I have coached a number of leaders who *listen* to an enormous amount of information from external sources but don't make enough space to *process* these podcasts. Take time out to think about the information you are absorbing, considering how it impacts your situation and how you might apply these ideas in practice.

Exercise is not just about physical fitness but mental alertness as well. You can maximise the benefits by allowing your mind to think, both during and after your workout.

DISTRACTION-FREE MEETINGS

Meetings are a bit like an evening meal, without the delicious food and drink. In today's work environment, almost everyone uses a phone, tablet or laptop when participating in meetings. This is effective most of the time. However, in some situations, it is not.

Psychology researcher Andrew Przybylski ran a series of studies to investigate the impact of smartphones on the quality of our conversations. People met together and talked about a variety of guided topics. For the experimental cohort, a phone was placed on a table, face down. For the control group, only a notepad was visible. When people rated the quality of their conversations, the presence of a phone inhibited 'interpersonal closeness and trust', and in particular, the ability to discuss 'personally meaningful topics'.[15] In a different set of lab experiments, led by behavioural economist Kristen Duke the mere presence of a smartphone impaired the ability of 800 participants to complete complex cognitive tasks. When participants placed their phone on a table in front of them, their 'ability to think and problem-solve' was reduced. This reduction was maintained, even when the phone was not touched, placed face down, and powered off.[16] If we extrapolate this research into our workplace context, it seems logical that we might choose to unplug for certain types of meetings – in particular, whenever we need to build relationships, foster trust, discuss personally meaningful topics or solve complex problems.

Here are a few tips to help you initiate distraction-free meetings:

- Determine the purpose or outcome of your meeting in advance. Consider the benefits of using digital technology, as well as the costs. In situations where technology is beneficial, use it to its full effect. When you need to converse without distraction, keep your devices out of sight.
- Silence your phone during meetings, and avoid answering calls unless absolutely necessary.
- When chairing a meeting or even having a one-to-one conversation, it is reasonable to ask for phones to remain off the table. Cultural norms will of course need to be considered. In some workplaces, answering phones and texting colleagues is normative behaviour. In others, it's not. In my mind, if people need to be at a meeting, it is reasonable to expect their full attention rather than using their phone.

- If you need to stay on top of incoming information, consider scheduling fifty-minute meetings rather than the habitual one hour. Most teams can achieve their outcomes in fifty minutes, leaving a pause of ten minutes between meetings to capture tasks, respond to urgent emails and think about upcoming conversations.

- Get creative by changing your environment. Nilofer Merchant suggests that 'if you want out of the box thinking you have to get out of the box'.[17] Walking meetings are a great way to generate new ideas. Stand-up meetings are valuable for making fast operational decisions. Close your laptop, be creative and shake things up.

Meetings are a fantastic way to strengthen relationships and synergise ideas as a team. Make space in some of your meetings without digital technology at hand, to gain the most out of your time together.

DISTRACTION-FREE COMMUNITY

Humans are social creatures. We look for social cues and copy the behaviour of others. Authors Dan and Chip Heath refer to a fascinating study in which social psychologists used peer pressure to solve a business problem. In an attempt to save costs, a hotel manager tried to encourage their guests to reuse their towels rather than leaving them on the floor. But it wasn't working. Their environmental signage 'save water by reusing towels' was ineffective. To change majority behaviour, researchers suggested a new approach – to harness the power of *herd thinking*. And it worked. By changing the hotel signage to say, 'The *majority* of guests at this hotel reuse their towels at least once', (italics mine) patrons became 26 per cent more likely to follow the establishment's desired behaviour.[18] This is the power of community. When people around us think and act in healthy ways, it is easier to make and maintain good habits. This is true when staying at a hotel. It is also true when decluttering our digital lives.

We need like-minded friends and family to support us in making positive digital choices, moment by moment. Here are some tips to help you get started:

- Peer support is extremely helpful when seeking to build new habits. This is why we buddy up with friends when starting a new diet or a challenging fitness regime. If you want to develop better digital habits, find a trusted friend and share the journey. Talk about your goals and break these down to pause in meaningful ways. Then cheer each other on when you succeed.

- Ask a friend if they are interested in starting a Spacemaker practice with you, for example, the weekly day of rest. You could meet at the pub on Friday after work, have a drink and turn off your devices. Or get competitive. Who can keep the longest streak of days in a row without checking Instagram? Get creative and share the joy of making space with others.

- Find ways to discuss the benefits and challenges of digital media with your community. Conversations shape culture, leading to a change in behaviour. Try encouraging your friends to read and discuss a chapter of this book or view a thought-provoking movie such as *Her*, *Ex Machina* or *The Social Network*. For an interesting documentary, discuss *The Social Dilemma*.

- If you are raising children, share struggles and learnings with others. Most parents feel perplexed about how to encourage positive digital behaviours in their children, myself included. Be brave in asking questions: *Is it healthy to let my toddler use an iPad? When do I give my child their first smartphone? Is it reasonable to ban social media for tweens? How do I talk about addiction with my teenager?* As the saying goes, talk regularly and talk often (about digital technology), and do this together. As parenting communities, let's support and learn from one another, to raise socially aware and digitally resilient children.

Life is better together, and together we can support one another to make space in the digital age. Share your challenges. Ask for help. Encourage others and be accountable to positive change.

DISTRACTION-FREE DEVICES

The last (and most effective) way to minimise distractions in the whirlwind of life, is to make our devices less distracting. This means eliminating apps and disabling notifications from our phones, tablets and other smart devices. In recent years, consumers have started to demand custom solutions to reduce the addictive nature of new media, leading to a range of new capabilities to track usage, block applications and disable alerts. Rather than provide an in-depth analysis of various 'do not disturb' features, which are ever changing, the following principles will help make your devices less exciting, and therefore, less distracting:

- Take an overarching look at the number of devices you own. Do you need all of them – a tablet, smartwatch, digital television, gaming console, fitness tracker? If not, sell these gadgets and remove a level of complexity from your life.
- Next, get serious about decluttering your phone. Fewer apps mean fewer distractions. Think about your habitual behaviours. What are the most addictive apps, the ones that capture your attention when you have a quiet moment – in bed, on the toilet, at the bus stop? Some of these need to go! Social media apps, news apps and mind games were my jam. Deleting these from my phone felt painful, but it improved my productivity and restored my attention. If you are in two minds about deleting an app, remove it anyway. You can always download it again in the future.
- Keep games and entertainment to a minimum or download them at special times, such as holidays. Be aware that games are designed to reward you so that you use them more and more.

- Uninstall social media apps from your phone – Twitter, Instagram, Facebook, Pinterest, Linked In – these are particularly addictive. You don't have to unsubscribe from these platforms. Just make it harder to log in. You will be far less likely to habitually scroll if you remove these infinity apps from your phone.

- Go to the notification centre on your phone, and remove the notifications from almost all of your apps. Don't display badges or banners or bells. Aim to only keep essential notifications, such as text messages, phone calls and calendar reminders.

- Consider activating greyscale mode to make your phone feel boring. Photographs are still taken in colour but will display in greyscale on your device. This idea may seem extreme, but it reduces the allure of your smartphone. To find out how to do this, type 'how to change your phone to greyscale' in an internet browser.

- If email is your biggest distraction, disable notifications from all devices, including laptops, tablets and smartphones. Reduce email volume by unsubscribing from companies that don't provide significant value. If you are feeling bold, unlink your email account from your phone. I haven't personally taken this final step, but a few of my clients have found this to be extremely liberating.

Decluttering your phone is not something you do just once. If you're anything like me, you'll download apps on the run, get obsessed and find yourself back where you started. There are times when I'm winning, and times when I'm losing. When I catch myself acting in addictive patterns, I analyse where I'm getting stuck, and declutter again.

A HUNDRED THOUSAND CHOICES

James Clear said, 'What is life, if not the sum of a hundred thousand daily battles and tiny decisions to either gut it out or give it up?' [19]

Making decisions to guard space in our day is never easy. As human beings, we tend to favour short-term rewards over long-term gain. But as Spacemakers, you and I know that a few simple habits can make a tremendous difference. This is why we pause each day. This is why we stop and think. Our attention is worth fighting for, moment by moment, one tiny habit at a time.

IN SUM

● When given the choice, many people prefer to receive painful electric shocks than to spend six to fifteen minutes alone by themselves. People prefer doing something rather than nothing, even if that something is unhelpful.

● The daily pause involves knowing when to use and not use our digital tools, in order to be healthy, focused and productive. It is not a single practice but a series of small decisions to maximise the space available to us each day.

● There are a series of practical tips and lifehacks that can help you to achieve distraction-free sleep, distraction-free meals, distraction-free exercise and distraction-free meetings, in a supportive community. There is also value in making your devices as distraction-free as possible, by deleting applications and removing notifications.

SOMETHING TO THINK ABOUT

What is one thing that stands out to you from this chapter?
What is the next action?

SPACEMAKER PRACTICES

Practices are where the rubber hits the road in our quest to slow down and make space. Spacemaking practices are informed by the paradigm of technology and the timeless principles of SPACE. We need annual, weekly and daily practices to unplug, unwind and think clearly in the digital age.

Rather than a summary of content, we finish this part with a checklist to help you commit to practical change.

Don't attempt to do everything at once, but commit to at least one next action. Select a habit, implement it, make refinements and return to this checklist to add another practice. Bit by bit, practice by practice, you will peg back clutter and experience the precious, wonderful, generous and life-giving satisfaction of a life with more space.

ANNUAL PRACTICES

○ **Book your holidays first**
Look at your calendar as a whole, and lock in your annual leave in advance. Consider the type of holidays you want to have. Align your holidays with times when you are traditionally in need of rest.

○ **Book a seasonal day to think**
Schedule four days in the year to 'give attention to what you need to give attention to', that is, a day away every summer, autumn, winter and spring to ruminate. Where will you do your day of

thinking? How will you spend your time? Who do you need to communicate this with?

○ **Book a digital detox**
Book a significant period of time away from your normal routine – let's say five days in a row – to experience a digital fast. You might combine your detox with an annual family holiday or book a dedicated digital retreat. Unplug from all devices. Recalibrate your routines. If you are heading away with children, you may need to communicate creatively to ensure that everyone experiences a digital-free retreat.

WEEKLY PRACTICE

○ **Design a weekly day of rest**
Design an intentional day of rest, once a week, to remain independent of digital technology. The aim is to orientate your activities, both mental and physical, around the pillars of rest and reflection. Rest involves activities that are genuinely life-giving, outside of the patterns of your work. Reflection is time spent thinking about meaningful things that nourish the soul. To plan your weekly day of rest, refer to the worksheet in Appendix 1, and plan your five Ds (day, dinner, disconnect, dos and don'ts).

DAILY PRACTICES

○ **Make space for a daily refresh**
Start a twenty-minute routine at least once a day, to refresh your mind, body and soul away from a screen. There are myriad ways to do this, depending on your personality, beliefs and season of life. To get you thinking, consider activities such as reading, journaling, playing an instrument, meditating, praying, walking, jogging, riding, swimming, painting, drawing or napping. Choose a place

to refresh, design a pattern in your schedule and create a plan to begin. You will need to adapt and modify how you approach this practice as time goes by.

Select a daily pause strategy

The daily pause is not a single practice but a series of small decisions to maximise the space available to us each day. Think about where quick wins can be found, related to distraction-free sleep, meals, exercise, meetings and community. You can also find quick wins by eliminating and disabling features on your devices. If you are unsure where to start, consider one of these high-value strategies: a) charge your phone outside of your bedroom, b) eat dinner without devices, or c) find a form of physical activity that allows you to think without a screen. Alternatively, choose a different action from the bullet points in the previous chapter, write it down and make a start.

CONCLUSION

In the Jewish history books, there is a strange but beloved story about a war between the gods.[1] It is a very old story, set in a time when Israel was ruled by a weak king named Ahab and his cruel wife, Jezebel. Together, these rulers hunted down and murdered priests and prophets throughout the country, zealous in their worship of the storm god Baal. In response, the God of Israel became angry and withheld the rain. Drought and famine destroyed the land. People starved and became desperate.

Enter Elijah, the hero of the story, who led a rebellion against the monarchy in a most unconventional way. He climbed to the top of a mountain and challenged 450 prophets of Baal (on the side of Ahab and Jezebel) to a god-duel.

To the modern reader, this showdown between Elijah and the prophets of Baal is hard to grasp. Even at the time, it was an unusual way to do battle. Each party constructed an altar, one for God and one for Baal. A sacrificial bull was laid on each altar, surrounded by dry wood. After this, it was time to wait. Rather than light a fire, the first altar to spontaneously burst into flames would be declared victorious, with accolades going to the most powerful god.

As unusual as this showdown seems, the story gets stranger. The prophets of Baal danced and shouted and ritually cut themselves to call fire down from heaven. As they danced, Elijah taunted them with a series of sarcastic remarks: 'Maybe your god is sleeping?' or 'Maybe he is on holiday?' Among the chaos, Elijah dug a large trench around his altar and poured out twelve large jars of water, enough to fill the trench. When the wood surrounding the altar was sufficiently soaked, he prayed to God, and fire immediately fell from heaven. His altar was consumed by fire. Elijah was vindicated. The prophets of Baal were destroyed. Across the land, clouds turned grey, and it began to rain.

Huh? What does this story have to do with the making and meaning of space?

I stumbled upon this story at a time when I was particularly stretched and overwhelmed by the volume of work hitting my desk. Despite being highly organised and focused at work, none of my habits were making life less exhausting. My calendar was booked months in advance. I had no time for myself outside of work. I was constantly chasing my tail and had no time to think. I am not sure why I was drawn to this story. It isn't that I enjoy this narrative – the opposite is true. The event bothers me. It is illogical. It is counter to the way our world works. In this story, the land was deep in *drought*, and yet Elijah poured out *water* on the altar. He poured out so much water that it soaked the ground. But where did the water come from? Why would he waste such a rare and precious commodity? After reading this story, I thought about this conundrum for days. I know this is odd, but something about the act of sacrificing water bothered me, and I couldn't shake the feeling. Intuitively, I knew within Elijah's battle, and his frivolous act of wasting water, lay hidden an answer to the problem of space I had been struggling to solve.

Then it struck me – Elijah poured out what he did not have in order to bring the rain. He sacrificed what he lacked most and trusted in a miracle. This was a profound discovery, which changed my perspective on work and life. I realised that I had been managing time using an insufficient paradigm. I had been assuming that discipline, organisation and methodology would fix my lack of space. Stuck in conventional thinking, I was trying to be productive by guarding my space (rather than pouring it out). If, rather than water, time was my most precious commodity, what would it look like for me to take the illogical path? What might it look like for me give up control of my time, to make space and trust in 'rain'?

So this is what I did. Rather than squeeze as much work as I could into a seven-day week, I poured out time that I did not have in the pursuit of prioritising space. I took my most productive day and sacrificed it. Every Monday morning, rather than opening up my schedule to others, I made space for myself, as a priority. For the next twelve months, Monday morning was off limits. Rather than open my computer, I walked on a mountain with a packed lunch and a thermos of ginger tea. It was bliss. I assumed that losing my most productive day would destroy my productivity, leaving me stretched and frazzled, but like the story of Elijah, the opposite occurred. I ended up achieving more in four and a half days than I had previously achieved in five, six or seven days. I found myself with more time to think and dream. My inbox got under control, my calendar normalised and my business continued to grow. When I needed more work, clients came to me. When I needed more space, projects slowed down. It was strange and unexplainable but exhilarating. Making space, I discovered, is an art, a belief, a matter of trust. This discovery led me to prioritise space in other areas of my life, leading to the annual, weekly and daily patterns contained within this book. I still don't fully understand how space works, but I do know this – whenever I pour out time that I do not have, in faith, I counter-intuitively make space.

In my mind, our struggle for space is not purely practical but spiritual. It begins with a desire for something greater, more meaningful, more human, and beckons us to examine our passions, priorities and purposes. If we are honest with ourselves, we will always desire more space and grapple with clutter. This struggle is not ultimately about a lack of time but a search for meaning. We are all running out of time. We will eventually run out of space. If our tension with time compels us to ask deeper questions of ourselves and our priorities, this can only be a good thing, for our battle with space is the battle to know ourselves.

By examining our paradigms, embodying true principles and seeking better practices, we can learn to appreciate the value of our life in a fresh way. And if we get stuck, we can return to the messages in this book. Each part offers a diagnostic tool that unpacks the root causes of clutter. Are misinformed beliefs or unexamined mindsets the main source of our distraction? If so, revisit the paradigm, and unlock better thinking. Are we exhausted and distracted because our priorities misalign with reality? If so, there is value in returning to the SPACE principles. And of course, if better skills are needed, we can recommit to the practices. Be persistent. Spacemaking is a journey. It may be, in the end, that our battles remain the same – the battles to focus, to think clearly and stay on top of our demanding workloads. But there is value in the struggle itself because over time, our character and resilience are strengthened.

Spacemaking is not something you do. It is someone you become. It is less about your habits and more about what you learn along the way. My hope is that this book not only enables you to discover better practices but encourages you to set time aside to reflect on who you really are, with and without your technologies. Be intentional. Be creative. Be disciplined. Be optimistic. Lean on the principles and practices embodied within this book. Pour out what you do not have in faith. Make space and enjoy the adventure.

WEEKLY DAY OF REST WORKSHEET

The Sabbath is not only an idea. It is something you keep. With other people. You can't just extract lessons from it.

JUDITH SHULEVITZ

WHEN WILL YOU MAKE A PLAN?

Book 1.5 hours in your calendar to design your weekly day of rest. Choose a time and place to focus without distraction (such as 1–2.30 p.m. next Saturday in a café).

REST AND REFLECTION

Follow these steps to map out a day of rest and reflection using the five Ds.

STEP 1: SELECT A DAY

What is the best day for you to practice a weekly day of rest?

- ☐ Friday evening to Saturday evening?
- ☐ Saturday evening to Sunday evening?
- ☐ All day Saturday?
- ☐ All day Sunday?
- ☐ Other:

STEP 2: FACTOR IN DINNER AND PREPARATION

- **Preparation**
  What do you need to do to prepare for your weekly day of rest
  (such as clean the house, prepare meals, set out candles, even hire
  a cleaner)?

  When will you set aside time to prepare for your weekly day of rest
  (such as 4–5.30 p.m. on a Friday afternoon)?

- **Ritual**
  Can you design a ritual to initiate your weekly day of rest (such as
  lighting candles, pouring wine, eating food, reading poetry, practising thankfulness, sharing a highlight of the week, playing or
  listening to music, reading liturgy, praying together, sharing stories, observing silence)?

STEP 3: DISCONNECT FROM YOUR DEVICES

How will you unplug from your devices to make space for restorative rest and reflection? (You might turn off laptops, tablets, phones, smartwatches, game consoles and other new media. If turning off your phone is unworkable, you might be able to disable applications and remove access to the internet or buy a 'dumb' phone for the weekend or create a phone-free period throughout the day.)

Be as specific as possible.

STEP 4: DEFINE YOUR DON'TS

What activities look and feel like work to you? Write a list of activities you plan to reduce or remove during your weekly day of rest? (Include activities that trigger your mind to engage in work-like thinking, and social expectations that are stressful.)

STEP 5: DEFINE YOUR DOS

- **Extrovert or introvert**
  What is your personality type (what energises you?) and how does this impact the way you rest and reflect as an individual? How does this differ from others in your family? What might it mean for you and your family to coordinate rest?

- **Active or inactive**
  What types of activity are restful for you? What types of inactivity are restful for you?

- **Season of life**
  What is your current season, and how does it impact your capacity to rest and reflect? (A single person with a roommate has different pressures and possibilities than a family with children in nappies, or a single mother with teens, or a retired couple. Deep rest is hard to experience in some seasons of life. Be realistic, flexible and kind

on yourself. Adopt practices and expectations that are helpful for your particular season.)

- **Rest**
  Write a list of activities that look and feel restorative to you (such as reading, painting, stretching, getting a massage, riding a bike, eating chocolate, napping in the day etc.). Be as specific as possible. These are your dos.

- **Reflection**
  Write a list of activities that enable you to lift your mind beyond the mundane, including contemplative, creative, self-development and spiritual activities (such as journaling, walking, visiting museums, writing, breathing, reading Scripture etc.). This completes your list of dos.

WEEKLY DAY OF REST EXAMPLE

Here is an outline of our family's plan to help us rest together in our current season of life (with three children between the ages of nine and fourteen years old).

STEP 1: SELECT A DAY

- Friday evening (6 p.m.) to Saturday evening (6 p.m.)

STEP 2: FACTOR IN DINNER AND PREPARATION

Our preparation:

- Grocery shopping on Wednesday for the week
- 'Stop work' alarm at 4 p.m. on Friday and home by 4.45 p.m. (Daniel)
- Buy bread in advance (Kylie)
- Prepare dinner (a double batch) (Kylie)
- Vacuum, sweep, fold clothes and tidy rooms (Daniel + kids)

Our ritual:

- Wash hands and sit down to dinner table
- Light two candles (for rest and reflection)

- Ask and answer two questions ('why do we rest?' and 'why do we reflect?')
- Say a thanksgiving prayer
- Pour wine / kombucha and break bread (communion)
- Eat together as a family
- Share a high-low-buffalo during dinner
- Pack up from dinner

STEP 3: DISCONNECT FROM YOUR DEVICES

- Turn off / put away laptop, iPad and phone at 6 p.m. (Daniel)
- Cover up and unplug the television (Daniel)

STEP 4: DEFINE YOUR DON'TS

- **To avoid or minimise:**
  - Email and phone (Daniel)
  - Achieving things from a to-do list (Daniel)
  - Cooking and preparing food (Kylie) (kids to prepare own lunch)
  - Cleaning and most housework
  - Must-do house jobs or fixing projects
  - Facebook and phone games (Kylie)
  - Reading (if work-specific)
  - Busy social engagements (we allow kids soccer in winter)
  - 'Emotional care' for friends and neighbours
  - Hard conversations about difficult issues, including politics
  - Overly violent or explicit movies (Daniel)
  - Homework and piano practice (kids)
  - Supermarket and other must-do shopping

- **Maybes:**
  - Social phone calls to friends and family if in the mood
  - Dishes and general tidy up (Daniel)

- Selective fun purchases (e.g. takeaway food, eating out)

STEP 5: DEFINE YOUR DOS

- **Rest:**
  - Reading non-work-related books
  - Eating fun food and sweets (especially kids)
  - Coffee with friends (especially Kylie)
  - Family outing (e.g. pool, walk, beach, soccer, bike ride, movies, etc.)
  - Board games
  - Socialising with close friends (low effort)
  - Chainsawing and brush-cutting (Daniel)
  - Gym, walking, mountain bike riding or swimming (Daniel)
  - Painting, drawing or sewing (Kylie)
  - Some television or electronic games (in morning for kids)
  - Playing music (guitar or keyboard)
  - Outdoor firepit
  - Sleeping in and early nights

- **Reflection:**
  - Journaling
  - Praying / listening
  - Reading Scripture
  - Daily devotions (our kids)
  - Reading life-enriching books
  - Silence
  - Listening to and playing uplifting music
  - Contemplative exercise, such as walking solo (Daniel)

PRINCIPLES IN PRACTICE

Our annual, weekly and daily practices are built on the SPACE principles. This quick reference guide is designed to show you how they work together.

Practice 1: Start with holidays

- Set Limits – we do this by booking holidays in advance and making them non-negotiable.
- Plan Patterns – once a year, as an annual pattern, we lock in our leave.
- Assign Rest – as a matter of priority, our holidays (rest) are assigned before our work (activity).
- Cultivate Community – for most people, holidays are shared in close contact with the people we care most about, thereby strengthening relationships.
- Embrace Silence – we can give ourselves space for silence by setting aside quiet times when on vacation.

Practice 2: A day to think

- Set Limits – if we have the mindset that 'thinking is real work', we will stop, think and say no to reactive requests that keep us unnecessarily busy.

- Plan Patterns – four times a year, as a pattern, we make space to get away from the office to think.
- Assign Rest – thinking, as a form of rest, is prioritised when we adopt this seasonal practice.
- Cultivate Community – as a manager, we have an opportunity to empower our teams to think deeply, as a habit. We can also lean on others to help us through a difficult period of reset, informed by our Post-it note timeline.
- Embrace Silence – thinking needs silence; the two are intertwined.

Practice 3: Digital detox

- Set Limits – by setting an extreme limit of several days with no digital technology, we can make space and open up creative possibilities.
- Plan Patterns – a digital detox can help us break old patterns and start new ones, as we examine our habits from a different perspective.
- Assign Rest – given that rest is not just physical but mental and spiritual, prioritising time away from digital distraction can be a deep form of rest.
- Cultivate Community – when we remove digital media from our lives and enter a transitional space together, we often experience community.
- Embrace Silence – long periods of silence are experienced on a digital-free retreat, enabling us to examine our heart, head and habits.

Practice 4: Weekly day of rest

- Set Limits – to experience a weekly day of rest, we say no to work-related activities, both mental and physical, and unplug from digital technology.
- Plan Patterns – once a week, as a pattern, we rest from our work.

- Assign Rest – the first pillar of the weekly day of rest is 'rest', and our practice is oriented around this value.
- Cultivate Community – by unplugging from our devices each week, we make space for deeper relationships – we disconnect to reconnect.
- Embrace Silence – the second pillar of a weekly day of rest is 'reflection', which is an expression of silence.

Practice 5: Daily refresh

- Set Limits – we maintain twenty minutes as a daily discipline, to refresh away from digital technology – a small but significant limit.
- Plan Patterns – the twenty-minute patterns we set must be predictable – same time and place – if they are to stick.
- Assign Rest – defined as physical, mental and spiritual repose, the variety of expressions associated with this practice contributes to our well-being.
- Cultivate Community – the practices we choose are often inclusive of others. We need encouragement from friends to help us maintain our daily habits.
- Embrace Silence – many of these practices, from journaling to prayerful meditation, are expressions of silence.

Practice 6: Daily pause

- Set Limits – decluttering our devices is an example of setting limits. By eliminating unnecessary apps and notifications, we make space to focus on what matters more.
- Plan Patterns – if we habitually wake without digital activity or power down for a better night's sleep, we have created a predictable pattern.
- Assign Rest – rest is accumulative. If we pause regularly throughout the day, we incrementally improve our mental composure and sense of calm.

- Cultivate Community – when we share meals without technology or chair meetings without distraction, we are strengthening our relationships.
- Embrace Silence – disconnecting several times a day to pause can be a form of silence. When we pause and quietly think, *what is the best thing I can do next*, we can end up transforming our day.

NOTES

Introduction

[1] Amy is not my client's real name. Minor details have been modified to ensure anonymity.

[2] Research shows that we move through five identifiable stages before lasting change can be achieved: pre-contemplation, contemplation, planning, action and maintenance. Shifting habits takes time. We need knowledge to change our minds, and instruction to change our actions. See G. L. Zimmerman, C. G. Olsen and M. F. Bosworth, 'A "Stages of Change" Approach to Helping Patients Change Behaviour', *American Family Physician*, 61 (5), 1 March, 2000, 1409–1416.

1 Space and Pace

[1] I collected these observations of Lululemon's corporate culture after visiting the company's office in Collingwood, Melbourne. The goal-setting culture of Lululemon has been documented by others: Laura Schwecherl, 'A Look Inside Lululemon's Unique Goal-Setting Program', *Greatest*, 26 February 2013, https://greatist.com/happiness/lululemon-athletic-company-goal-setting#1.

[2] See, for example Dr Thomas Jackson, *The E-Mail Optimisation Toolkit* (London: ARK Group, 2009). This comprehensive summary of email research examines costs and practices from both an organisation and user perspective. Chapter 7, in particular, outlines the high cost of email inefficiency and cost benefits of implementing policies to reduce email volume and email interruptions. See also, Thomas Jackson, Ray Dawson and Darren Wilson, 'The Cost Of Email Interruption', *Journal of Systems and Information Technology*, 5 (1), 2004. By analysing employee habits, Jackson et al. recommend turning off email alerts and setting up email applications to check for email at no less than every forty-five minutes.

[3] A. Gupta, R. Sharda and R. Greve 'You've Got Email! Does It Really Matter To Process Emails Now Or Later?', *Information System Frontiers*, 13, 2011, 637–653.

According to simulation modelling, processing email in blocks of time, rather than continuously, is more efficient, and could save an organisation thousands of hours of lost productivity each year. See also Kostadin Kushlev and Elizabeth

W. Dunn, 'Checking Email Less Frequently Reduces Stress', *Computers In Human Behavior*, 43, 2015, 220–228.
When adults were randomly assigned to check their email three times a day, rather than continuously, they experienced significantly lower daily stress levels.

Part II: The Paradigm (Preliminaries)

1   Mic Wright, 'The original iPhone announcement annotated', *TNW*, 9 September 2015, https://thenextweb.com/apple/2015/09/09/genius-annotated-with-genius/#annotations:7767774.

2   Heather Whipps, 'How Gutenberg Changed The World', *Live Science*, 26 May 2007, https://www.livescience.com/2569-gutenberg-changed-world.html.

3   Andrew Sullivan, 'I Used To Be A Human Being', *New York Intelligencer*, 19 September 2016, http://nymag.com/intelligencer/2016/09/andrew-sullivan-my-distraction-sickness-and-yours.html. Sullivan proposes that the nature of humanity has changed as a result of the iPhone. A worthwhile read.

4   Jean M. Twenge, *iGen: Why Today's Super-Connected Kids Are Growing Up Less Rebellious, More Tolerant, Less Happy – and Completely Unprepared for Adulthood* (New York: Atria Books, 2017), 78.

5   Jean M. Twenge, 'Have Smartphones Destroyed a Generation?', *The Atlantic*, September 2017, https://www.theatlantic.com/magazine/archive/2017/09/has-the-smartphone-destroyed-a-generation/534198/.

6   Twenge, *iGen*, 51–52.

7   Twenge, *iGen*, 77.

8   Mark Dolliver, 'US Time Spent with Media 2019: Digital time Keeps Rising as Growth Subsides for Total Time Spent', *eMarketer*, 30 May 2019, https://www.emarketer.com/content/us-time-spent-with-media-2019.

9   Malcolm Gladwell, *David and Goliath: Underdogs, Misfits, and the Art of Battling Giants* (New York: Little, Brown and Company, 2013), 44–54. My appreciation goes to Malcolm Gladwell, whose insights into the inverted-U curve provided me with the knowledge I needed to understand the relationship between productivity and digital technology.

10 Cal Newport, *Digital Minimalism: On Living Better with Less Technology* (London: Penguin Books, 2019), XIV.

2 Technology

1   Adam Lefky, 'Number of Televisions in the US', *The Physics Factbook*, 2007, https://hypertextbook.com/facts/2007/TamaraTamazashvili.shtml.

2   Marshall McLuhan, *Understanding Media: The Extensions of Man* (Massachusetts: MIT Press, 1964).

3   Nicholas Carr, *The Shallows: What the Internet is Doing to Our Brains* (New York: W.W. Norton & Company, 2011), 3.

4   Alex Kuskis, 'We shape our tools and thereafter our tools shape us', *The McLuhan Galaxy*, 1 April 2013, https://mcluhangalaxy.wordpress.com/2013/04/01/we-shape-our-tools-and-thereafter-our-tools-shape-us/;   Lance   Strate, 'Marshall McLuhan's message was imbued with conservatism', *The Guardian*, 26 July 2011, https://www.theguardian.com/commentisfree/2011/jul/26/marshall-mcluhan-conservatism-medium-is-message.

5   'Digital Australia: Product Insights Report', *Enhanced Media Metrics Australia*, 2013, https://emma.com.au/wp-content/uploads/2013/10/digital.pdf.

6   Tim Challies, *The Next Story: Life and Faith After the Digital Explosion* (Michigan: Zondervan, 2011) 61–62.

7   Ibid, 36.

8   Ian Johnston, 'Apple guru kept his kids away from iPads', *The Bulletin*, 13 September 2014, http://m.centraltelegraph.com.au/news/apple-guru-kept-his-kids-away-ipads/2385871/.

9   Canela López, '7 tech executives who raise their kids tech-free or seriously limit their screen time', *Business Insider*, 4 March 2020, https://www.businessinsider.co.za/tech-execs-screen-time-children-bill-gates-steve-jobs-2019-9.

10 Rob Price, 'Apple CEO Tim Cook: I don't want my nephew on a social network', *Business Insider*, 20 January 2018, https://www.businessinsider.com.au/apple-ceo-tim-cook-doesnt-let-nephew-use-social-media-2018-1.

11 Doug Bolton, 'The Reason Steve Jobs Didn't Let His Children Use an iPad', *The Independent*, 24 February 2016, http://www.independent.co.uk/life-style/gadgets-and-tech/news/steve-jobs-apple-ipad-children-technology-birthday-a6893216.html.

12 Matthew Jenkin, 'Tablets out, imagination in: the schools that shun technology', *The Guardian*, 2 December 2015, https://www.theguardian.com/teacher-network/2015/dec/02/schools-that-ban-tablets-traditional-education-silicon-valley-london.

13 Everett M. Rogers, *Diffusion of Innovations* (New York: Simon & Schuster, 1995).

14 Neil Postman, *Technopoly* (New York: Vintage, 1993), as cited by Challies, *The Next Story*, 61–64.

3 Plasticity

1   Susan is not my client's real name. Minor details have been modified to ensure anonymity.

2   See the following research for more information. Colin Blakemore and Richard C. Van Sluyters, 'Innate and environmental factors in the development of the kitten's visual cortex', *The Journal of Physiology*, 248, 1 July 1975, 663–716; Bogdan Draganski, Christian Gaser, Volker Busch, Gerhard Schuierer, Ulrich Bogdahn and Arne May, 'Neuroplasticity: changes in grey matter induced by training', *National Library of Medicine*, 427, 22 January 2004, 311–312; Janina Boyke, Joenna Driemeyer, Christian Gaser, Christian Büchel and Arne May, 'Training-induced brain structure changes in the elderly', *The Journal of Neuroscience*, 28, 9 July 2008, 7031–7035.

3   'The Net causes extensive brain changes. The current explosion of digital technology not only is changing the way we live and communicate but is rapidly and profoundly altering our brains. The daily use of computers, smartphones, search engines, and other such tools stimulates brain cell alteration and neurotransmitter release, gradually strengthening new neural pathways in our brains while weakening old ones.' Carr, *The Shallows*, 120.

4   'Technology is biological. Our brains actually change in response to new technologies. The brain of a person raised in the age of print, a person who learned from books and who read books in time of leisure or study, has a brain that is markedly different from a person who has learned primary from images or who has watched videos in times of leisure and study.' Challies, *The Next Story*, 44.

5   Carr, *The Shallows*, 5.

6   Alana Mitchelson, 'Australians are spending more than one-third of their day in front of a screen', *The New Daily*, 19 April 2017, http://thenewdaily.com.au/life/wellbeing/2017/04/19/australians-screen-sleep-blue-light/.

7   Lonergan Research, 'Screen Time', March 2017, http://1v1d1e1lmiki1lgcvx32p49h8fe.wpengine.netdna-cdn.com/wp-content/uploads/2017/04/1366-Screen-Time-OPSM-FINAL-Report-31-03-2017.pdf.

8   In *Brain Rules*, John Medina says 'Multitasking, when it comes to paying attention, is a myth. The brain naturally focuses on concepts sequentially, one at a time.' 'To put it bluntly, research shows that we can't multitask. We are biologically incapable of processing attention-rich inputs simultaneously.' See John Medina, *Brain Rules: 12 Principles for Surviving and Thriving at Work, Home, and School* (Washington: Pear Press, 2008) 84–88.

9. Chris McChesney, Sean Covey and Jim Huling, *The 4 Disciplines of Execution: Achieving Your Wildly Important Goals* (London: Simon & Schuster, 2012), 26.

10. Kep Kee Loh and Ryota Kanai, 'Higher Media Multi-Tasking Activity Is Associated with Smaller Gray-Matter Density in the Anterior Cingulate Cortex', *PLOS ONE* 9, 14 September 2014, e106698. https://doi.org/10.1371/journal.pone.0106698.

11. Cal Newport, *Deep Work: Rules for Focused Success in a Distracted World* (New York: Hachette Book Group, 2016), 157.

12. Eyal Ophir, Clifford Nass and Anthony D. Wagner, 'Cognitive control in media multitaskers', *Proceedings of the National Academy of Sciences of the United States of America,* 106, 15 September 2009, 15583–15587.

13. Reynol Junco and Shelia R. Cotten, 'Perceived academic effects of instant messaging use', *Computers and Education*, 56, February 2011, 370–378.

14. Mark W. Becker, Reem Alzahabi and Christopher J. Hopwood, 'Media multitasking is associated with symptoms of depression and social anxiety', *Cyberpsychology, behavior and social networking*, 16 February 2013, 132–135; Jean-Yves Rotge, Dominique Guehl, Bixente Dilharreguy, Jean Tignol, Bernard Bioulac, Michele Allard, Pierre Burbaud and Bruno Aouizerate, 'Meta-analysis of brain volume changes in obsessive-compulsive disorder', *Biological Psychiatry*, 65, 2009, 75–83.

15. Carr, *The Shallows*, quoting Stanford professor Clifford Nass, 142.

4 Power

1. President John F. Kennedy delivered in person before a joint session of Congress 25 May 1961, 'Excerpt from the "Special Message to the Congress on Urgent National Needs"', *NASA History*, 24 May 2004, https://www.nasa.gov/vision/space/features/jfk_speech_text.html.

2. McChesney, Covey and Huling, *The 4 Disciplines of Execution*, 38–43.

3. Tibi Puiu, 'Your smartphone is millions of times more powerful than all of NASA's combined computing in 1969', *ZME Science*, 11 February 2020, http://www.zmescience.com/research/technology/smartphone-power-compared-to-apollo-432/.

4. Carrie Marshall, '10 amazing things you never knew a smartphone could do', *Tech Radar*, 26 August 2013, https://www.techradar.com/news/phone-and-communications/mobile-phones/10-amazing-things-you-never-knew-a-smartphone-could-do-1175046.

5. Andy Crouch, *Playing God: Redeeming the Gift of Power* (Illinois: Inter-Varsity Press, 2013), 133–148.

6   'Absolute power corrupts absolutely', Lord Acton's first letter to Bishop Mandell
     Creighton, 5 April 1887, can be accessed in 'Acton-Creighton Correspondence',
     1887, *The Forum*, http://oll.libertyfund.org/index.php?option=com_content&
     task=view&id=1354&Itemid=262.

7   Crouch, *Playing God*, 17.

8   J. R. R. Tolkien, *The Lord of the Rings* (London: Harper Collins, 1968), 34.

9   Robert is not my friend's real name; this detail was changed for anonymity.

10   Aleksandr I. Solzhenitsyn, *The Gulag Archipelago 1918–1956: An Experiment
     in Literary Investigation* (Vol. 2) (New York: Harper & Row, 1975), 615.

11   Newport, *Digital Minimalism*, 3–25.

12   'With great power comes great responsibility' seems to come from numer-
     ous sources. Major figures such as Lord Melbourne, Winston Churchill and
     Franklin D. Roosevelt have supposedly articulated versions of the adage. Stan
     Lee and Steve Ditko, the creators of *Spider-man,* were important in the popu-
     larization of the saying. Quote Investigator 'With Great Power Comes Great
     Responsibility', *Quote Investigator*, 23 July 2015, http://quoteinvestigator.
     com/2015/07/23/great-power/.

13   Michael Crichton, *Jurassic Park* (London: Random House, 1991), 306.

14   Ibid., 391.

15   Crouch, *Playing God*, 42.

5 Freedom and Choice

1   Steve Simpson, *Unwritten Ground Rules: Cracking the Corporate Culture Code*
     (Queensland: Narnia House Publishing, 2001), 40–41. I first read about 'Five
     Monkeys' in this book, a story that has been circulating in various forms for
     years and may be an urban legend. I have not been able to find a reference to
     an actual experiment, yet it is a great fable about how cultural norms develop
     over time.

2   Behind all systematic thought, is 'dogma' (or story) – presuppositions forming
     the basis of a person's belief system. Dogma cannot be proven, as all reason-
     ing needs a starting point (even science, which assumes that what is seen and
     reproducible is real). Next comes our 'plausibility structure' (which I call *rea-
     soning*) – the framework through which we determine what is plausible and
     implausible, based on dogma. Logic only exists within a belief framework.
     Without a plausibility structure – a filter through which one decides what is
     relevant and irrelevant – everything is overwhelming. We need a plausibility
     structure to form a logical opinion or rational argument, and make sense of
     the many 'facts' in our world. Our world view is therefore an expression of our

dogma, a complex interaction of creation stories, myths and untested assumptions that shape our external habits and behaviours. For more on this subject, consider reading Lesslie Newbigin, *The Gospel in a Pluralist Society* (Michigan: Eerdmans Publishing Co., 2000), 1–14.

3 I chose this example because it involves a clash of historical, cultural and religious stories. Our plausibility structures inform how we approach every area of life, including language, gender, money, power, politics, spirituality, sexuality, work, rest and technology.

4 Few people are truly irrational. We judge others, calling them ignorant or inconsiderate, without recognising the impact of our own dogma on our determinations. If a person believes in a divine being who reveals their plans through holy writings, then some facts become relevant and others irrelevant. Faith healings and supernatural experiences become plausible and moral relativity implausible. Such a person's conclusions may differ from our own, but they are not illogical. They are operating from a different plausibility structure. The same is true for all belief systems, including humanism, environmentalism and secularism. Our deepest stories inform our reasoning and shape our behaviours.

5 Oxford Dictionary, 'Freedom', 2020, https://www.lexico.com/definition/freedom.

6 Movies, as narratology, typically follow 'the hero's journey', a formula popularised by Joseph Campbell in his seminal work, *The Hero with a Thousand Faces*. In this narrative, a hero takes a journey from the known to the unknown. They are guided by a mentor, or helper, to overcome challenges or temptations. After entering an abyss, they confront themselves, return victorious and renew their community. In Disney and Pixar movies, however, we see a story within a story – a particular emphasis on our hero discovering themselves in opposition to their community. In the Western script, it is individual autonomy, rebellion from authority, the following of one's heart and feelings, that provides enlightenment for our hero. This is not always the case in cultural mythologies. See Jonah Sachs, *Winning the Story Wars: Why Those Who Tell – and Live – the Best Stories Will Rule the Future* (Massachusetts: Harvard Business School Publishing, 2012), 146–166.

7 *Frozen*, despite my critique of 'Let It Go', is well-rounded compared with most Disney movies. Sacrificial actions between siblings, rather than 'falling in love', is the path to freedom. That said, parents must die, and the community act intolerantly, before our hero can discover her true self – in line with the formula. In contrast, *Cars*, a modern Disney-Pixar movie, genuinely flips the freedom-narrative formula on its head. Lightning McQueen, an individualistic,

self-centred, self-made race car is forced to become part of a simple community, and in doing so discovers his 'true self'. In learning to sacrifice his own desires in service of a community, Lightning discovers freedom, which in turn, allows him to participate as a healthy individual.

8   I am not suggesting that we should *never* follow our heart or trust our feelings. It can be wise to 'let it go' – in some circumstances. My concern is the over-communication and over-simplification of this narrative in individualistic cultures, without deeply considering our context.

9   Heather L. Koball, Emily Moiduddin, Jamila Henderson, Brian Goesling and Melanie Besculides, 'What Do We Know About the Link Between Marriage and Health?', *Journal of Family Issues*, 31 (8), 2010, 1019–1040. 'Married people enjoy better physical and mental health than those who are not married, and have longer life expectancies than do members of single-parent or divorced families.'

10 Stuart is not his real name. Minor details have been modified to ensure anonymity.

11 Barry Schwartz, 'The Paradox of Choice', *TED*, July 2005, https://www.ted.com/talks/barry_schwartz_on_the_paradox_of_choice.

12 'The Size of the World Wide Web (The Internet)', *WorldWideWebSize.com*, 20 January 2020, http://www.worldwidewebsize.com/.

13 'Size Comparisons', Wikipedia, retrieved 17 January 2021, https://en.wikipedia.org/wiki/Wikipedia:Size_comparisons.

14 Schwartz, 'The Paradox of Choice'.

15 *The Holy Bible New International Version*, 1 Corinthians, chapter 10, verses 23–24.

6 Love

1   *The Holy Bible New International Version*, Psalm 115, verses 2–8.

2   David Foster Wallace, *This is Water: Some Thoughts, Delivered on a Significant Occasion, about Living a Compassionate Life* (New York: Little, Brown and Company, Hachette Book Group, 2009). Available from: David Foster Wallace, 'David Foster Wallace on Life and Work', *The Wall Street Journal*, 19 September 2008, http://www.wsj.com/articles/SB122178211966454607.

3   Fyodor Dostoevsky, *The Brothers Karamazov* (New York: Penguin Books, 1982), 278.

4   Tim Keller, 'The Strategies of Darkness', *Gospel in Life*, 24 November 1991, https://gospelinlife.com/downloads/the-strategies-of-darkness-5669/. I first heard this question posed by Tim Keller in this talk on the realities of evil.

5   Steve McAlpine, 'When Ground Floor Projects Are Pushed One Floor Up', 2 July 2018, https://stephenmcalpine.com/when-ground-floor-projects-are-pushed-one-floor-up/.

6   Wallace, *This is Water*.

Part III: The Principles (Preliminaries)

1   Winston Churchill, 'Address to Britain's National Book Exhibition', 1949, cited in Lawrence A. Machi and Brenda T. McEvoy, *The Literature Review: Six Steps to Success* (California: Corwin Press, 2016), 156.

2   Stephen R. Covey, *Principle Centered Leadership* (New York: Simon & Schuster, 1990), 22.

3   H. H. Farmer aptly stated, 'If you go against the grain of the universe, you get splinters.' Cited by Eugene H. Peterson, *A Long Obedience in the Same Direction: Discipleship in an Instant Society* (Illinois, Inter-Varsity Press, 1980), 117.

7 Set Limits

1   Daven Hiskey, 'Dr. Seuss Wrote "Green Eggs And Ham" On A Bet That He Couldn't Write A Book With 50 Or Fewer Words', *Today I Found Out*, 24 May 2011, http://www.todayifoundout.com/index.php/2011/05/dr-seuss-wrote-green-eggs-and-ham-on-a-bet-that-he-couldnt-write-a-book-with-50-or-fewer-words/.

2   Dr Seuss, *Green Eggs and Ham* (New York: Random House, 1960).

3   The man's real name was Hsieh, but for readability, I have used a pseudonym of Chen.

4   Katie Hunt and Naomi Ng, 'Man Dies In Taiwan After 3-day Online Gaming Binge', *CNN online*, 19 January 2015, http://edition.cnn.com/2015/01/19/world/taiwan-gamer-death/.

5   Simon Parkin, *Death by Video Game: Tales of Obsession From The Virtual Frontline* (London: Serpent's Tail Books, 2015), 13–16.

6   Michael Sullivan, 'South Korea Says About 20% Of Its Population Is At Risk For Internet Addiction', *NPR*, 30 July 2019, https://www.npr.org/2019/07/30/746687204/south-korea-says-about-20-percent-of-its-population-is-at-risk-for-internet-addi.

7   Jerald J. Block, 'Issues for DSM-V: Internet Addiction, American Journal of Psychiatry', 165:3, 2008, http://ajp.psychiatryonline.org/doi/pdf/10.1176/appi.ajp.2007.07101556.

[8] Elias Aboujaoude, Lorrin M. Koran, Nona Gamel, Michael D. Large, Richard T. Serpe, 'Potential Markers for Problematic Internet Use: A telephone survey of 2,513 adults', *CNS Spectr*, 11, 2006, 750–755.

[9] American Psychiatric Association, *Diagnostic and Statistical Manual of Mental Disorders, Fifth Edition (DSM-5)* (Washington, DC: American Psychiatric Association Publishing, 2013). In 2013, Internet Gaming Disorder (IGD) was included in Section III of the DSM-5 as a '"condition warranting further study". It was the first time internet gaming was recognised as a mental health disorder, albeit tentatively, in psychiatric nomenclature.' Although IGD is not an 'official' disorder in the DSM-5, the APA encouraging further research does highlight the growing concerns of internet addiction globally.

[10] The Cabin Sydney is a specialised outpatient addiction treatment centre in Sydney, Australia, offering services for cyber-sex addiction and cyber-relational addiction. Their website is https://www.thecabinsydney.com.au/internet-addiction-treatment/.

[11] According to its website, reSTART has a mission to enable 'sustainable digital media use for people and the planet', https://www.netaddictionrecovery.com/.

[12] Maggie Yu and Jennifer Baxter, 'LSAC Annual Statistical Report: Australian Children's Screen Time and Participation in Extracurricular Activities', *Growing up in Australia*, 2015, https://growingupinaustralia.gov.au/research-findings/annual-statistical-report-2015/australian-childrens-screen-time-and-participation-extracurricular?_ga=2.196322732.1085852583.1566189230-83019648.1563508864.

[13] 12 hours x 365 days x 68.9 years (removing our 10 earliest years of life, as we don't spend 12 hours online a day as toddlers) = 301,782 hours over lifetime, or 34.45 years. Mark Dolliver, 'US Time Spent with Media 2019', *eMarketer*, 30 May 2019, https://www.emarketer.com/content/us-time-spent-with-media-2019; Vision Direct, 'How Much Time Do We Spend Looking At Screens?' 30 June 2020, https://www.visiondirect.co.uk/blog/research-reveals-screen-time-habits.

[14] Directed by Patty Jenkins, *Wonder Woman* (Warner Bros. Pictures, 2017).

[15] Joan Borysenko, *Fried: Why You Burn Out and How to Revive* (USA: Hay House Publishers, 2011), 3–4.

[16] Grace Marshall, 'Is Your Schedule Demanding Perfection From Others?', 23 June 2014, https://grace-marshall.com/is-your-schedule-demanding-perfection-from-others/.

8 Plan Patterns

1. Edward Gibbon, *The History of the Decline and Fall of the Roman Empire* (London: Penguin Books, 2000).

2. Ashley Barker and John B. Hayes, *Sub-Merge: Living Deep in a Shallow World* (Maine: GO Alliance, 2002), 49; Christian History Institute, '#201: Benedict's Rule', 2018, https://christianhistoryinstitute.org/study/module/benedicts-rule/; Rod Dreher, *The Benedict Option: A Strategy for Christians in a Post-Christian Nation* (New York: Penguin Random House, 2017).

3. Dwight Longenecker, *St Benedict and St Thérèse: The Little Rule and The Little Way* (Indiana: Our Sunday Visitor Inc, 2002), 24.

4. Emanuel Paparella, 'Medieval Monasticism as Preserver of Western Civilisation', *Metanexus*, 31 May 2008, https://www.metanexus.net/medieval-monasticism-preserver-western-civilization/; Melissa Snell, 'Preserving Middle Age Information', *ThoughtCo.*, 8 December 2019, https://www.thoughtco.com/the-keepers-of-knowledge-1783761.

5. August Turak, *Business Secrets of the Trappist Monks: One CEO's Quest for Meaning and Authenticity* (New York: Columbia University Press, 2013), ix. Turak writes: 'Although much has been written about the tremendous intellectual debt that Western civilisation owes monasticism for preserving Greek philosophy and drama during the Dark Ages, very few have explored the highly successful business methodologies that the monks have preserved and prospered for centuries.'

6. Rodney Stark, *The Victory of Reason: How Christianity Led to Freedom, Capitalism, and Western Success* (New York: Random House, 2005).

7. Hugh Halter, *BiVO: A Modern-Day Guide for Bi-Vocational Saints* (Colorado: Missio Publishing, 2013), 74–75.

8. Charles Duhigg, *The Power of Habit: Why We Do What We Do and How to Change* (London: Random House, 2012), xvi.

9. James Clear, *Atomic Habits: An Easy and Proven Way to Build Good Habits and Break Bad Ones* (London: Random House Business Books, 2018), 41.

10. I first heard this analogy used by John Mark Comer at the Rebuilders Conference in Melbourne, September 2017.

11. Alan is not my client's real name; this detail was changed for anonymity.

12. Simpson, *Unwritten Ground Rules*.

13. Reed Hastings and Erin Meyer, *No Rules Rules: Netflix and the Culture of Reinvention* (London: WH Allen, 2020), 18. Details about how Netflix use written and live 360-degree feedback is in the chapter, 'A Circle of Feedback', 189–205.

14 Laurel J. Kiser, Linda Bennett, Jerry Heston and Marilyn Paavola, 'Family Ritual and Routine: Comparison of Clinical and Non-Clinical Families', *Journal of Child and Family Studies*, 14, 2005, 357–372; Mary Spagnola and Barbara Fiese, 'Family Routines and Rituals: A Context for Development in the Lives of Young Children', *Infants and Young Children*, 20 (4), 2007, 284–299.

15 Angela K. Salmon and Teresa Lucas, 'Exploring Young Children's Conceptions About Thinking', *Journal of Research in Childhood Education*, 25:4, 2011, 364–375.

16 Mick Breen and Sally Breen, *Family on Mission: Integrating Discipleship into the Fabric of our Everyday Lives* (South Carolina: 3DM Publishing, 2014), 79.

9 Assign Rest

1 Sara Robinson 'Why We Have to Go Back to a 40-Hour Work Week to Keep Our Sanity', *Alternet*, 25 April 2018, https://www.alternet.org/2018/04/why-we-have-go-back-40-hour-work-week-keep-our-sanity/.

2 Rowan Cahill, 'On Winning the 40 Hour Week', *Illawarra Unity*, Vol. 7, Issue 1, October 2007, http://ro.uow.edu.au/cgi/viewcontent.cgi?article=1083&context=unity.

3 Sarah G. Carmichael, 'The Research is Clear: Long Hours Backfire for People and for Companies', *Harvard Business Review*, 19 August 2015, https://hbr.org/2015/08/the-research-is-clear-long-hours-backfire-for-people-and-for-companies; Erin Reid, 'Why Some Men Pretend to Work 80-Hour Weeks', *Harvard Business Review*, 28 April 2015, https://hbr.org/2015/04/why-some-men-pretend-to-work-80-hour-weeks.

4 Evan Robinson, 'Why Crunch Modes Doesn't Work: Six Lessons', *igda*, 12 February 2005, https://igda.org/resources-archive/why-crunch-mode-doesnt-work-six-lessons-2005/.

5 Daniel Cook, 'Graphing Productivity and Overtime', 28 September 2008, https://lostgarden.home.blog/2008/09/28/rules-of-productivity-presentation/. This concept diagram has been reproduced with the permission of Daniel Cook. His diagram, based on Evan Robinson's research of game developers, can be found in the Rules of Productivity presentation on his Lost Garden blog.

6 *The Business Roundtable*, 'Scheduled Overtime Effect on Construction Projects', November 1980, http://web.archive.org/web/20090824001133/http://www.curt.org/pdf/156.pdf.

7 James Clear, 'The Science of Sleep: A Brief Guide on How to Sleep Better Every Night', https://jamesclear.com/sleep.

[8] Stephen Covey, *First Things First: Coping with the Ever-Increasing Demands of the Workplace* (New York: Free Press, 1994), 13.

[9] Mike Breen, *Living in Rhythm with Life* (South Carolina: 3DM Publishing, 2006), 55.

[10] Newport, *Digital Minimalism*.

[11] Ibid, 168.

[12] Joshua Becker, 'A Helpful Guide to Becoming Unbusy', *Becoming Minimalist*, 2014, https://www.becomingminimalist.com/un-busy/.

10 Cultivate Community

[1] See the full story in *The Social Network*. Directed by David Fincher, *The Social Network* (Columbia Pictures, 2010).

[2] Text from the Facebook Sign-Up Page, July 2019, https://www.facebook.com/.

[3] Julianne Holt-Lunstad, Timothy B. Smith and J. Bradley Layton, 'Social Relationships and Mortality Risk: A Meta-analytic Review', *PLoS Medicine*, 7 (7), 2010, 14. This meta-analysis reviewed 148 studies across 308,849 participants and concluded that 'individuals with adequate social relationships have a 50% greater likelihood of survival compared to those with poor or insufficient social relationships. The magnitude of this effect is comparable with quitting smoking and it exceeds many well-known risk factors for mortality, such as obesity and physical inactivity'.

[4] Susan Pinker, *The Village Effect: Why Face-To-Face Contact Matters* (London: Atlantic Books, 2014), 7–9, 23–28.

[5] Pinker, *The Village Effect*, 23.

[6] Graph adapted from Figure 6, Holt-Lunstad, Smith and Layton, 'Social Relationships and Mortality Risk', 14.

[7] Edson C. Tandoc Jr, Patrick Ferrucci and Margaret Duffy, 'Facebook use, envy, and depression among college students: Is Facebook depressing?', *Computers in Human Behavior*, 43, 2015, 139–146, https://www.sciencedirect.com/science/article/abs/pii/S0747563214005767?via%3Dihub; Emily McDool, Philip Powell, Jennifer Roberts and Karl Taylor, 'Social Media Use and Children's Wellbeing', *IZA Discussion Paper No. 10412*, 2016, https://ssrn.com/abstract=2886783; Jessica C. Levenson, Ariel Shensa, Jaime E. Sidani, Jason B. Colditz and Brian A. Primack, 'The association between social media use and sleep disturbance among young adults', *Preventive Medicine*, 85, 2016, 36–41.

[8] Heather Woods and Holly Scott, 'Sleepyteens: Social media use in adolescence is associated with poor sleep quality, anxiety, depression and low self-esteem',

Journal of Adolescence, 51, 2016, 41–49, https://pubmed.ncbi.nlm.nih.gov/26791323/; Twenge, *iGen*, 93–118.

9   Ethan Kross, Philippe Verduyn, Emre Demiralp, Jiyoung Park, David S. Lee, Natalie Lin, Holly Shablack, John Jonides and Oscar Ybarra, 'Facebook Use Predicts Declines in Subjective Well-Being in Young Adults', *PLoS ONE*, 8 (8), 2013.

10 Morten Tromholt, 'The Facebook Experiment: Quitting Facebook Leads to Higher Levels of Well-Being', *Cyberpsychology, Behaviour and Social Networking*, 19 (11), 2016. A similar study was undertaken in the USA by Holly B. Shakya and Nicholas A. Christakis, 'Association of Facebook Use With Compromised Well-Being: A Longitudinal Study', *American Journal of Epidemiology*, 185 (3), 2017, https://academic.oup.com/aje/article/185/3/203/2915143.

11 Leslie J. Seltzer, Ashley R. Prososki, Toni E. Ziegler and Seth D. Pollak, 'Instant Messages vs. Speech: hormones and why we still need to hear each other', *Evolution and Human Behaviour*, 33, 2012.

12 David A. Baker and Guillermo P. Algorta, 'The Relationship Between Online Social Networking and Depression: A Systematic Review of Quantitative Studies', *Cyberpsychology, Behaviour and Social Networking*, 19 (11), 2016.

13 Pinker, *The Village Effect*, 30, citing Eysenbach, G. et al. 'Health Related Virtual Communities and Electronic Support Groups: A Systematic Review of the Effects of Online Peer to Peer Interactions', *British Medical Journal*, 328 (7449), 2004, https://www.bmj.com/content/328/7449/1166.

14 Norman Nie, D. Sunshine Hillygus and Lutz Erbring, 'Internet Use, Interpersonal Relations, and Sociability: A Time Diary Study' (Chapter 7) in Barry Wellman and Caroline Haythornthwaite (ed.), *The Internet in Everyday Life* (Massachusetts: Blackwell, 2002).

15 Jaron Lanier, *You Are Not A Gadget: A Manifesto* (New York: Vintage, 2010), 53.

16 'Less is more' was a phrase adopted by architect Ludwig Mies van der Rohe in 1947, https://en.wikipedia.org/wiki/Less_is_more.

17 Philippe Verduyn, David Seungjae Lee, Jiyoung Park, Holly Shablack, Ariana Orvell, Joseph Bayer, Oscar Ybarra, John Jonides, Ethan Kross, 'Passive Facebook usage undermines affective well-being: Experimental and longitudinal evidence', *J Exp Physiological Gen*, 144 (2), 2016, 480–488, https://pubmed.ncbi.nlm.nih.gov/25706656/.

18 News Feed Eradicator, https://west.io/news-feed-eradicator/.

11 Embrace Silence

1   Sarah Dessen, *Just Listen* (New York: Penguin, 2007).

2 Raymond M. Kethledge and Michael S. Erwin, *Lead Yourself First: Inspiring Leadership Through Solitude* (New York: Bloomsbury, 2017).

3 Susan Cain, 'The Power of Introverts', *TED*, February 2012, https://www.ted.com/talks/susan_cain_the_power_of_introverts.

4 Wayne E. Oates: *Nurturing Silence in a Noisy Heart* (New York: Doubleday, 1979), 3.

5 Rae Jacobson, 'Metacognition: How Thinking About Thinking Can Help Kids', *Child Mind Institute*, https://childmind.org/article/how-metacognition-can-help-kids/.

6 Viktor E. Frankl, *Man's Search for Meaning* (New York: Pocket Books, 1959), 164–166. 'We don't invent our mission, we detect it.'

7 Newport, *Digital Minimalism*, 104.

8 Strong's Concordance: *erémos*, https://biblehub.com/greek/2048.htm. 'The words "wilderness" (erēmos) and "peaceful" (ēremos) are very similar in ancient Greek, suggesting a connection between the two concepts. The word erēmos ("deserted, remote and uninhabited wilderness") is synonymous with ēremos (being "peaceful, quiet and tranquil").'
   The Strongest NIV Exhaustive Concordance (Michigan: Zondervan, 1999), erēmos (2245), ēremos (2475).

9 *The Holy Bible New International Version*, Luke, chapter 5, verses 15–16.

10 Ibid, Luke, chapter 8, verses 43–48.

11 Ibid, Mark, chapter 3, verses 9–10.

12 Ibid, Mark, chapter 4, verses 35–41.

13 Ibid, Matthew, chapter 14, verses 13–21.

14 Ibid, Luke, chapter 4, verses 1–2.

15 Ibid, Luke, chapter 6, verses 12–13.

16 Ibid, Mark, chapter 14, verses 32–36.

17 Martin Luther King Jr, *Stride Toward Freedom: The Montgomery Story* (New York: Harper & Brothers, 1958), 125.

18 Mother Teresa and Thomas Moore, *No Greater Love* (California: New World Library, 2002), 8.

19 'Solitude can be your most powerful thinking tool', *Entrepreneur*, 23 January 2015, https://www.entrepreneur.com/article/242059#:~:text=As%20the%20great%20Thomas%20Edison,has%20been%20done%20in%20turmoil.%E2%80%9D&text=No%20distractions%2C%20just%20you%20and,is%20food%20for%20the%20soul.

20 Jordan B. Peterson, *12 Rules for Life: An Antidote to Chaos* (London: Penguin Random House, 2018), 178–185.

[21] Blaise Pascal, 'Pascal's Pensées', Thought #139. This is one of the more common of the many English translations of this phrase.

[22] Parker Palmer, *A Hidden Wholeness: The Journey Toward an Undivided Life* (San Francisco: Jossey-Bass, 2004), 58.

[23] Ronald Rolheiser *The Holy Longing: The Search for a Christian Spirituality* (New York: Doubleday, 1999), retrieved from Ryan Dueck, 'We Are Distracting Ourselves into Spiritual Oblivion', *Rumblings*, 21 September 2011, https://ryandueck. com/2011/09/21/we-are-distracting-ourselves-into-spiritual-oblivion/.

[24] Ruth Haley Barton, *Strengthening the Soul of Your Leadership* (Illinois: Inter-Varsity Press, 2008), 51.

[25] Ibid, 47.

Part IV: The Practices (Preliminaries)

[1] David Allen, *Getting Things Done: The Art of Stress-Free Productivity* (New York: Penguin Books, 2015), 97.

[2] Stephen R. Covey, *The 7 Habits of Highly Effective People* (Melbourne: The Business Library, 1989), 95.

[3] Allen, *Getting Things Done*, 51–52, 154–163; John P. Kotter and Dan S. Cohen, *The Heart of Change: Real-Life Stories of How People Change Their Organizations* (New York: HBS Press, 2002), 25.

12 Start with Holidays

[1] James is not my client's real name. Minor details have been modified to ensure anonymity.

[2] Barbara Pocock, Natalie Skinner and Philippa Williams, *Time Bomb: Work, Rest and Play in Australia Today* (Sydney: New South Publishing, 2012), 185.

[3] Adewale Maye, 'No-Vacation Nation, Revised', *Centre For Economic And Policy Research*, 2019, https://cepr.net/images/stories/reports/no-vacation-nation-2019-05.pdf.

[4] Jossy Chacko, *Madness!: One Man's Crazy Idea to Transform Asia and Beyond* (Melbourne: Empart, 2008), 53.

13 A Day to Think

[1] Marcus Buckingham, *The One Thing You Need to Know … About Great Managing, Great Leading and Sustained Individual Success* (New York: Free Press, 2005), 188.

2 David Allen, *How to Make it All Work* (New York: Penguin Books, 2008), 73.

3 Terry Walling, 'Staying on Trac™ Coaching System: Creating Your Post-It Note Time Line', 2010, https://www.leaderbreakthru.com/timeline/; Dr J. Robert Clinton, *The Making Of A Leader: Recognizing the Lessons and Stages of Leadership Development* (Second Edition) (Colorado: NavPress, 2012).

14 Digital Detox

1 A. A. Milne and Ernest H. Shepard, *Pooh's Little Instruction Book* (London: Egmont UK Ltd, 1996).

2 If you think the idea of a home digital detox is hardcore, have some compassion for Susan Maushart and her teenage family. This journalist unplugged her teenage family from all digital devices for a period of six months and wrote a book about it. It's worth a read for the entertainment value alone; Susan Maushart, *The Winter of Our Disconnect: How Three Totally Wired Teenagers (and a Mother Who Slept with Her iPhone) Pulled the Plug on Their Technology and Lived to Tell the Tale* (London: Penguin Books, 2011).

15 Weekly Day of Rest

1 Abraham J. Heschel, *The Sabbath* (New York: FSG Books, 1955), 28.

2 Judith Shulevitz, 'Bring Back The Sabbath', *The New York Times*, 2 March 2003, https://www.nytimes.com/2003/03/02/magazine/bring-back-the-sabbath.html.

3 *The Holy Bible New International Version*, Exodus, chapter 20, verses 1–17.

4 Walter Brueggemann *Sabbath as Resistance: Saying No to the Culture of Now* (Kentucky: WJK Books, 2017), 3–6; *The Holy Bible New International Version*, Exodus, chapter 20, verses 8–11.

5 Judith Shulevitz, *The Sabbath World: Glimpses of a Different Order of Time* (New York: Random House, 2011), xxvi.

6 Shulevitz, 'Bring Back The Sabbath'.

7 Heschel, *The Sabbath*.

8 Peter F. Drucker, *Classic Drucker* (Boston: Harvard Business Review School Publishing Corporation, 2006), 13.

9 Judith Shulevitz, *The Sabbath World*, 74.

10 Susan Cain, *Quiet: The Power of Introverts in a World That Can't Stop Talking* (New York: Random House, 2013), 255.

11 Alex Pang, quoted in 'Get More Done By Working Less', *Farnam Street*, https://fs.blog/2017/04/get-more-done-by-working-less/.

12 Brueggemann, *Sabbath as Resistance*, 43.

17 Daily Pause

1 Timothy D. Wilson, David A. Reinhard, Erin C. Westgate, Daniel T. Gilbert, Nicole Ellerbeck, Cheryl Hahn, Casey L. Brown and Adi Shaked, 'Just Think: The Challenges Of The Disengaged Mind', *Science*, 345 (6192), 2014, 75–77.

2 Wilson et al., 'Just Think', 75–77, citing the 'American Time Use Survey', *Bureau of Labor Statistics*, U.S. Department of Labor, 2012, www.bls.gov/tus/home.htm#data.

3 Ibid, 75–77.

4 Clear, 'The Science of Sleep'.

5 Abbey G. White, Walter Buboltz and Frank Igou, 'Mobile Phone Use And Sleep Quality And Length In College Students', *International Journal of Humanities and Social Science*, 1 (18), 2011, 51–58.

6 Live Love Spa, 'The A-Zzz's Sleep Guide To Wellness: An Infographic', https://www.dailyinfographic.com/wp-content/uploads/2014/05/sleep-640x2153.jpg.

7 Jan Van den Bulck, 'Television Viewing, Computer Game Playing, And Internet Use And Self-Reported Time To Bed And Time Out Of Bed In Secondary-School Children', *Sleep*, 27 (1), 2004, 101–104; Susan McLean, *Sexts, Texts and Selfies: How to Keep Your Children Safe in the Digital Space* (Australia: Viking, 2014), 53–81, 113–120.

8 Pinker, *The Village Effect*, 112.

9 Duhigg, *The Power of Habit*, 109.

10 Pinker, *The Village Effect*, 112.

11 Maushart, *The Winter of Our Disconnect*, 267.

12 Carol S. Dweck, *Mindset: The New Psychology of Success* (New York: Ballantine Books, 2008), 235.

13 Gladwell, *David and Goliath*, 97–124.

14 Dr John J. Ratey and Eric Hagerman, *Spark: How Exercise Will Improve the Performance of Your Brain* (London: Quercus, 2009), 35–56.

15 Andrew K. Przybylski and Netta Weinstein, 'Can You Connect With Me Now? How The Presence Of Mobile Communication Technology Influences Face-To-Face Conversation Quality', *Journal of Social and Personal Relationships*, 30 (3), 2012, 237–246.

16 Kristen Duke, Adrian Ward, Ayelet Gneezy and Maarten Bos, 'Having Your Smartphone Nearby Takes A Toll On Your Thinking', *Harvard Business Review*, 20 March 2018, https://hbr.org/2018/03/having-your-smartphone-nearby-takes-a-toll-on-your-thinking.

[17] Nilofer Merchant, 'Got A Meeting? Take A Walk', *TED*, February 2013, https://www.ted.com/talks/nilofer_merchant_got_a_meeting_take_a_walk?language=en.

[18] Dan Health and Chip Heath, *Switch: How to Change Things When Change is Hard* (New York: Broadway Books, 2010), 228–229, citing Noah J. Goldstein, Steve J. Martin and Robert B. Cialdini, *Yes! 50 Scientifically Proven Ways to Be Persuasive* (New York: Free Press, 2008), chapter one.

[19] James Clear, 'Motivation: The Scientific Guide On How To Get And Stay Motivated', https://jamesclear.com/motivation.

Conclusion

[1] *The Holy Bible New International Version*, 1 Kings, chapter 18, verses 1–46.

ACKNOWLEDGEMENTS

Writing is a team effort. I am grateful for the incredible team of people who stood alongside me, supporting, critiquing and guiding this manuscript to become more than I could have penned alone.

To start, I would like to thank my wife, Kylie, who is my dearest friend, companion and life coach. Thank you for giving me the space to write, despite the personal costs. I am also thankful for my three children, Naomi, Caleb and Jethro, who are an integral part of my story.

Next, is my team at Spacemakers, in particular Tim Hynes and Mikala Grossë, who believed in this project from the beginning and encouraged me along the way. I am grateful for Matt Bain for challenging me to write a 'brave' book. And for Tom Smith and Mark Kuilenburg, our motion graphics team, for the colour and vibrancy they bring to our story.

Thank you, Christina Aitken, for reviewing this manuscript when I had almost given up. Your generosity and encouragement kept the book moving.

And more recently, my incredible team at 100 Movements Publishing, who saw a diamond in the rough and made it shine. In particular, thanks to Anna Robinson for your constant encouragement, wisdom and deep insights to make *Spacemaker* what it is today. You made this process a joy.

Lastly, I want to thank our broader tribe who resonate with our vision to see a world where busy people have space to think, breathe and become their better selves. This book is for you.

INDEX

ABOUT THE AUTHOR

Daniel is the co-founder and director of Spacemakers®, a productivity consulting group for busy leaders. As a trainer, coach and keynote speaker, he has worked with CEOs, executives, and other senior professionals throughout Australia and beyond, ranging from global corporations and businesses to universities and non-profits. He has a broad professional history, including leadership roles in physiotherapy, health management, project management and Christian ministry.

He is the founder of a number of globally accessible productivity courses such as Email Ninja®, List Assassin®, Priority Samurai™, which in total have more than 15,000 students online and offline.

Daniel lives in Tasmania, Australia with his wife, Kylie, and their three children, Naomi, Caleb and Jethro. He also keeps fourteen Barnevelder chickens who eat too much grain and lay too few eggs.

To learn more about Daniel and his work at Spacemakers, please visit www.spacemakers.com.au.

CPSIA information can be obtained
at www.ICGtesting.com
Printed in the USA
LVHW040313050521
686501LV00001B/2